# From Straight-laced
# to
# Cross-dressed

*A childhood diary and an adult in therapy*

Douglas Baign

"From Straight-laced to Cross-dressed," by Douglas Baign. ISBN 978-1-949756-07-4 (softcover); 978-1-949756-08-1 (eBook).

# Dedicated to

My two therapists, presented here as Sherry
My wife Anne, whose love supported me through therapy
The movie *101 Dalmatians*
My VP Sharon, who challenged me to write this
My editor, who diligently worked with me to get it done.

The people and life events in this memoir are all quite painfully real. To protect the identity of all concerned and that of the author, all names have been changed (except for some celebrities), as well as associated dates and places. With rare exceptions, place names have no connection to real locations. For obvious reasons, author privacy is requested.

Contents of this book may be disturbing to some readers.

Inspired by *The Diary of Anne Frank*

# Contents

# Foreword

Author Douglas Baign weaves together threads from actual diary entries and letters exchanged by high-school sweethearts as well as from logs recounting psychologist sessions when an adult to untangle the web of childhood trauma. Inspired by Anne Frank's diaries, Douglas documents his pain and confusion. The names and places have been changed but the events presented in this poignant, disturbing memoir are true.

*From Strait-laced to Cross-dressed* would seem to begin with the family idyll of charming, hard-working, brilliant parents whose lives revolve around the Fundamentalist Church and their own dedicated teaching careers. An artistic mother wins national magazine approval as woman of the year and looks beyond her own family to aid needy children abroad. A father steeped in science and math tutors his three children, ensuring they are light years ahead of students their age.

Yet for the careful observer, suggestions of trauma slowly reveal themselves. We find an accident-prone sister; a gifted, seemingly coddled older brother pressured to perform; a toddler with a speech impediment abandoned to a grandmother's care. The parents first focus on their own college studies, eke out a modest living, then begin teaching at a private, Church-affiliated school. Apart from churchly matters, the parents seem to afford little real family time.

Enter the unconventional grandmother, divorced from a sometime criminal. Her curious sampling of the seven deadly sins would seem the stuff of Hollywood drama, not far from the southern California setting, for a childhood gone off the rails.

While the close-knit Fundamentalist community keeps watch on its flock, it dismisses any muted cries of despair. A few teachers mock the stuttering boy in his early years. In later years, a youth counselor in nearly every situation bends a Bible verse to punish or praise.

In this hothouse environment, Doug stumbles head-on into adolescence confused about sex and love, betrayed by those who ought to nourish and protect him. Since his church and church school discourage intellectual exploration, demand impossible perfection, and paper over human suffering with insistence on unthinking joy, he is unable to move forward or back.

To an outsider, there would seem to be elements of cruelty and stunting in such a culture. A church camper who fails to memorize that day's Bible verse is not permitted to eat. And there is the head-spinning perception, right or wrong, that Fundamentalist elders favor rote memorization over reason and rely on literal meanings that ignore the vagaries of language, translation, distance, and time.

Although circumstances may vary, Doug's story shares many troubling aspects of coming of age in 1970s America, amid the sexual revolution, rock music, and youthful rejection of social norms. The contradictory cultural standards young people then faced, and still face, remain doubly disturbing for Fundamentalists. Like many young men, Douglas confronts the conundrum of sex, perhaps best expressed in the symbol of female purity and danger, the neatly coiffed perfection of the Barbie doll, sexualized yet untouchable. Barbie, the icon of idealized womanhood, appears unmoved by those who would love her. Only a perfect Ken doll may stand beside her.

How then does one rediscover the self as each shell, layer, successive Russian doll of one's being disrobes and reveals another self? The same but different, the multiple but singular self, not a plaything or a curiosity, but the man himself sits inside, waiting to be discovered.

How does anyone undo the ravages of child sexual abuse? *From Strait-laced to Cross-dressed* shares one man's story.

J.G.

# Prologue

# 1962

*March 10, 1962, at home*

Douglas rarely risked going out the front door onto his family's red brick porch. Instead, he favored the side door to enter and leave the same world that was different.

The porch really was made from genuine red brick. That was the first thing you noticed when you walked up to the house. A tidy walkway slid past a well-kept lawn to the broad, inviting, red brick porch. The red set off the white trim of the window frames of the gray stucco house. It suggested stalwart, wholesome Americana, packed into a small but lovely home.

If you knocked on the front door, the lady of the house would greet you, or perhaps a small child. Peering inside, you would see the living room graced with a large woven rug and an old Philco vacuum-tube radio. You could hear a wooden mantle clock with its merry chime every quarter hour. In the dining room, you might glimpse the dinner table set for five.

Later that evening, you might see the father take his three children outside to trace the constellations across the sky. He teaches them the composition of stars and galaxies. Then the mother explains that the constellations are personified into the gods of myths and how El Greco and Van Gogh stained the sky upon their canvas.

The family pitches a tent in the front yard to sleep in that night, looks for shooting stars then sings themselves to sleep. In the morning, the tent comes down and everyone scampers into the house for breakfast and a shower.

You hear the chime. It's time. The father backs the old Ford Fairlane down the driveway and leaves for work. The mother walks with her oldest son toward the bus stop. The middle child, a girl, trots out the front door, then turns the corner toward the elementary school nearby. The parents appear to be in their late twenties, the oldest child about 9 or 10, the girl slightly younger.

But where's the youngest, a tow-haired boy about five years old? He's old enough for kindergarten at least. Puzzled, you discover a side

Douglas Baign

door and a path leading from the house to a small granny cottage out back, up against an alley. Then you spot Douglas.

# 2001

Depression was a constant darkness around him. It felt like living in Beijing, breathing smog and smoke with never enough oxygen. Every day was a struggle to breathe, to walk through each moment. Nothing was clear, nothing was pure. Nothing was holding onto him—just the grey, ever-present smog.

His arm felt itchy at work one day, so he took a pushpin to scratch it. A few minutes later, it felt itchy again and he absentmindedly scratched it again. An hour later, same thing. By the end of the day he was curious about why he was still itchy and so took a look at his arm.

It was bloody. Very bloody. He'd been cutting himself with the pushpin.

It's difficult to describe severe depression to anyone who hasn't been suicidal or isn't a psychologist. But perhaps one good way is to contrast depression to the ordinary. For example, if you're depressed it feels strange to sleep well or to enjoy a good dinner.

His meds hadn't kicked in yet and he was driving back home down the mountain, a 1,000-foot drop in 10 miles down a steep and windy road with no barriers. Just a single twitch, he thought. That's all it will take. And then I can drop forever and get rid of this thing.

He continued driving straight. Maybe it's that Sicilian chicken sandwich, he thought. Damn, that was good. If I stay alive, maybe I can take another bite then let it melt slowly in my mouth. He didn't normally swear, but being suicidal felt like a special occasion.

It'd been the best sandwich in his life: moist chicken, fresh onions, a delicious sauce of mayonnaise and Dijon, tasty cheese and a bit of lettuce all on this gorgeous sesame-seed Kaiser roll. It was fantastic!

But at the same time, it felt wrong to enjoy a sandwich, his old fundamentalist background coming back to haunt him. Had he sinned somewhere? He felt like something weird was going on. Why was he enjoying anything at all?

When he felt closer to normal, there was an overwhelming guilt at the cascade of beauty: a wilted flower, just one, a raindrop, the smell of pumpkin pie and whipped cream, or even a fly buzzing by. Sometimes he got so fascinated by the bewildering paths they follow that he didn't want to swat them anymore.

A fly is such a tiny thing. But a chicken sandwich saved his life once and if a sandwich can, maybe a fly can. The universe is a compendium of many tiny things and some of them brought Douglas joy.

# Bridges

# The Westfield Bridge

*March 17, 2001, standing on the bridge*

Douglas missed death by just three seconds, that's how long it takes to hit the ground once you jump from the Westfield Bridge. Suicide-wannabes do that all the time. Simply step past the railing and let yourself fall.

It started for him on the freeway. There he was on the road driving along wondering if there were any way to keep driving south into the northbound lanes in such a way as to make himself dead without killing anybody else. And he decided . . . probably not. "So . . . how else can I do myself in?" he thought.

Guns are too messy. Besides, he didn't own one.

Hanging himself sounded attractive. "I have plenty of bed sheets or bathrobe belts for a rope," said the Voice. "I can tie a good knot, and Anne and I have a nice strong rafter in our master bedroom. Terrific!"

But it seemed cruel for Anne to find his dead rotting body swinging from the rafters when she walked into the bedroom. Scratch that idea.

So he took a walk to Westfield. Good walks are a great way to think through life's little problems, and Douglas had a tough one on his hands. What was the best way to kill himself? It had to be effective (after all, he wanted to be dead) and not directly hurt anyone else, especially Anne. Douglas wanted her to find his cold body in the morgue, not the bedroom, because that's where dead bodies belong.

He found himself on the bridge looking down and thinking: Hey, this will work great! The idea cheered him up, so he glanced and calculated it out: 32 feet per second per second and Douglas is good with math: 3 seconds. 1 thousand . . . 2 thousand . . . 3 thousand . . . SPLAT! Sometimes it's not easy to just cross a bridge.

Considering suicide is serious business (well, duh). You want to die right now, and the logistics of a good suicide are hard to solve with only the items on hand. It takes common sense to figure out how to kill yourself and that's usually sadly lacking at the time. Douglas knew. Been there, hadn't done that, or at least not yet. The bridge still beckoned.

Interstate bridges are often beautiful and attractive to a suicide wannabe. You don't have to do any planning in advance. Just take a casual stroll and find yourself in the right place at the right time.

Then jump.

The zoo saved him. Douglas went there a lot as a kid and once he watched a snake eat a mouse. A small feeding door in the snake enclosure popped open and a hand dropped in a free lunch. The mouse squeaked in terror then swelled up and stuck its white fur out. At first, the snake just ignored the mouse, it wasn't going anywhere. Then it wiggled its tongue and slithered closer. The mouse squeaked again, eyes sparkling and backed into a corner, barking. It made as much fuss as possible, to live just a second longer, but soon enough, it was down the hatch.

Animals will fight to save their lives, even mice, even when they have no chance. And by God, Douglas was going to fight to save his. He didn't know why he was depressed, but was alert enough (barely) to know something else: it doesn't matter. Depression alone can literally kill you.

*March 28, 2001, in session*

Sherry's office was more interesting than Douglas expected. First, it was right next to a small courtyard full of lovely green trees. That was an automatic plus–he liked trees. Second, a few scientific and psychological magazines were scattered among the usual pop-culture rags. Douglas rang the buzzer to notify Sherry and began to read an article on ziggurats. It was interesting.

He hadn't gotten too far when Sherry came out and asked, "Douglas?"

"That's me," he said. He put the magazine down then gave her a glance. His first impression was that she was tall, perhaps 5'7" or 8", about as tall and a bit older than he was and good-looking. She had short, dark hair and wore a white blouse and tan pants with a green necklace. He thought the necklace might be real silver and jade but wasn't sure.

Douglas stopped to admire a photo of a distant beach, then sat down on the sofa. Sherry settled into the therapist's chair nearby.

"Hello. How can I help you?" she said. There weren't too many introductions.

"I want to kill myself," Douglas responded.

"OK. How serious are you about it?"

"How do I judge?" It was the obvious question.

"There's different scales but the one I use is 1 to 5. A '1' is just a brief thought about it and that's normal behavior. A '2' is when you start to obsess about it, '3' is when you plan a suicide, '4' is a half-hearted attempt, like OD-ing on pills but not enough to kill you and '5' is a very serious attempt that you somehow manage to survive."

Douglas thought about it a moment, "I guess you could say I'm a '3'. I certainly obsess about it and I planned ways to kill myself. The problem is that I don't really see any need to make a half-hearted attempt. If I don't get help, which is why I'm here, then I'm likely to just jump from a 2 or a 3 to a 5. Preferably off a bridge or building high enough that I won't survive."

"All right," said Sherry, making a few marks on her notepad. "That's pretty serious. Why do you want to commit suicide?"

"I don't know. I can't talk about it."

"Why don't you want to talk about it?"

"No," Douglas corrected, "It's not that I *don't* want to talk about it. After all, I'm here, but that I *can't* talk about it."

Sherry raised an eyebrow, "You can't talk about it," she reiterated.

"Right."

"So how do you propose to get started?"

Doug rubbed his face. "Let me sketch my family very quickly then tell you three things up front."

"That makes sense," she agreed. "Go ahead."

"I was born at a very young age . . ." Douglas gave a lopsided grin. Sherry just sat and waited.

"No, seriously. My parents are Bill and Annette Baign; I have two older sibs John and Rose to make for a nuclear family of five. John's the oldest. He and Rose are both married now with kids (my wife Anne and I never had any), so I've got five nephews and nieces instead and now some of them are married and have kids. Aargh. Tempus fidgets.

"Mom died from cancer about 24 years ago." He paused a second. It had been a slow, painful death and he didn't like talking about it. It wasn't just the emotional closeness but the disruption, and the death of a link to the foggy memories of his childhood. Then Doug collected himself and kept going.

"Dad remarried right after that so I have a step-mom named Gwen. Nice lady, but she's not my mom. I'll have to talk more about my real mom at some point; that is, Annette, later, but let's continue the overview. *Eppur si muove*, as Galileo said. The world kept going after she died.

"Mom's got two sibs, four if you count her two half-sisters, dad has one sister and at one point every single grandparent, aunt, uncle and cousin lived within a day's drive, plus several second cousins. Which was way cool! There was such a diversity of interest and opinion in my family while growing up. Mom's cousins were farmers and my uncle was a military analyst. It was fun to talk to them all."

Doug paused again while Sherry took notes. "There's too much to talk about," he finally added.

5

Sherry nodded, "Yes. That's a common problem. There's never enough time. What are the three things you wanted to tell me up front?"

"OK. First, I grew up in the conservative environment of both my family and my church."

"How conservative?" Another obvious question.

He frowned and thought a second. "Extremely. Here's a very short description of my ex-church. I can't say that we were as far to the fundamentalist right as you can go without falling off a cliff. But that's only because the church had *already* fallen off the cliff. There was nothing farther to the right at all, at least not in Santa Brisa.

"So when I finally left the fold, I had to run *left* in order to get to the cliff they'd already fallen off of. Then I had to start climbing *up* the cliff. And it wasn't easy. I'm not that good of a rock climber.

"Then once I struggled up there, I was simply back to the starting point — as far to the right as you can go without falling off the cliff. I *still* had to keep running far left."

Sherry nodded, "That's very conservative. Go on. What's the second thing I should know about you?"

He shrugged. "I'm not sure how relevant it is, it just comes to mind. The second thing is that I've been on the Internet since 1980 or thereabouts. All this fad madness about chat rooms and email and so on. It's all old hat to me. In fact, IM is primitive compared to what I'm used to.

"Maybe it's not all that important but whatever. I guess what's important is to let me know if I use an acronym or Internet term that you're not familiar with. They just come natural to me."

"I can do that. What's item #3?"

"I've got a speech impediment." Doug said. "You can't usually tell now because I had two looong years of speech therapy in junior high twice a week. Did wonders for my social skills," he added sarcastically. "But back when I was a kid, I stuttered, whistled 's', used 'sh' instead of 's' mixed up 'c' and 'k' and Lord knows what else. It sounded a bit like . . ."

He sat there a second, trying to put himself back into 3rd grade then spoke in a whispy voice.

"M-m-om. Looce, th-the s-(whistle)elver c-cat shat d-down near th-the kair," he said.

"I don't notice anything now," said Sherry.

"Right. The speech therapy fixed much of it. But I can still wander or say the wrong word entirely. For example, I'm a history buff and I started to tell Anne yesterday about Hanoi, North Korea's policy towards Saigon during the 'Viet-man-aise' war. For two minutes, not just a single slip.

"Confused her totally. I swear I was thinking "North Vietnam", and my tongue said "North Korea" anyway. And I have to think carefully if I'm going to pronounce "Viet-nam-ese" war correctly. Then the week before that episode, someone asked me about my accent. It's native Californian with a small speech impediment."

That someone, who had probably moved to California when Douglas was 15, had treated him as an out-of-town tourist. Douglas wasn't sure if that was funny or sad. His family had lived near Santa Brisa since 1930.

"Anyway," Douglas continued, "my speech was bad enough that I was in all the 'slow' groups by 3rd grade and my teachers started asking how retarded I really was. Should I be put back a grade? Yeah. They discussed this right in front of me and used the word 'retarded'; 1965 was not exactly politically correct."

He paused. Sherry waited a bit then asked, "What school was that?"

"Taft Elementary."

"What happened next?"

"Well, the teachers reluctantly decided to keep me at my grade level, which was 4th grade, but they put me into the Bluebirds instead. And even the Bluebirds knew they were the slow group. I mean, get real— the Bluebirds, Yellowbirds, and Redbirds?"

Douglas's eyes looked distantly into the memory.

Mrs. L—"Her real name reminds me of 'Looney,'" he told Sherry— scanned the class with a practiced eye. It was a classic 7-10 split with lots of slow Bluebirds or advanced Redbirds, but not very many in the middle. How to even things out? Maybe it was time to move someone up, so she motioned towards the Bluebirds.

"Douglas, there are not very many Yellowbirds today. Let's move you over to that group just for today."

It was easy to read the doubt on Mrs. L's face and Douglas swallowed hard. He liked his fellow Bluebirds. They didn't laugh at him and he talked as little as possible.

But the problems were getting too easy. 'Dad's math problems are funner than this,' Douglas thought ungrammatically. His father taught 8th-grade science, and he'd been playing with Douglas lately, giving him tricks to make math simple, like how to memorize the squares from 1-50 in your head. Dad made that easy too. Verbal answers made Douglas nervous but he thought he could do OK. Everything is a table, Douglas reassured himself, and tables are square.

Douglas looked up from reminiscing.

"Dad's always believed that it's the results that count, not the way you get there, so he taught me all the shortcuts. If I got the right answer with my own approach, then I got the right answer, didn't I?

"Which attitude came back to bite me by the time I attended Jonathan Edwards Christian University, what I called JECU. What is it about Christian colleges? They want to make you stop thinking or something? I can understand why they might want to object to biology and evolution or whatever, but math? How is mathematics sinful?

"Never mind. I'll have time to be bitter about JECU later. Right now, I'm still in Mrs. L's 4th-grade math competition, and my brain wasn't the problem. My tongue was the problem. But you don't have to talk much during a math test, even a verbal one. You just do the math and 'lithp' the answer. Slowly, to make sure the teacher understands you."

Mrs. L explained the rules. "Each group will stand in a line. I'll ask the first person in the line a math question. If you get the question right, then you go back to the end of the line. If you get it wrong, you'll sit down. The winner is the last person left. Let's get started." No one minded when Douglas went to the back of the Yellowbird line.

"Bluebirds: What is 4 x 7?"

Douglas's Bluebird friend Ron Miller answered correctly, but nonetheless his other Bluebird friends sat down straight away. Douglas had hoped for some help, so he didn't have to represent the whole team. His new Yellowbird teammates hung on a bit longer, but all too soon they were gone too, except for Douglas. Only one Redbird had sat down.

The Redbirds got rotating questions, moving to the back of their line every time they got something right. But Douglas was the team, the only Yellowbird left. He had to answer every question right.

And Douglas just knocked everyone down like 10 pins, the entire Redbird team by himself, one-at-a-time. He was hotter than blazes and making them sweat. One poor Redbird wiped his forehead in relief as he answered his question correctly and walked back to the end of his line, which was getting shorter, too. Chop, chop, chop.

Douglas just smiled at him then trounced him the next time he came up.

He-he-he.

Mrs. L finally stopped the competition when the 4th-grade math class was up to 8th-grade algebra. You had to learn it on the spot then answer the question. The top Redbird and Douglas were the only ones left--another boy. Douglas knew that he could take him down. The rest of the class, or at least, the bottom two-thirds of it, wanted more. They were cheering him on, one of their own. There was blood in the water and he was the shark. But Mrs. L said she had one winner for each group and that was the end of it.

"Oh, but I could taste the blood myself," Douglas told Sherry. "And I've always wondered who I would have been if they had simply let me keep going. No matter; I knew I had won.

"From that point on, my teachers put me into the Redbirds of each and every grade where I was always one of the best of the best. By the time junior high rolled around, I attended the 1960s equivalent of a GATE school.

"I started childhood by befriending the Bluebirds, by joining the Yellowbirds then by beating all the sharks. This damn retarded Bluebird done good."

Sherry smiled. "That's a good start. But we're out of time for now and will have to continue next week." They finished the paperwork then Douglas found himself ushered out the door. Right before he left Douglas turned around and said, "I think I know why that story is important."

Sherry nodded and said, "Go ahead, but make it quick."

"I can do that," Douglas responded. "Maybe I remembered that story 30 years later," he continued, "the other day when I found myself looking down from a bridge and counting out the three seconds it would take for me to die. After all, I'm good at math and can calculate the odds.

"But I came from the bottom to win. And if I can do it with my head, then I can do it with my heart."

# Building a Bridge to Trust

*August 22 and September 5, 2001*

Five months later he wasn't so sure. "The good news is that I'm finally on meds that help me out," Douglas wrote to Jacky that day. "That gives me hope to keep talking with Sherry, trying to bang my way into myself." The letter was a good summary—drug adjustments and talk therapy. The drugs worked. Therapy hadn't, at least not yet.

His wife Anne had had to live with him while Dr. H fiddled with the dosages. Zoloft made him sleepy. "But hey," Douglas wrote, "That's better than being dead! Thank you, God, for making Zoloft!"

He stayed awake on Prozac, possibly because of his weird body odor. This really happened. You could smell him coming from 20 feet out and he felt allergic to himself. Anne certainly was; talk about strange side effects.

Luvox just plain sucks. It felt like holes in his mind, little rips in his psyche. One day Douglas's boss asked him, "How are you doing, Douglas?" and Douglas wanted to smash his teeth in for being so obnoxious. How dare he ask him how he was doing! He felt violent and what's more, he wanted to be violent.

He didn't smash his boss's teeth in that day. Instead, Douglas went to the MD and switched meds. Sometimes it takes courage just to do the obvious.

Dr. H finally settled on Lexapro as the anti-depressant of choice. In terms of good effect (keeping him alive) and side effects (Douglas's boss still had a full set of teeth and Douglas still had a job), Lexapro was a much better choice. For the moment, the side effects were bearable.

However, it'd been a year of therapy and Douglas still didn't understand the source of his depression. Staying alive was all well and good, but he didn't like himself and didn't always feel in control of his behavior. All he could do was to keep coming in to see Sherry, despite the slow progress. At least his arm wasn't bleeding.

He still abused himself, but not as frequently. He was also cross-dressing and the two felt related somehow.

The myth is that folks in therapy just open up the innermost self and start solving troubles right away. Alas, a mentally ill person is too

10

confused to even know who the innermost self is, so how do you open it up?

Answer: you don't. Therapy has a matryoshka doll feel to it or perhaps it's more like the veils of Salomé. You open up the outer self to look inside for you and there you are again! It's you! Then you open up the inner self to finally talk to the innermost self and there you are again! It's you!

Or as that great philosopher Buckaroo Banzai once put it: "No matter where you go, there you are."

There are three reasons why finding your own matryoshka dolls can make therapy difficult, perhaps more:

- It's confusing to peel away the dolls backwards, but that's what you have to do.
- You have to track which matryoshka doll is which.
- You keep finding damaged or mis-sized matryoshka dolls and you have to make everything fit together.

Oy vey! Like archaeology, digging layer upon layer with little discovery, therapy is a slow, tedious and dirty affair. Still worse, the crumbled matter you discover along the way doesn't always fit together with the cracked, ancient pottery of matryoshka dolls you expect to find and you end up thinking: how did that get there? ("Gack," said Douglas, pantomiming coughing up a hairball.)

At $130 an hour, this made for some intriguing therapy sessions. "Hmmm," Douglas would mumble, tears stream down his cheeks. "I hurt. I hurt a lot. Pain! Pain! Pain! (sob, sob)."

"Time's up! That'll be another $30 co-pay, please."

"It helps to have a sense of humor in this universe," he told Sherry in the next session. "Folks occasionally joke that they'd be dead without one, but you know, maybe I would be."

Sherry smiled, something she did rarely. It looked good on her. "Do you remember more of early childhood?"

He shrugged, "Not much, really. It's kinda a blur until I was nine or so, when I won that math competition."

That seemed late to be developing solid memories, so she pressed him. "Anything at all?"

"Just fragments. Uhhh . . . like when my grandmother made me a stuffed Dalmatian, or when Junior and I sat on the porch and stared at pedestrians."

"Who's Junior?"

"I dunno. That's just the name that comes to mind. Some young guy in a black suit and fedora who showed up with some other older guy in a black suit and fedora. The other dude was important somehow and was talking to my grandmother, so the one I chatted up was Junior. But that's about all I remember. We sat on the porch and looked at people walk by the house."

"Do you know why?"

"Nope. No clue."

"Do you know why the important dude was talking with your grandmother?"

"Nope. Still no clue."

"OK. Tell me about the stuffed Dalmatian."

"Well, that I can do, a bit anyway. That's a good memory," Douglas paused.

"*101 Dalmatians*, one of my favorite movies," he added, "came out in early 1961, a few months after I turned three. Momma May, that's my grandmother, put her professional sewing skills to work soon after and made me my own Dalmatian stuffed animal. I wanted it so bad that I helicoptered, watching her every stitch like a hawk. As soon as she was done with the body and head, but not the face, I snatched it then ran away as fast as I could.

"'Wait!' Momma May called after me, 'I haven't put the eyes on yet.'

"'It's got eyes all over its body,'" I called back and kept running. She just laughed.

"Remember, I had a speech impediment," Douglas reminded Sherry. "So what I'm really saying is 'It's(whistle) ga-ga-gawd eyes(whistle) aw-awl over its(whistle) b-bawdy.' But you'd go nuts if I did that for every childhood quote of mine, so let's just stick with translations. I was hard to understand outside of my family. And that just contributed to the loneliness and the mocking at school.

"But that's how I felt. I had eyes all over my body, waiting and looking for people to avoid and places to hide. But the Dalmatian was someone else to watch and guard, to talk to, to give me company. I loved that toy so much."

❦❦❦

That session had made a little progress; most didn't.

Fine. The direct approach didn't work, so a few months later Douglas decided it was time to try something else. He couldn't talk about his past big problems, so he started talking about small ones now, anything to keep himself talking. The idea was that talking about his current small problems now would help Douglas talk about the bigger middle problems that were rooted in past problems that caused the current problems.

And if you can follow that then you're ready to learn recursive programming languages like LISP. But bottom line, it's just a matryoshka doll. There's always something to talk about in the here and now.

Say, annoying co-workers. Douglas's boss Jim is cool and he's not one of them. But Mike is one of the few people Douglas had met who really is an ignor-anus, an idiot too stupid to realize what an asshole he is.

For example, Mike was so destructive to the company one six-month review cycle that Douglas decided to undermine him for the next six months. Douglas had to trash his own project to do it, but Jim knew this. The idea was to stop the madness.

It worked too. Douglas ran into Jim in the men's room just before Douglas's review came up.

"Hey, Jim!" he called. "We need to tell you our most significant accomplishments over the past six months, right?"

"Right," responded Jim. The two of them enjoyed a moment of companionable silence.

"Well," added Douglas, "my most significant accomplishment during the last six months has been preventing Mike from having any significant accomplishments."

Jim stifled a guffaw. But Jim couldn't get rid of Mike either. On the other hand, Jim was quite happy that neither Mike nor Douglas had gotten anything done at all. Hot damn! Nothing happened!

The alternatives when Mike 'accomplished' something were much, much worse. Oh yeah. Douglas could talk to Sherry about Mike. There were, however, more pleasant things to talk about. Say, rotting maggots feasting on a three-day-old corpse.

But Douglas's mind went blank when he tried to talk about anything substantial. Or he'd stutter or cry so hard he couldn't talk. Some sessions he just sat there on autopilot, "Hi. My name's Douglas. How are you today, Sherry? How are your sons doing?" She's got two of them. The fact one was an archaeologist explained her science magazines.

"Time's up! That'll be another $30 co-pay, please." Then he'd come in the next session and Sherry would ask him again, "Why do you want to kill yourself?"

But he dinno. He couldn't talk about it. The repeated episodes reminded Douglas of a definition in the Nerd Dictionary. "Endless loop: *see* loop, endless. Loop, endless: *see* endless loop." At the end of a full year of therapy, Douglas still didn't know why he wanted to kill himself.

But by the end of the year, he began to realize that it had something to do with sex and fear.

*September 11, 2001, at home*

*Dear Jacky,*

Forgive me, Jacky, if I ignore the Twin Towers. When I first heard about it I thought the world might be crazier than I am. Then I remembered, I can't take the world with me to my therapist—I can only take me.

My own problems seem very big to me right now. I heard about people jumping out of buildings today and my most coherent thought was that I wanted to join them. I wanted to die. Of the many strange things about 9/11, perhaps the strangest is that I have to pretend it isn't here, lest I too join the dead.

I can't let myself think about 9/11 because I'm mentally ill. It's just that I can write fairly well while I'm in the middle of insanity. I can't prevent the victims from being killed. They were dead before I even woke up here in Santa Brisa. I can only keep from killing myself.

Thus, I'm far more worried about my session with Sherry tomorrow than about terrorism today. I have a session tomorrow and perhaps that's the only thing keeping me together. There is, in fact, a tomorrow.

I can't solve 9/11. It's hard enough for me to gather the will to just stay alive. And trust me; that's really, really hard.

*Love,*

*Douglas Baign*

*September 12, 2001*

The more Douglas realized his problem was sexual, the more afraid he was of his therapist. Then fear became terror. Douglas became so afraid that he decided the only way he could talk to Sherry was if he dressed like a little girl and hid behind the sofa. If he didn't, Douglas believed Sherry would tie him up, crack him with her belt, then rape him. Isn't hurting little boys what women want to do?

So maybe he should be a little girl instead. Douglas was 43 years old and male. And he was deathly afraid of his therapist. But that's the first step of therapy: you gotta do whatever it takes to heal. If acting like a little girl would help him heal, then he would be a little girl.

Two things made the process easier.

First, Douglas began to trust his therapist. It took a while, but Sherry gradually coaxed him out from behind the sofa. Of course, he still sat on the floor wearing his pink skirt, white blouse and pumps and fussed with the pretty pink bow in his hair. but progress was made. He could flutter his eyelids and act like a little girl while answering questions like a man.

Second, Douglas attended an adult church group on the Song of Solomon, which is far more crucial than it sounds. Yea. Douglas was 43 years old the first time he heard sex discussed openly in his religious environment.

Douglas finally told Sherry a story about sex at the next session. He'd presented a paper at an IEEE conference one night, came home and dressed like a girl the next morning, wanting to punish himself. But 15 minutes in front of the mirror wasn't enough, so he primped and cooed and put his hands behind his back to be tied, then curtsied and begged to be spanked. So he fluttered his eyebrows, put a pretty, pink bow in his hair, spanked himself then masturbated.

And it still wasn't enough. He wanted to do it all over again: to feel shallow, pretty and feminine, to flutter his eyebrows and mince and giggle. Then punish himself and punish himself and punish himself over and over again.

He cut his arms, bought some Barbie dolls in advance, and held a tea party. Wouldn't you like some tea, dear? Then let me bash your face in. He stabbed the dolls with a screwdriver. Hard enough to put holes in the floor. Then he smashed the dolls into the ground, ground their faces into the dirt, and finished by masturbating three more times. Then he cut himself again the same afternoon at work. Ahhhhh! Yummmm! Feels good!

"The Barbie dolls probably represent someone in particular." Sherry commented. "Who are they?"

Douglas thought it over. "Dunno. But I was doing this like every morning, OK?" he told Sherry. "Then the next day I'd start it all over again; and again, and again, and again—*Groundhog Day*. Trust me. This behavior is not conducive towards good mental health."

"And before you say anything, yeah, I know I'm making jokes about it, OK? But that's also the only way that I can talk about it at all, even this much. And I gotta talk about it. It was a very serious problem and it just about killed me. Do I have to really jump off the bridge to prove that I'm serious?"

"No, you don't," Sherry said. "Of course not. Besides, I can tell."

This may have been the second step of therapy. Douglas could talk about sex without actually having sex. He could act like a girl without being a girl. For heavens' sake, Douglas had wanted to throw a tomato at Bill Clinton for years now, thinking of sex and girls, but he didn't have to do it, did he?

Wanting is not doing, which is perfectly obvious when you're sane and terribly difficult to see when you're not. For Douglas, accepting the obvious was a strong step forward, especially given his religious background.

Let's illustrate the point. A pastor once told Douglas about Mr. X from Douglas's old church, Lands Baptist. Being careful not to name names, the pastor explained that Mr. X had just married a hot babe—a complete sex bomb—a few weeks before he sought counseling. To make matters happier, his wife just could not keep her hands off him.

The reason to seek counseling? Mr. X couldn't get it up, not even on his honeymoon. He thought he was sinning. As the pastor told Douglas, why are you getting married if you don't want to make love with your fiancée before marriage?

But Mr. X thought desire *after* marriage was a sin. Lands Baptist took things that seriously partly because, as the pastor pointed out, they had lost the distinction between desire and act. 'I looked at beautiful women, didn't I? Then I had lust in my heart,' said Brother Jimmy in *Playboy.*

"If I could wave a magic wand at the traditional wedding ceremony," Douglas told Sherry next session, I'd change only one word, nothing else. After the vows are exchanged, after the pastor blesses them deeply, after they get up from kneeling to pray, after that beautiful shining moment that comes to many of us, I'd have the pastor smile, let them wander into each other's eyes, bless them once again and say:

"'You may now fuck the bride.'"

"Or the bridegroom for that matter. Marriage, after all, is God's permission to fuck like rabbits. Isn't that one of our highest expressions of love? Why doesn't the Church just admit the truth and be done with it?

"Never mind; that's rhetorical. But I can't help but wonder: how much difference would it make?"

"Let's leave the Church aside for the moment and stick with sex," Sherry suggested. "Otherwise there are just too many variables. Why can't you just be a man who enjoys cross-dressing?"

"The answer is twofold," said Douglas, "First, it's controlling me. I'm not controlling it. It's difficult to concentrate, almost impossible. I don't want to write or play the piano or work or take a walk. I just want to play computer games so I can forget that I want to be a little girl and stare at myself and giggle. Or conversely, I want to obsess about it, to compulsively act like a girl. But whether it's avoidance or compulsion, I'm not controlling my own behavior.

"Second, there's more to it than just cross-dressing. The problem is the ritual self-destruction, though I'm still not quite sure why I'm doing it. I don't cross-dress; I cross-dress then punish myself for being female."

The session broke a taboo, and suddenly Douglas realized he could talk, at least about some things.

*September 19, 2001–September 2, 2002, a year in a nutshell*

Now that the barrier had been broken, sex seemed like the only thing Douglas could talk about. It takes two to tango, so sex with whom? Sherry made a list:

1.   Talk about Douglas's mom.
2.   Talk about the first girl he could remember.
3.   Talk about the second girl he could remember.

And so on—you get the picture. Douglas spent the next year in therapy, sometimes still ducking into a restroom to change into a skirt and blouse before session then changing back into street clothes afterwards. In session, he'd start fussing with his pretty pink bow then talk about each woman he knew: mom, Maureen, Rachel F., Rebecca, Robin, Dawn, Rachel B. and Lorraine—lots of "R's" there during the first 17 years of Douglas's life. He hadn't hit major issues, but he was moving forward. Still, the constant lasciviousness was exhausting.

"Sex, sex, sex," he told Sherry one session. "I really get sick of talking about sex. I'm sure President Clinton felt the same way. There are other things in life, you know. Let's talk about something fun today.

"Say, ice cream. Yummy stuff! My favorite is straight vanilla with chocolate and caramel sauce with candy sprinkles. Just divine! So simple and yet so pure and refreshing. What's your favorite, Sherry?"

Sherry smiled. "Neapolitan. But are you sure you want to spend $30 talking about ice cream?"

"God, yes!" Douglas exclaimed. "I just gotta take a break. I can't say I never had an ice cream I didn't like. Dad bought concord grape sherbet back when I was 10 or 11 and it was just awful. We teased dad for days wondering which was worse—concord grape or the rum raisin he bought the next week.

"Concord grape was absolutely gross but my vote still went for rum raisin. There's something just plain yuck about finding this mushy little raisin inside rock hard rum-flavored ice cream. They freeze at different temperatures. The worst all time ice cream I've had the displeasure of trying. Hideous!

"But anyway. I obviously don't have any hang-ups about ice cream. I do have hang-ups about sex. I mean, I just about killed myself one day thinking about Deirdre, not ice cream. I have to talk about my sex life, not cousin Bill's."

"Who's Deirdre?" Sherry asked. "She's not on the list."

Douglas whacked his head. "Just a sec. We talked two sessions ago about taking Lorraine to the junior/senior banquet back when I was a junior, right?" Baptists don't have proms because there's dancing.

Sherry consulted her notes. "Correct. Then last week we talked about dating Linda."

"Right." Douglas took a deep breath. "But what I didn't tell you is that there's a four year gap between dating Lorraine in '74 and Linda in '78. And I'm not quite sure why I skipped it. The Earth didn't suddenly jump four loops in its orbit, did it? *Eppur si muove.* The Earth still moves. Regularly. Stuff happened between 1974 and 1978." Then he thought about it. "Even if it was the '70s," he amended.

"And you dated Deirdre between Lorraine and Linda," Sherry surmised.

"Yeah. I fell seriously in love with Leanne before Deirdre. I've not talked about Leanne or Deirdre at all. Plus I'll have to tell you about L'Abri. Wow! That's gonna be a long story. More than one," he added.

"Leanne and Deirdre will have to wait until next session," said Sherry. "That'll be a $30 co-pay, please."

"Just one more thing. It's short. You know those three Barbie dolls I've been abusing?"

"Sure."

"You asked me who they were a few weeks back. I named two of them Leanne and Deirdre."

*September 3, 2002, at home*

*Dear Jacky,*

It's quite the fad to talk up the first 9/11 anniversary. Anne pointed out the sign on the Vineyard Church when we picked up groceries. "September 11 memorial service, September 8," with a big U.S. flag nailed to the church building. She was amused by the sign. The Vineyard's not heard of a mid-week service? Ha!

I was amused by the flag. Seeing U.S. flags in a church always reminds me of a prank I played when I was in college at JECU. Fundamental churches (or schools) display both the U.S. flag and the Christian flag at the front of the sanctuary, the Christian flag in the place of honor–duty first to our religion.

So I snuck into the main chapel late one night (it wasn't locked) and reversed flag positions. He-he-he. Had to roll these big heavy flag stands to do it too, but trust me, I observed all the proper flag protocols.

The question du jour, of course, is "have you changed?" and I have, but it's got to do with Sherry not 9/11. OTOH, I'd hate not to have changed over the course of a year. You make a mistake if you fail to grow.

I chose to cross the Westfield Bridge instead of jumping from it. I can cross the L'Abri bridge too.

I'm still here.

*Douglas Baign*

*P.S.* Sometimes there's so much day-to-day stuff going on, like 9/11, that it's too hard to think about serious stuff. But the only way that I can see to prevent life from continuing to intrude is to end it. Aargh!

*September 14, 2002, at home*

*Dear Jacky,*

I told Sherry today that my wanting to commit suicide has something to do with Leanne and Deirdre. What exactly that is, I dunno, but one step at a time. All I'm doing now is opening up the next matryoshka doll. And surprise! There I am again, but this time with Leanne and Deirdre the day after I got back from L'Abri.

Talking things over with Sherry just wears me out. I simply don't have the emotional stamina to talk about everything all at once. It's one little bit at a time, which means therapy takes forever! But what else can you do but try? Beats suicide, I guess. Being dead would ruin my plans to be World Dictator.

Snort. The one thing about therapy is that it gives you confidence. After all, you don't need to worry about saying or doing something crazy because you really *are* crazy. Though I'm certainly not crazy enough to be World Dictator . . .

At any rate, whatever is going on with me that I can't talk about has to do with something that I can talk about, at least a little. That's the day Leanne covered Deirdre's derriere while Deirdre stabbed me in the back. The day Leanne told me not to get mad that Deirdre had betrayed me. The day I came back from L'Abri.

Yeah. That Leanne. And yeah, that Deirdre. The girls I wrote you about 25 years ago. Twenty-five years and I've not yet dealt with those relationships. Well, if I wait any longer it'll just be 26 years—might as well get on with it.

Thanks for listening!

*Love,*

*Douglas*

# Up and Down the L'Abri Bridge

*September 17, 2002, in session*

There was a lot to cover before Douglas could talk to Sherry about L'Abri. What was it, for example? Sherry knew that L'Abri are the French words for "The Shelter," but she didn't know what it was as an organization. What did it mean to "go to L'Abri"? And why did he want to go?

But he didn't know how to talk about L'Abri without talking about Deirdre first, and he didn't know how to talk about Deirdre without talking about Leanne first. In fact, he didn't even know how to talk about Leanne without talking about his church first. Everything kept going backwards so far that Douglas felt like Fitzgerald's Benjamin Button or Merlin from *The Sword in the Stone,* living life in reverse from death to birth.

The heart of the story was why Douglas felt betrayed by L'Abri, Deirdre and Leanne, in that order. So Douglas decided that the other questions could be answered by talking about that. Or at least, he'd get a good start.

L'Abri, he told Sherry at his next session, is a Christian organization founded by Francis Schaeffer in the '60s. Between writing books on apologetics, Schaeffer designed L'Abri as a shelter for any hippie looking for God. L'Abri is a place in Huémoz-sur-Ollon, Switzerland, where one could talk about the meaning of the universe without being in a church. Definitely Douglas's kind of place, as he was angry back in the '70s, too.

"I lacked direction," Douglas said. "I was confused. That's part of what you are when you're 20 anyway, but for me things were much worse. My mind was spiraling in 1977 and it wasn't upward. It doesn't seem like it now, but being an Independent Baptist in the '70s meant Jerry Falwell was just too liberal."

Sherry raised an eyebrow. "Who's Jerry Falwell?"

Douglas was impatient. "Just think of him as famous conservative pastor; really, really conservative—pro-life, anti-gay, traditional families. He supported prayer in schools and preached against Martin

Luther King Jr. and opposed desegregation in the 1950s and 1960s. By the 1970s, he'd lightened up, had a token black in his church choir and in a great display of love, even let someone play a guitar during a worship service."

Douglas blew a raspberry.

"That's conservative," Sherry commented.

"Yeah. But my church was Independent Baptist, so we thought Falwell was liberal. I mean—playing a guitar in church? That's counter-culture. Besides, everyone knew that God cursed blacks with the "Mark of Cain" because their ancestor killed Abel. And no, I'm not kidding. Gar! It'd make more sense to me if the "Mark of Cain" was being white instead of being black, all that melanin helps prevent skin cancer, but never mind. Clearly Brother Jerry had backslid from The Faith."

Douglas added a Southern drawl to his accent. He was obviously still upset about it.

"OK. So what does Jerry Falwell have to do with L'Abri?" Sherry queried.

Douglas thought about it. "Oh, I didn't tell you that, did I?" His brain knew the connection, but again the question was actually saying it. The speech impediment not only meant that he mispronounced words, but that he sometimes used the wrong words entirely or thought he'd said something when he hadn't.

Sherry smiled, "No, you didn't tell me."

"OK. Falwell was a . . . a benchmark. My church was more conservative than Falwell. That meant I was having trouble both at church and in high school because the church conflated conservative politics with conservative theology. More on that later, but even in high school that didn't make any sense to me because there's just too many ways to interpret the Bible."

"OK," Sherry asked, "Why did you go to L'Abri?"

"Several reasons." Douglas responded. "The big one was that no one seemed to have any answers. I had lots of questions, lots of issues I wanted to deal with and no one seemed to care. The church didn't, JECU didn't, my parents were tied up in their careers.

"The only way out seemed to reject Christianity entirely and I was still Christian. L'Abri felt like a good compromise. I could get away from the traditional church and explore my own beliefs and why I believed them. In one way, L'Abri was the court of last resort."

Douglas hesitated. He hated to bring up the next topic. But just then Oscar Wilde's quote came to mind: "The only thing worse than being talked about is not being talked about." Or as we say now, "Negative publicity is still publicity." For Douglas in therapy, the quote reversed.

The only thing worse than talking about pain is not talking about pain, because then it just builds up and the only way out becomes suicide.

"I was pretty messed up back then, even without thinking about God and politics. I had anger problems, still do now but much less so, and felt hostile."

"Who were you angry at?" asked Sherry.

"Back then?" Douglas replied. "Dunno. PD, I think, a few folks at the Church. That's harder to talk about because I keep hitting The Block. That is, the things I can't talk about because I can't talk about them."

The capital letters were apparent even in how he said it.

"The only thing I can tell you for sure," he continued, "is that my anger was back when I was still in love with Leanne, even after we stopped dating. I wrote Jacky about it and I've got a copy of the letter."

Paper rustled. "This is dated May 24, 1976, two years before I went to L'Abri. I was 19 years old." Douglas read the diary entry out loud.

> *May 24, 1976*
>
> *Dear Jacky,*
>
> *I was angry last night, frustrated. Leanne stood so full of joy and peace. And there I was tearing my heart out and thrashing it into the ground against my will. I'm my own worst enemy. I couldn't accept the fact that Leanne was two laps in front of me in a two-mile race. I felt frustrated and humiliated having to be helped by someone younger than I, someone who has more pressures than I do.*
>
> *Humiliated, dirty, desperate, despairing, angry. I can't accept the fact that I am me and that I am behind, and that I do need help. I'm not supposed to need help; I'm not supposed to be less spiritual than other people.*
>
> *I'm supposed to be an example, a leader, someone to look up to. But I'm not. So why can't I just accept the fact and go on? I need help, but I can't need help. I can't be perfect and need help. But I'm not perfect, but I have to be perfect. Why? Because I exist only as I struggle towards perfection.*

Douglas finished reading from that 1976 diary entry.

"I may have been suicidal before I even started dating Deirdre," he said. "I was certainly depressed. Another reason I went to L'Abri was to find out why and to do something about it.

"But I can't tell you why I was depressed *before* I went to L'Abri now any more now than I could tell you then." Douglas felt frustrated. I have to start with what happened *at* L'Abri. Whether I like it or not, L'Abri is my bridge between now and then."

"Good. Talking about L'Abri will open the next phase of therapy," Sherry commented.

Douglas was curious "And what's that?"

She elaborated "You started therapy because you were suicidal. That phase helped you learn you had a problem with sex and fear, even if it was still vague or generalized. Then you acted out your problems; you cross-dressed and played with dolls, using my office as a safe environment until you learned to trust me. Now you're narrowing it down. You're going to talk about a specific story about sex and fear."

Douglas just shook his head. "And that's why they pay you the big bucks," he complimented. "Thank you. I didn't realize that's what I was doing until you mentioned it."

"You're welcome," Sherry smiled. "But if I'm going to help you in the next step, I'll need you to be an adult. Do you think you can show up next week without cross-dressing?"

Douglas was still in his skirt and blouse. He thought about it. He was still a little nervous about it, but Sherry had alleviated most of his fears. So he simply said, "Yeah. It's time to move on to the next agenda item."

It was on that note that they ended the appointment—time for Douglas to get to work.

*October 2, 2002, in session*

Douglas opened the next session, wearing his normal street clothes, abruptly. "I still don't understand why going to and leaving L'Abri has to do with wanting to kill myself before I went there in the first place. But hey, you gotta start somewhere—one matryoshka doll at a time. So let's just tell the story."

Douglas dropped out of school in 1977 to earn the money for L'Abri. He missed the social contact but got some anyway because he was dating Deirdre at the time.

It was a good match. Deirdre and Douglas pulled each other up when one was down and thought enough alike that they could see the pain behind the pretense: touching, loving, sharing. The only reason he didn't propose to Deirdre was because he was just mature enough to realize that he wasn't mature enough.

His moods slid like a rollercoaster; almost like a manic-depressive way with tenderness one moment and screaming the next. Both Leanne and Deirdre warned him to deal with his anger or lose their friendship, or in Deirdre's case, her girl-friendship. A few months later, they both agreed that he had in fact been working on it, but he needed more work.

"I kept yelling," Douglas told Sherry, "so something was obviously wrong. I didn't know what was wrong, but that's one reason I wanted to go to L'Abri—to sit down, discover the problem, then build a solution.

"Going to L'Abri was a search to find both God and myself as a person. What was making me so angry?"

Douglas and Deirdre did some serious making out in the back of his dad's car on the way to LAX. There was fire to it. They were dead serious at the time and her hair and smell melted into his arms. Whoa, baby! ("Damn her worthless hide," Douglas interrupted his reminiscing with a curse.)

The jet made a quick fuel stop in Seattle and took a polar route to Denmark. 'Watching ice floes is interesting', he thought, admiring the view. Douglas changed flights in Copenhagen and someone asked him for directions in German. He looked Nordic!

The flight instructions on the next jet to Geneva were in French first, then German, and finally badly accented English–not in Kansas anymore. Douglas understood the French pretty well.

He took a train from Genève to Lausanne all the way by Lake Genève. "God, I gotta go back there," Douglas told Sherry. Then he booked a good hotel room overnight. By then he had endured a full day of travel and had serious jet lag. A small voice in his head was telling him to rest up a few days.

But the next morning Douglas decided there wasn't any difference between being sick in a Lausanne hotel and being sick in a Huémoz pension. And in Huémoz, he'd at least be where he most wanted to be. On he went.

Big mistake. On the other hand, he couldn't have known that at the time. Still, the difference was in how rational he was while making decisions in Huémoz—or irrational, as the case may be. At any rate, Douglas hopped on a bus up the hill to L'Abri, a Swiss 'hill' being something like 10,000 feet straight up.

L'Abri, of course, was overbooked.

"Huémoz is a ski resort," he told Sherry, "and this was like February in Switzerland, you know?"

Douglas had anticipated this and was prepped to stay a few nights nearby. A few weeks even. He made arrangements, laid out his stuff, then promptly came down with *la grippe.*

After a few days of sneezing and putting too much saccharine in his tea, someone in L'Abri finally gave Douglas a tour and explained how things worked. Study Schaeffer or Udo Middleman in the morning; shovel snow at night or vice versa. There seems to be a lot of snow in a Swiss ski resort during February.

Again, Douglas had anticipated this and it didn't bother him. That's what he was there for, but he was curious about their approach. All L'Abri had done was lay out lots of cassette tape recorders (this is the 1970s) and Schaeffer books to read. Where was the discussion group? Socratic dialog helps to explore.

Douglas had done his homework before class. He knew the Bible thoroughly ("Imagine that," he told Sherry in yet another aside. "Guess what happens when you attend a fundamentalist church for 19 years?"), was comfortable with philosophy, and had read all of Schaeffer's books in advance. Or rather, he'd studied them backwards and forwards. Douglas had read all the C. S. Lewis books he could get his hands on and to be honest about it he thought Schaeffer was a more interesting and better philosopher.

Yup. Homework's done; where was the class? Where was the method to find answers? Douglas knew the questions already, thank you very much, and had a good grasp of Schaeffer's universe. Well and good.

But what was his part in it? Douglas knew quite a bit about *The God Who Is There,* the title of a Schaeffer book, and desperately wanted to know "The God Who Is Here." The question was not *How Should We Then Live* (to cite another title) but rather "How Shall I Then Live".

If he could choose, he would choose God. If he could give, then he would give freely. But to whom? If there is to be passion and living, then let me be fire, he thought, but how?

Douglas was 20 years old and desperate to know God. Why should he sit and listen to Schaeffer's books on tape for 4 hours a day? He just about knew them by heart by now anyway. What did the material mean? And mean to him?

They told Douglas to sit down, shut up, and read another book. Right. After 19 years of Sunday school, he was familiar with that approach, duh, and frankly it wasn't working. Why the heck did he travel to Huémoz in the first place?

To Douglas's surprise, the L'Abri worker agreed with him. They were discouraging people from coming to Huémoz as they'd been oversold, but folks were flooding in anyway.

But somehow this didn't seem like the correct approach. Any org can work towards building a better communications net, even in the '70s, and if you can't stop the flood then you'd better start sandbagging. The only saving grace was that yes, they did discuss the texts, usually over dinner. Would he like to attend one?

You betcha.

Dinner was scheduled another day or so away, and he just couldn't get the right amount of saccharine into his tea while he sneezed and waited. Douglas would drop in a pellet or two in, take a sip to find it bland, blow his nose and add just one more pellet and end up with egg flower soup. Reading the tea leaves did not bode well. The trip was feeling absurd.

There were 16 or 17 people at dinner that night. Douglas sat almost exactly halfway around the table from the host Tom and the discussion started when Tom asked each person going around the table what they thought of L'Abri so far (this was newbie night).

And the discussion sounded like dialogue from a *Leave It to Beaver* episode. Everything was fine! Everyone was so excited to be here! Everyone was so happy to be listening to the Schaeffer tapes!

Talk about saccharine. *The Stepford Wives* kept gushing away until, oh, say about halfway around the table. Then Tom asked Douglas. What did he think of L'Abri?

"It doesn't make sense to me," Douglas responded. "Is this all there was to it? The prefab lectures don't address individual issues; it's all stuff you can find in the books. What does God really mean in my life?"

"Well, what did you expect?" said Tom, "Mrs. Schaeffer to give you a cup of tea as you stepped off the bus?"

YOW! God had answered Douglas's prayer. He'd asked God who he was and God told him. He was worthless. God didn't love him. Of course, God didn't hate him either. It was disdain.

Douglas could literally feel the shock driving in to lodge poison in his heart. He died that day. He died that moment: again and again and again. There is simply no way to tell you the size of *The Wasteland*. It's still the single most devastating moment in Douglas's life. "Well, what did you expect? Mrs. Schaeffer to give you a cup of tea as you stepped off the bus?"

Douglas paused to grab a Kleenex. Every therapist has a large supply.

"I won't shit you, Sherry. One single sentence and he hits all my buttons all at once. It's been 24 years and God that fucking hurts! Maybe it shouldn't. Maybe I should blow it off. Maybe I'm immature. Maybe I'm holding a grudge.

"Yeah, maybe I am.

"But therapy starts with knowing where you're at and that's where I'm at. I'm sitting at the table hearing Tom crucify me publicly for believing in a personal God, in his personal God. I was a Christian, and God, that really, really hurt.

"'If you meet the Buddha on the road, kill him.'"

He paused again to wipe his eyes. Sherry just waited. He finally continued.

"But I'm not one much for killing, so I decided to leave L'Abri, though this was probably another mistake. Francis Schaffer wasn't there at the time and maybe I shoulda waited until he was there then fuss loudly enough to get a chance to talk to him. Should I take Tom's statements as L'Abri's official position?

"Or another idea: stay there and play the game . . . then twist it. Say, read books two hours then spend the next two hours writing a paper based on Schaeffer books proving L'Abri violated his own philosophy.

"But I wasn't there to get nasty. I was there to get answers and I certainly had mine. God wasn't going to treat me as a person; He was going to publicly humiliate me instead. My duty in life was to be God's whipping boy.

"No one would give me a cup of tea as I stepped off the bus, with or without too much saccharine."

Douglas looked at the green trees outside gently swaying in the breeze. There was a small flower in Sherry's office and he found the trees and the plant to be calming, soothing. The plants and flower became his touchstone and he just sat and stared.

It was fortunate that a minute or two was still left in the session, because Douglas didn't continue. He needed the time to compose himself, settle the paperwork then leave for home.

*October 9, 2002, in session*

"And so I left L'Abri," Douglas told Sherry as he walked in, starting abruptly again. "Of course, what happened when I got back from L'Abri was just as bad, if not worse, but I'm getting ahead of myself."

"I walked down the mountain in a blinding snowstorm. Visibility was bad, maybe 15 feet, but all I really had to do was follow the road and drop altitude.

"It cleared lower down the mountain, enough to see Lake Genève shining before me, glistening like the jewel it is. The mountains beckoned to me, their snow calling my name, too bright to see, too white to miss. There were no deer leaping through the snow.

"I vowed to return. Then I walked the rest of the way to Lausanne and boarded a train to Paris to visit my friends in the Clayton family." Douglas settled down in the couch and continued to reminisce.

Trains are a good slow way to start, and this one retraced Douglas's steps back to Genève.

> *There are seven pillars of Gothic mold*
> *In Chillon's dungeon deep and old.*
> —"The Prisoner of Chillon," Lord Byron

The train takes you right past Castle Chillon and it's outrageously beautiful. Douglas felt like Lord Bryon, too, such a strange mix of torture and love. Different emotions running through him all at once: awe, confusion, anger at the debacle in L'Abri, but also wanting to stop to explore, as well as wanting to get out of there.

Douglas was deeply religious and he was losing his God.

The train passed Genève then wandered into Alsace-Lorraine. Rolling hills dusted in powdery white, soft villages in the distance. The roads were slow black lines against the white, circling hither and yon. Douglas's great-great-great-great-great grandpa was from the Alsace, and it felt like a home, a pretty one at that.

He slept a few hours and woke up in La Gare Nord (the name sounds terribly romantic but it really just means "The North Train Station") then took the Metro to the Claytons. The Claytons were missionaries in Paris and he'd met the family through church many moons ago. Their eldest, David, was Douglas's age.

Douglas paused.

"It was free room and board or anyways nearly free," he told Sherry. "Yeah. In Paris. It's easy now to attack myself for not staying longer. Duhhhhh . . . cheap tourism! But I wasn't there to tour, I was there to learn about myself and L'Abri was such a disaster to my self-esteem."

Then he continued the story.

The Claytons held a Socratic dinner almost every night. Douglas found this disturbing. The normally proselytizing missionaries were holding a discussion group. The L'Abri philosophers were proselytizing.

At least the constant conversation brought a rapid improvement in his French. One Parisian remarked on Douglas's drawl and asked if he were Swiss. He-he-he. That was one of the great compliments received in his life. In Paris, that's much better than being called American. He couldn't help but thank his great-great-great grandpa Schneider.

He told Mme. Clayton what happened at L'Abri, and she felt God had brought him there as a consequence. Stay here, practice French, visit some sights and just keep showing up for dinner. Douglas thought about it while Pierre, Jean-Paul, the sisters and I played Triple Cranko. ("Don't ask!" Douglas told Sherry in an aside. "Just take it as a fancy game. You can google that name now, but our rules are far more complicated than what you'll find on the Web.")

He thought about Mme. Clayton's advice some more when walking in the Tuileries. It made a lot of sense to him. Did it really matter if he found the Holy Grail in Paris instead of in Switzerland?

He was in the most beautiful city in the world with a cloud following him wherever he went. So much happens in Paris, above and below. Have you ever seen Notre Dame? Have you ever walked through the City of Lights? He spent one day looking at l'Arc de Triomphe then walked down L'Avenue des Champs-Élysées.

"Thank God the Nazis walked around L'Arc de Triomphe," Douglas remarked to Sherry, "not under it! It's difficult to see Nazis with any sensibilities but they must have had them.

"Wait. I lost my place. Where was I?"

"Walking down the Champs-Élysées," said Sherry.

"Before that."

Sherry consulted her notes, "In the Tuileries."

"Oh yeah, right—in the Tuileries."

Yet it seemed that fate kept getting in the way. Douglas accidentally stuck his fingers into the blades of a radio-controlled hovercraft while he was in the Tuileries. Some kids were playing around, lost control of it and he tried to save them some trouble by picking it up. Ouch!

Mme. Clayton's offer made sense but several ideas kept coming back to bite him, just like the hovercraft blades. The wound at L'Abri had been too deep and Douglas didn't feel ready to listen. It didn't make sense to just give up either, but he wanted to talk his problems over with the friends that knew him the best, Leanne and Deirdre. Deirdre was his girl. Leanne was his best friend. Leanne and Douglas salvaged a friendship after they broke up; then she introduced him to Deirdre.

Maybe he just needed Deirdre to hug him and say, "Poor baby." We all need that sometime. Or maybe it was because, for as much as he liked the Claytons, they didn't know him as well as his friends did. He wanted to ask Deirdre basic questions, like "If L'Abri isn't the right approach, then what is the right approach?"

Was he even looking for the right thing? There was no use finding the Holy Grail in Paris if he ended up finding the wrong one. So what was he really looking for? What was he so seriously missing in his life? Did he need counseling or dialogue? Douglas was willing to try anything as long as it gave him answers. Answers always come from inside, but sometimes it helps to talk with friends.

Mme. Clayton offered to chat, too, but it just didn't feel right. Evening discussions were fine, but the days were painful and depressing. The Madame ran a house with four kids, a missionary hubby, and a constant stream of visitors. Every time Douglas talked with her he had to follow her around like a kitten batting at a ball of catnip.

Enough of being the Little Lost Lamb. Douglas decided to go back to the States so that he could talk to Deirdre. Perhaps another mistake, but again, there was no way to know that in advance.

It was easier to do than he anticipated. Board the metro, board the train, stare at the city for an hour while wondering if you're making the right decision ("I still don't know if I was or wasn't," Douglas told Sherry); then stand in line to trade in his Geneva to L.A. ticket for Paris to L.A. He saved some money in the process. Board the airplane.

But he couldn't sleep much on the flight and his dreams became delirium. To be honest about it, he probably still had a fever from the flu he picked up at L'Abri. Deirdre showed up in one dream and said that she'd already broken up with him by telepathy. And Douglas said, "No, you can't do that. Telepathy is of the devil." He still believed in a conservative God.

Predicting the future (correctly) is painful. When the future becomes "now," you feel like a puppet of your own premonition. Nothing you do can prevent the future from being now so you lose control while everything stumbles into disaster. It's like being paralyzed and tortured in front of a mirror.

He decided: if he couldn't prevent the fire, then he could at least burn himself as fast as possible. He got all the way to JECU (very expensive!) then simply walked onto campus, strolled into her dorm (separated from the male dorms, of course) and asked the front desk if he could speak to Deirdre. Burning yourself is easy to do. ("I've done it," he told Sherry. "And I do mean literally.")

This is the '70s. This is JECU. This is a Christian college and this is a women's dorm. Douglas is of course male, so he found a comfortable sofa in the waiting room and tried to fight the jet lag; Paris one morning, California the same morning. California was clear and sunny. It might have been 10 o'clock.

And Leanne walked into the room instead of Deirdre. Say what? Something had to be wrong because Leanne and Deirdre were suite mates at the time, Douglas's girlfriend and his ex. It was just too big of a coincidence.

"Don't get mad," said Leanne. She didn't say, "Hi" or "Hello." She didn't say, "So what are you doing here?" She said, "Don't get mad." To this day Douglas can't help but wonder if things would have gone better if he'd gotten a simple, if somewhat confused, greeting.

It didn't happen, though it's not clear it would have helped anyway. This is the day Leanne covered Deirdre's derriere while Deirdre stabbed him in the back. The day Leanne told Douglas not to get mad at the fact that Deirdre had betrayed him—the day he came back from L'Abri and he was trapped by his own foreknowledge.

Leanne gently explained that Deirdre had been seeing someone else while Douglas was gone. In fact, she'd been, ah, more or less seeing all of him since school started five months before. His name was Ratfink. Douglas had met him once or twice.

Douglas liked Sherry's office. There was always something calming to look at, whether it was the trees outside, a picture of the beach inside, or just the white tiles in the ceiling. He looked at the tiles now, tilting back and letting the emotions wash through him.

"So on week #1," Douglas summarized, "L'Abri tells me that I'm insignificant and that God won't treat me as human. On week #2, I learn my girl's been sleeping with someone behind my back. Deirdre had been two-timing me all along."

*October 16, 2002, in session*

Sherry was wearing pants this time. She looked good in them but then Douglas thought she looked good in almost anything. He took some time just resting before Sherry started.

"How do you feel about L'Abri?" She asked.

Douglas fumbled for a second. He couldn't quite get his emotions under control. Then he continued. "Let's go back to Deirdre sleeping with someone else instead. That's the second part of the same story anyway."

"OK."

"I'd had the same opportunity as Ratfink and turned Deirdre down. To repeat myself (repeat myself), this was the '70s. I was a Christian. This was JECU. One does not fuck before marriage. Would I have been a better boyfriend by fulfilling my lust and violating my conscience? Certainly didn't violate Deirdre's.

"And Leanne just justified it. Well, maybe she didn't, but it sure sounded like it. 'Girls will be girls, you know. It's just those hormones running.' Yeah, right. Seems like I've heard that one before. But if it's not OK for men, it's not OK for women. And if 'just hormones' are a good excuse for girls, then they're a good excuse for boys.

"How do I feel about it? Rotten. But it's very hard to talk about. I did, however, write about it once. I have the poem with me today."

Douglas rustled through his belongings then finally pulled out the right sheet of paper. He'd brought it just in case.

31

# Dear Deidre

*I used to love you like hot chocolate.*
*You were sweet and warm and*
*I would wrap my hands around you to sip deeply,*
*to taste your richness.*
*But how am I to love you now? Can I even let you be my*
*friend?*
*Or will you betray my friendship as you once betrayed my*
*love?*
*Am I to give up my trust? Am I to deny my love?*

*I loved you. You betrayed me.*
*I needed you. You lied.*
*I cherished you. And you slept with him behind my back.*
*Such a short, deep stab when you told me once so long ago.*
*But every moment, every eye every stretch of hair I see*
*reminds me*
*of you.*

*Am I to forgive you? Or hate you?*
*Does my forgiveness justify your actions?*
*Does my hatred bring back tenderness?*
*Does my anger feed my love?*
*My love, my love. My love for you.*
*You are my love.*

*I hurt so much inside that*
*I am afraid to touch it, or to let it go.*
*Betrayer.*
*I would strike you, my love, but could not.*
*And so I struck myself.*
*Am I better now that I am insane?*
*Am I kinder now for my own self-destruction?*

*I never knew how much I loved you*
*until I let myself feel the pain.*
*I never knew how much I loved you*
*until it turned to hate.*

"So clearly I *wrote* about this. But remember Leanne had said not to get mad, and I couldn't talk about L'Abri without my anger whipping out of control. So I didn't talk about it. At all, though I doubt this is what Leanne intended.

"I didn't talk to anyone about L'Abri and Deirdre. Ever.

"You, Sherry, are the first person I've ever told the entire story to, while I keep the Kleenex division of the Kimberly-Clark corporation in business. And it's taken me more than 20 years to get here—20 years.

"I spent the first seven years nearly insane, Sherry, or maybe really insane. Looking back, it's hard to know, it's that confusing. I lost my God. Then I lost my girl. And I'm not sure which I lost first. Then I lost trust in Leanne to boot. My anger was justified and there Leanne was telling me it wasn't."

"But to this day I don't understand Leanne's motives. Why did she tell me instead of Deirdre telling me? If Leanne had really wanted to help, then she needed to butt out and make Deirdre fess up to me right up front. So what's Leanne's angle? Preventing a scene? Helping a friend? It was too much the busybody."

Sherry made a suggestion. "Maybe she just wanted to retaliate. Leanne was your ex, right? So maybe she was saying, 'You could have picked me but you got Deirdre the slut instead.'"

"Maybe," responded Douglas. "But coating the knife in your back with 'hormones' adds poison, not butter."

"Or maybe Leanne felt differently. I dunno. All I know is that I wasn't exactly feeling rational at the time and I didn't. Lose my God, lose my girl, lose my best friend and Leanne had been my best friend. Got my parents mad at me on top of that. I'd gone to L'Abri to find and heal myself and that's what I found instead."

He paused.

"*The End.*" He was remembering the song by The Doors. The darkness and anger seemed appropriate.

"OK. Not really. But there's a gap in my memory. I was one person until that moment, another person afterwards. Or at least that's what it feels like. I can't remember what happened in that gap. Flashes of talking with Leanne on a dirt road somewhere, another flash of talking to Deirdre while hot white fire ripped my stomach, killing me, blinding me."

He paused again.

"Damn."

Douglas remembered the snow of L'Abri, white like the tiles in the ceiling above him. He still didn't know why, but the snow was important: clean, refreshing. Thinking about it gave him the strength to continue.

"Let's get back to my smashing dolls, such a fun topic to talk about. Remember I've named two of my three Barbie dolls Leanne and Deirdre.

So the worse of it is that Leanne and Deirdre are only two-thirds of my problem. I went to L'Abri because I was a mess to begin with. Deirdre betrayed me after I got back. I've given the third Barbie doll a name but my mind doesn't let me know what it is. But Leanne and Deirdre point to something.

No, I don't know who or what that is, nor why I think this story has something to do with the third Barbie doll. But I guess I don't need to. All I really need to know is that L'Abri is where things began. It's the first matryoshka doll.

"And that gives me an idea about how to proceed to open up the second: talk about Leanne and Deirdre, starting from when I met Lee."

"You don't want to talk about your childhood?" Sherry confirmed.

"I can't," Douglas replied. "I'll just have to work backwards from being 19 at L'Abri towards childhood. But heck, I guess time travel's part of therapy in the first place. You open the first matryoshka doll then you open the second."

"OK," Sherry smiled. "We can start talking about it next week."

Douglas rolled his eyeballs, but they finished the session and he went off to work.

# The Marathon Run
# Away from the Church

# Planning Stages

*October 20, 2002, at home*

*Dear Jacky,*

I've started sorting my letters to you, but it's confusing and I've got lots of gaps. Unfortunately, I've lost all the letters before April 1975 and anything after 1977. Rose might have some but then again she might not. You've seen her garage! All I've got left is May 1975 through December 1976.

Still, the fact that I have anything at all is pretty amazing. I somehow managed to keep your address through 3 years of craziness after L'Abri, 5 different cities, a week of being homeless in L.A., dozens of different homes and 30 very odd years.

But precious jewel that it is, and precious that you are to me, my Jacky, for you've stayed with me. And the story of Leanne and Deirdre has something to do with whatever was wrong with me in May 1976.

But I'm not sure a chronology is the best way to approach these letters. By now I've reread through the next 10 or so and am beginning to think I need to discuss themes, not each individual letter in sequence. But how to do so? I'm not yet quite sure of the themes or where each letter fits.

This is painful. Not only because I have to admit my mistakes, but because my mistakes caused pain to people I love. It helps that I've worked in computer programming. My urge is not to 'find the good and praise it,' as my friend Tabitha might say. My urge is to find the bad and kill it—to remove the bugs, even if they are in me.

*With Love,*
*Douglas*

*October 23, 2002, in session*

"I want to talk about Leanne today," Douglas began, "but there's something I want to cover first."

"What is it?" asked Sherry.

"Let's go back to the day when Lee told me that Deirdre was seeing someone else."

"All right."

"Remember that I was still quite feverish at the time, so maybe I was making up the entire incident."

Sherry frowned. "I doubt it. Leanne's behavior is consistent."

Douglas pondered that, "Maybe. Or maybe it didn't happen at all and I imagined it in a fever dream. At any rate, it doesn't matter too much one waaay or the other." It's gonna getcha, getcha, getcha, he thought. "The most important thing for now is that I *believed* it. That matryoshka doll cracked then shattered," he said.

Sherry probed further. "True. Do you have any idea about how that influenced wanting to commit suicide later on?"

"No, not really. The whole thing still doesn't make any sense to me. But if I talk through my relationship with Leanne maybe something will come to me. And that's another long story." Douglas gave a lopsided grin. "I seem to collect them."

"All right," said Sherry. "You'd better get started."

Douglas folded his legs beneath him and curled up on the couch.

They met at a church high school retreat at Big Bear in December of 1974. Leanne's father, a captain in the Air Force, had just transferred to Santa Maria and her family started attending Lands Baptist. Douglas's first impression was that she was a little young, but he wanted to get to know her better. She seemed interesting.

The next time he saw her, she was holding hands with Randy. She knocked him off his pins, anyway.

Leanne was the only girl Douglas knew who scored 12 on his 10-point scale, the most radiant girl he ever met, just incredible. It wasn't just her sexiness or curves. There was something about her aura, the smile and charisma, the way she handled herself. Leanne was playful, solemn, bewitching, gracious, sexy, fun to be with, a lady in every sense of the word. Douglas adored her from that moment on.

And she was holding hands with Randy. In a way, that was freeing to Douglas. Randy and Douglas were good friends at the time and it gave Douglas a chance to just get to know Lee. The three of them hung out while he tried to sort out hormones from loyalties—mostly successfully. Douglas was fixated on Rachel back then, even after it was clear she didn't return the favor. It was a great defense mechanism. Randy liked Leanne, Douglas liked Rachel, end of story.

Douglas interrupted himself, "I've got a chicken-and-egg problem, Sherry."

"What is it?" she asked.

"How do I describe what happened to me without describing my fundamentalist background? The two feed off each other. So do I talk about Leanne or talk about my church?"

Sherry was unsympathetic. "You tell me."

Douglas frowned and thought a second. "I already mentioned that my church was ultra-fundamentalist. I need to talk about that more later by itself, but I think I can talk about both Lee and my church simultaneously. Leanne and I were both at one of Pastor Dan's (PD's) religious activities, several, in fact."

Go on," Sherry encouraged.

Douglas settled deeper into the couch and let his mind drift back.

"The first one was Pastor Dan's one-week trip to Lake Powell during spring break," he said. "PD's getaways—I mean, Pastor Dan but we called him PD or Pettie—seemed like they were choreographed by Torvill and Dean: colorful, precise, crammed full of lively elements, and timed to the second.

"Which is great when you're talking Olympics ice dancing, but this was high school. A little more chaos would have been useful. Like . . . maybe a lot more chaos.

"Here's a typical day at Lake Powell. Leanne and I both attended."

Douglas and Randy woke up at 6:30 a.m. on the male side of camp, becoming the first boys to rise and gaze at the glory of Dawn. A few girls on the other side of the camp were already awake.

Douglas dressed and groomed, then sat down to refresh himself on the day's Bible verses. This was day #3 of the trip, so he needed to know Romans 5: 1-9—three verses a day would complete the chapter in a week. He'd already memorized them last night but reviewed them once before asking Randy to quiz him.

> *Romans 5*
> *1 Therefore, since we have been justified through faith, we have peace with God through our Lord Jesus Christ,*
> *2 through whom we have gained access by faith into this grace in which we now stand. And we boast in the hope of the glory of God.*
> *3 Not only so, but we also glory in our sufferings, because we know that suffering produces perseverance;*
> *4 perseverance, character; and character, hope.*
> *5 And hope does not ashame us, because God's love has been poured out into our hearts through the Holy Spirit, who has been given to us.*

*6 You see, at just the right time, when we were still powerless, Christ died for the ungodly.*
*7 Very rarely will anyone die for a righteous person, though for a good person someone might possibly dare to die.*
*8 But God demonstrates his own love for us in this: While we were still sinners, Christ died for us*
*9 Since we have now been justified by his blood, how much more shall we be saved from God's wrath through him!*

"Nope," said Randy. "That's not it."

"What do you mean that's not it?" Douglas was astonished.

"Verse 5. It's not 'does not ashame us'. The verse says 'does not put us to shame.'"

"What difference does it make?" Douglas was petrified. Shame felt close by and hope felt very far away.

"The difference," Randy said pragmatically, "is that you can't eat until you have everything perfect word-for-word through verse 9 in the King James version. And I'm hungry. Now start over from the top."

It took once more, but then Douglas had it perfectly. After that, he turned around and checked Randy. Randy preferred memorizing in the New American Standard, but otherwise it was the same process. Those were the only two translations allowed.

Leanne joined Douglas and Randy for breakfast at 7:30. PD asked each person if they'd been checked on their verses (on the honor system), and they settled down to enjoy milk, eggs, and pancakes. Randy and Leanne held hands and the three friends discussed what to do until lunch, finally settling on trying to water ski.

Fun! The boat could only handle one water skier at a time, so Leanne and Douglas talked whenever Randy took his turn. They got to know each other.

They all ate lunch at 12:30 p.m., repeating back the same set of Bible verses to each other before eating. Charlie S. had trouble with the verses, and Douglas was worried that Charlie would have to skip a meal. But he finally got it right a few minutes before the portable kitchen closed.

There was a devotional after lunch. The church youth group studied a different one each trip, usually something like *Dealing with the Devil* or *The Practice of the Presence of God*. Max Lucado wasn't around back then, but any of his books would fit right in.

Next, several folks confessed their sins. Finally, at about 3:30 that afternoon the group was free to goof off and collect more sins along the way. Several boys confessed that Dawn really did think she was alone when she went skinny-dipping. Yup. Wake up early enough and you'll see the glory of Dawn. The episode became legendary. So did Dawn.

Dinner was at 6:30 p.m. By then Douglas had memorized verses 9-12 and recited back the entire segment (1-12), this time to Leanne. He usually only had trouble memorizing the verses for breakfast.

In the evening, the group sang songs around 7:00, listened to a skit or testimonies, then PD gave a short message. Afterward the teens just chatted or reviewed their verses for tomorrow before returning to their respective sides of the camp and drifting off around 10 or 11.

Next morning: different day, different verse, quite literally. By the end of high school—Douglas attended a private Christian one—he could recite the entire books of Galatians; Ephesians; Philippians and Colossians; I, II, and III John; I and II Timothy; Titus, Philemon; James; and Jude, plus six complete chapters in Romans, six chapters in I and II Corinthians, three more in Hebrews, large chunks of I and II Thessalonians, parts of I and II Peter, several chapters in Psalms and Proverbs and, of course, pieces of Matthew, Mark, Luke, and John.

Perfectly, word-for-word in the King James version. Later in life, the local Renaissance Faire was a snap. Douglas already spoke their language. Plural, 'faires', Interesting to go to one, at least once.

Time passed.

The Lake Powell trip was in March. Douglas's junior/senior banquet would be in early June. He didn't have a date, though he was thinking through three possibilities. Douglas was close enough to Leanne by then that he could chat with her about A, B, and C without naming names. But he couldn't decide who he should take.

Then Leanne flirted with him. Every once in a while, Douglas felt like Lee was looking at him, not Randy. Was she an unexpected "X" in his equations? It felt dangerous. One does not steal a girl from a friend.

Ah, the wonders of high school.

# Stretching Out

*October 30, and November 6, 2002, in session*

Douglas's weekly therapy sessions began to create a routine. He came in, took a moment to get his bearings, explained how he felt about last week's story, and then told a new one. If there was still time, he'd comment on the current story.

This week was no different. Douglas came in, admired the picture of the beach, then talked about memorizing the Bible in high school.

"Twenty-five plus years later," he began after the session's amenities, "I never carry a Bible to church —everyone else probably thinks I'm a heretic—and I rarely even read it at all. Maybe just to look something up.

"I mean, why bother? I'll know if (and sometimes when) a pastor reads things that just aren't in there. There's something truly scary about this, Sherry. I mean, what did I really learn by memorizing a stadium full of Bible verses? That I can ace several *Jeopardy* categories?"

Sherry laughed, "Do continue."

"I didn't go to church so I could know *about* God," Douglas elaborated, "I wanted to know *God*. Church and the Bible, or for that matter, L'Abri, are only useful as means to that end. Somewhere around the Lake Powell trip I began to wonder for as much as I know the Bible, is my church helping me to know God? What's written in your head isn't necessarily written in your heart.

"My church was writing on the wrong parchment. This is a radical thought when you're an Independent Baptist. It's fundamentalism. In fact, the act of thinking is itself a radical thought when you're a fundamentalist Independent Baptist.

"To hell with them."

Douglas paused. The feelings were there but like any other ex-Fundamentalist, he wasn't good at swearing. That he tried to swear now meant that talking about leaving the Church was obviously still painful.

Then he shook himself and continued. "Cursing them won't help me," he said. "So let's keep going. It'll give me a chance to talk about Lee and to describe my church at the same time, anyway.

"The trip to Lake Powell was in March of '75 . . ."

In April, the church high school group visited a sister church near L.A. where they were to put on a fair for an elementary school. By coincidence, Las Ramblas Evangelical Free—what we called "Ramble Free" or "Bramble Free" for short—was Leanne's old church, and she was looking forward to seeing her old friends. Naturally, both Douglas and Randy were going as well.

After all, Douglas was president of the church high school group, or at least, one of two presidents. He wasn't tagging along with Randy and Leanne. Douglas and Kevin, his counterpart from Bramble Free, were nominally leading the entire event.

The bus trip up to L.A. was dull but uneventful, which was unusual because the Rad Red Rocket was named both for its color and for its pronounced tendency to explosively shed engine parts. PD was the driver as well as the youth pastor. Douglas felt guilty about being glad he wasn't called up front to pray for the bus to hold together long enough to reach the next machine shop.

He used the respite to chat with Leanne and Randy. The most interesting item was that Leanne's dad could be transferred to D.C. in six months, taking his family with them. Douglas's own dad had been in the Navy before he was born, so he understood. Friends were secondary to family.

Douglas wanted to talk to Leanne about his possible dates to the junior/senior banquet (A, B, and C), but not in front of Randy. Instead, he left Randy and Leanne alone and went to the back of the bus to talk to Dawn. He'd known Dawn at church since kindergarten and they confided in each other a bit.

Douglas explained C's mysterious actions to Dawn without naming names and asked, "Do you know why 'C' doesn't like me?"

"It isn't that," she said. "Some girls just like to tease." It was something Douglas had never considered. Maybe I'm not really able to handle a relationship with a girl, he thought to himself.

Several folks from opposite churches hugged each other once Douglas arrived and introductions were made all around. He was surprised by how many people seemed to know each other already. He'd been at Lands Baptist literally his entire life and hadn't met these folks.

The children's fair festivities began right away. The Bramble Free booths were built in advance, so Douglas and Kevin called everyone together, held a short prayer, then everyone ran to their assigned tasks. The Lands Baptist high schoolers were mainly there to provide manpower and support.

Douglas's job (and Kevin's) was to monitor everything and pitch in when needed. At first this seemed boring but then he noticed that the younger kids were dragging for no apparent reason. On the other hand, the kids watching the play were having a good time.

Douglas pondered the problem a moment and become so engrossed that he didn't notice when Rachel started flirting with him. If the fair was really as God-given as the organizers asked him to believe, then he had to be sinful to notice that it wasn't. And why would any good God-fearing girl be interested in a backsliding sinner?

He thought about the fair again while playing Ping-Pong later that night. ("Which no doubt," he told Sherry, "is one reason why I got my butt kicked. I'm usually a very good player.") Then he realized that the fair booths were too far apart. The younger kids got tired of walking between booths and the critical mass for pleasant mingling was never reached. Conversely, the play worked well because the children were collected and rested.

But that was something he couldn't tell anyone. To mention the issue, even to say 'this' would get more of what was wanted than 'that,' would be to criticize the adult organizers. And criticism was the same as saying they were ungodly.

Sherry interrupted, "That they were ungodly? I don't follow the logic."

Douglas asked, "How much time do we have left?" He could see the clock for himself but knew that Sherry and he had different senses of time. "It might take me awhile to explain."

"Five minutes."

Douglas gnawed at a fingernail, "Not enough time. Let's just say that trying to criticize the leaders was a very bad idea and I'll explain why later. You're right it's important, and I need to talk about it more but it'll take too long to explain. I'd rather talk about how I felt about the fair."

"OK," said Sherry, "how do you feel about it?"

"Felt about it," corrected Douglas. "I wrote this in 1975." He pulled out one of his letters to Jacky. He routinely brought a few into session if he thought they might be relevant, "Let's see here."

"April 13, 1975, Dear Jacky," he began. "Uh, skipping down, yadda yadda yadda . . . Ah. Here we are."

> *Girls don't usually like boys who are introspective, moody, and a bit weird. So I've never asked a girl out if I'm that serious about her. I always check to make sure I don't offend her. Back-check, front-check, side-check. I try to make things too perfect and girls don't like it. I'm too idealistic and ideal*

*structures don't exist. It's just exhaustive analysis. I don't think any girl can like me.*

*My emotions are too unstable. If I did overcome my obstacles and managed to date only one girl, I'd probably still like another. I should be able to stabilize to like one girl first.*

"So the Bramble Free fair has two themes," summarized Sherry, "your relationship to women and your relationship to church leaders."

Douglas was startled, "Yeah. That's a very good point. Thanks! The two themes first connect at the fair. And I need to talk about how they developed and interacted during my relationship with Lee."

"Good," said Sherry. "That's a good stopping point. I'll see you at the same time next week."

They said good-bye and Douglas once again headed to work.

*November 13, 2002, in session*

"I said there was a lot going on in April of '75," Douglas opened at the start of the next session, "but there's a lot more than I realized."

"Go on," Sherry encouraged.

"But let's finish off what happened at the Bramble Free fair before telling the story of the trip back home. Then I can get to the rest of the stuff that happened that April, like my sister Rose almost dying or my fight with PD. Grr," Douglas gnashed his teeth. "This is a long story."

Sherry just nodded. She didn't say too much in session except to clarify, which just made her occasional comments worth listening to.

"OK," explained Douglas . "Last week you pointed out two themes at Bramble: my relationship with women and my relationship to church leaders. Let's get back to how I saw women for a second. That's important to explore before talking about dating Lee because it colored that relationship."

"Go on," was all Sherry said. Douglas continued by pulling out the same letter.

"The letter I read last week said: 'I don't think that any girl can like me.'

"I wrote that the same evening after Rachel flirted with me. And I didn't notice, possibly because I was putting too much pressure on myself."

He skipped down a paragraph or two.

*I wonder if Michael, John or Jeff like girls other than their girlfriends? If they do then I would too and I'm not ready to date. And if they don't, they are probably mature enough to be married.*

Michael dated Judy, John dated Janice, and Jeff dated Laurie. Of course, Michael and Judy broke up right after this trip, John and Janice married then divorced, and Jeff married Sue. Douglas knew this was a possibility at the time but wasn't interested. He felt like he had to consistently like only one girl before he even started dating her. He had to make a perfect choice immediately. That had to do with Gothard's idea of courting, but that was too long a story to discuss with Sherry right now. He'd have to get to who Bill Gothard was later.

Still, Douglas's ideal romance in '75 may have been unhealthy even for a teen. Too much pressure. It was ironic that he had these ideas in his head while his own romance with Leanne was just developing. Leanne had just split up with Randy, though Douglas didn't know that yet, and she had her eyes on him.

"Literally," added Douglas. "But I haven't gotten to that part of the story yet; more on that next week. Right now I want to swing back to my relationship to the church leaders to talk about the two things that didn't happen on the trip up."

"That didn't happen?" queried Sherry.

"Yeah," Douglas confirmed. "Things that didn't happen, which was odd because they usually *did* happen. I mentioned the first already—the bus did not break down. But I glossed over how I felt about it in '75. What did I say again? Uhhh . . . I felt guilty that I was happy not to be called up front to pray for the bus, awkward phrasing, that."

Sherry glanced through her notes. "Right. I was going to ask you about that last week but decided to let you keep going. What were you trying to say?"

"Several things.

"First, I know it's probably anthropomorphic to pray for the bus, but I didn't really think anything about it at the time. If God's going to be acting in your life, it might as well be for one thing as for another, buses included.

"Still, part of me was annoyed on the one hand that my church simply didn't solve the problem by buying a new bus. They'd just bought a honking chunk of property out in Rancho Pedro, and you're telling me they didn't have enough money for a new bus? Rancho Pedro?"

"Remember, I can't criticize the adults (more on that later, but let's continue with this story first); so on the other hand, another part of me felt pressured. I couldn't just be a teenager out having fun. I was supposed to be . . . a pastor-in-training, an acolyte. And I got tired of being Mr. Spiritual."

"So I was glad not to have to play the part for a change. But on the third hand, the expectations to be Mr. Spiritual were just so high that I felt guilty I wasn't going to cut it this time around. I wasn't going to pray for the bus. I was going to just chat with friends. Very proletarian, you know. Not the type of things a super spiritual high school president should be doing. At the very least, I could memorize more scripture or something."

"That's three hands," Sherry commented. "How did you manage that?"

"I cloned myself," grinned Douglas, "then killed my clone (after all, it's my own body, right?) then stitched the third hand into my side. Can't you see it? I keep the rest of the body parts in my freezer just in case. No rejection problems neither."

Sherry smiled back, "You said there were two things that didn't happen. What was the other?"

"Right. Pastor Dan wasn't reading and memorizing scripture while driving the bus."

"Excuse me?" Sherry was startled.

"You gotta remember that we're all supposed to have scripture memorized or we can't eat. Right? Well, that rule applied to the guy who made it—Pastor Dan. But PD had lots of other responsibilities too; he is, after all, the model Mr. Super Spiritual, and he was constantly running out of time. So he'd read and memorize his section of scripture while driving the bus. One of my responsibilities was to be the guy that heard him recite scripture and clear him to eat lunch."

"What joy!" Douglas added. "I seem to be saying that a lot these days."

"Wow!" said Sherry.

"Yeah. Not sure how distracted driving makes someone more spiritual. I was always worrying that PD'd have an accident while I'm there helping him to be even more spiritual, that'd be kinda silly, you know, but that's only part of what caused his accident later on."

"What!?"

"Aargh!" Douglas grimaced. "PD caused a bus accident after I left high school. But there's simply too much to talk about and I want to get back to the trip, if that's OK. I feel like I'm off track."

"Certainly."

"We're talking about things that did not happen, weird as that may be. PD did not memorize scripture while driving up to Ramble Free because it was really Ramble Free's event, not ours. We were invited guests so Rabbi PD (Or is that Mullah PD?) hair-split that since it wasn't our event, no one had to memorize scripture. Besides, it was only a one-day event, up and back."

He shrugged. "That was just so much sophistry, if you ask me. Either you're gonna memorize scripture every trip or you don't. All the time means all the time. But I was just the leader. Pisses me off. They had

'God's law' down pat. But had no clue of 'God's mercy'; everything in the Old Testament and nothing in the New."

Douglas added, "I was starting to feel the hypocrisy." He paused and glanced at the clock.

Sherry did the same and summarized the session. "There was little or no flexibility at your church. You felt like you had to be perfect with women in advance of dating, and you felt like you had to be perfect with the church leaders before becoming one. Assuming you wanted to be one."

"Yeah. Thanks!" said Douglas. Then he added, "I wrote Jacky something about perfection that evening in '75. I'll find it eventually, but we're out of time for now, aren't we?"

"Correct," Sherry confirmed. "We can continue next week."

Douglas said good-bye and all too soon it was time to loop around the rest of the mall. Traffic was never too bad but it was still a pain to get to work.

*November 20, 2002, in session*

Douglas was typically at least 5 minutes late everywhere and today's appointment with Sherry was no different. But he finally got there and still felt uncomfortable.

"I feel out-of-sorts," he started. "I usually start by talking about last week's story and tell a new one last. Every week. But there's more to last week's story to tell."

"Why not just reverse the pattern?" Sherry queried.

It was the obvious solution, but it felt difficult. Douglas liked doing things the same way every week not just because it was a security blanket, but because it freed mental resources to do something more interesting.

"I can try," he said doubtfully.

"Why not?" challenged Sherry. Douglas thought about explaining but decided it wasn't worth the effort. Besides, finding new patterns was one reason he was there, especially since the last patterns he'd tried had dead ends, almost literally. So . . . why not?

"Yeah," Douglas said. "I was gonna talk about the trip back the next day." He settled down and started telling the story.

"I kept looking at Lee on the way back from Ramble Free . . ."

. . . Doug was trying to understand why Leanne would go with Randy when she knew her dad could move to D.C. Finally, Leanne let Douglas stare directly into her eyes for 5 or 10 seconds. He felt that eyes tell a lot about the person and soon discovered that her eyes were phenomenal.

He didn't even notice her face, just her eyes. They were deep and real. Douglas saw her as a strong and wonderful individual. She was aware that she was alive. Looking at her dark brown eyes convinced him that she liked Randy in particular, and admired the characteristics Randy had. ("Silly me," said Douglas to Sherry, "but yeah, that's what I was thinking back then.")

Douglas thought he could tell she was a Christian. He could see the quiet peace and joy in her. She was wise and her eyes were loving, kind, compassionate, and deep. The deepest part was in her white spot. It felt mystical.

Randy was unimpressed when Douglas told him and pointed out that it was just light reflecting. Douglas told him that was no doubt true, but added that he thought it was more than that. Douglas couldn't stop look at her eyes; they were beautiful. "I can see them still now," he added to Sherry.

Douglas finally apologized to Leanne because he felt so rude.

"I still feel troubled about it," Douglas ended. "At the time, it was clear that Leanne was Randy's girl and I was just a friend. Lee told me later that she'd decided to break up with Randy by then, but it still felt like I was cutting in, which I didn't really want to do. I had no idea then, and still find it lovely now, that looking into someone's eyes can be that powerful."

"I wrote Jacky about it that evening—not about the eyes but I riffed off individuality." Douglas pulled out the appropriate letter.

*April 15, 1975, at home*
*Dear Jacky,*

*Are individuals important? If God loves all of us equally, then does any one person matter? If I seek to become better in God's eyes, then do those people who aren't better in God's eyes lose their importance? If society never changes, the individual is lost and faceless. But an individual rarely changes the group. I can't do what I want to do. And no matter what, the individual is lost.*

*Some individuals are never happy being ruled. But if you don't require that, then the group loses. No matter what you do, someone is going to end up being unhappy.*
*Love,*
*Douglas*

"What were you driving at?" Sherry asked.

Douglas struggled to find the right words. "I remember feeling unhappy and trapped when I wrote that," Douglas finally said. "'Some individuals are never happy being ruled.' Well, maybe Pastor Jeff can be, he ran cross-country and track with me in high school and by coincidence he's now the pastor at our soon-to-be-ex-church. Got a long list of those. But never mind.

"Anne told me the other day that Jeff lives in a meringue tower, all sweetness and light. My own towers are iron and stone, maybe something like Notre Dame.

"But in high school it felt like I was supposed to live in the same meringue towers as Jeff and that didn't make sense. 'I can't do what I want to do,' to quote from my letter to Jacky again. Chapter 7 of Paul's Epistle to the Romans was probably in the back of my head."

Douglas leaned back and quoted the verses verbatim from memory.

> *19 For the good that I would I do not: but the evil, which I would not, that I do.*
> *20 Now if I do that I would not, it is no more I that do it, but sin that dwelleth in me.*

"My feelings went past St. Paul's angst," Douglas added. "There was so much pressure to conform. If I saw that something was wrong with the church fair, was it really sin that 'dwelleth in me' if I said so? But I didn't feel like I could express my doubts directly, even to Jacky, so I obfuscated."

He continued. "The constant pressure for perfection felt like a . . . I can't find the right word here . . . a girdle? A corset? A straightjacket? Too restrictive."

"Very much so," Sherry agreed. "But why did you feel that you had to be perfect?"

Douglas waved his hands, trying to find words. "It's back to memorizing Bible verses. You had to be perfect or you couldn't eat. Lots of negative reinforcement there, but PD thought it was biblical, as if everything had to be, but never mind. 'Be ye therefore perfect, even as your Father which is in heaven is perfect' which is in Mathew 5, if I remember correctly."

Again, He quoted the verse, perfectly, word-for-word in the King James version, without hesitation. But he certainly didn't feel like a pillar of the spiritual community. He'd seen too much life to see it through rose-colored glasses. I, he thought to himself, will never be Jeff.

Sherry glanced at the clock. "And that's all the time we have for today."

Douglas was annoyed. "Grr," he groused. "I'm not done talking about the letter."

But Sherry was adamant. "It'll just have to wait for next week."

Douglas muttered under his breath, but that was the end of the session.

# Training

Douglas felt embarrassed every time he walked up the stairs to Sherry's office. There was no reason for it but he still felt out of place. Everyone else he saw probably worked there and he felt like an intruder. But no one arrested him for trespassing or called the police. It was just his normal paranoia—not something he enjoyed, but it was much easier to deal with than depression. As long as no one was pulling out a gun and shooting at you, you were probably fine. And if that were the case, find cover.

The usual paranoia was small. But the depression was dragging at him, the hooded demon pulling him down. The meds helped a lot but he had nasty migraines at the larger dose he needed. The doc was trying to find a workaround but nothing had come up yet. Time to focus on therapy, not drugs.

Another unremarkable day.

Douglas slumped down in his usual seat and got started.

"Where were we last week?" he asked.

"Talking about perfection. You talked about memorizing the Bible word-for-word."

"Right." But Douglas felt dissatisfied with that paradigm. "I need a better example than memorizing Bible verses perfectly," he said out loud. "Or maybe 'perfection' isn't the right word."

The word he wanted was "valued" not "perfect." Douglas hadn't felt valued by his church because only the veneer of perfection was valued. Instead, the Church's mores reminded him of how the Soviet Union handled protest. The Soviets often put dissenters into insane asylums because communism was perfect. If you criticized the State then you must be insane.

The same logic applied to Lands Baptist. The church leaders were holy and their plan to guide you was sent by God. So if you disagreed with their plan, then you were sinful.

But thinking this is one thing, putting words on your tongue is another issue altogether, then or now.

52

So Douglas stared outside the window, looking for words. Today's sky was overcast with nary a sketch of blue in sight. Douglas's rule-of-thumb was "Gray outside, gray inside." The dullness made it easy for happiness to escape him, although he thought he'd settle for mental well-being.

Unfortunately, the words escaped him, too. Sherry left him alone for a moment then called him back. "Can you think of a better example?"

"Yeah. I think so," Douglas's consciousness came back into the room. "A few months back, my wife Anne joined a women's group at church to help produce a play. She looked at the script, which was just awful (I had the mis-pleasure of looking at it myself after Anne came home) and she made the mistake of asking the group, 'Who wrote this crap?'

"Not the most diplomatic thing to say, mind you, but that doesn't justify what happened next. Anne took it upon herself to at least correct the spelling and grammar then edit some of the worst places, without changing a word of the treacly message—just basic clean up.

"But when Anne got part way into it, word got around to the group leader about what Anne was doing and the proverbial fecal matter hit the AMD."

"The what?" queried Sherry. Douglas's mind routinely bounced here and there.

"The AMD," Douglas explained. "Air-moving device. It's a faux-tech acronym for a computer 'fan' so the manufacturer can justify jacking up the price. The fecal matter hit the AMD."

"Ah," said Sherry. "What happened next?"

"The leader (PD's wife Ellen, but how she got there is yet another long story, so let's not go there) called Anne and started screaming at her. And I do mean screaming. I know because I was in the next room and could hear both sides of the conversation. Or rather, both sides of the scream fest.

"Ellen's gist, if you eliminate the fundamentalist equivalent of swear words, was: 'How dare you change the words of godly women?' alternated with 'WHAT KIND OF A REBELLIOUS DISOBEDIENT WOMAN ARE YOU?' For 30 minutes.

"Bear in mind that the authors weren't church members. Nor had they copyrighted their doggerel. Also bear in mind that Anne wasn't changing the semantic meaning, just cleaning up the grammar, spelling and syntax. Nevertheless, Ellen spent half an hour on the phone screaming at my wife."

The steam was still visible on Douglas's face and he took a slow breath.

"I empathize with Cain, my Apeman ancestor, 'Attack my mate, will you?' But never mind."

"I'm not sure why Ellen didn't have more important things to do, but never mind that, too. Apparently, it's OK for church leaders to scream at you," he continued, "but not for you to scream at them. Never could figure that out but never mind that three–the point."

He took another breath and tried to slow down.

"You can't criticize church leaders like Ellen or the 'godly' authors of a women's play. To criticize implies their words are less than perfect or godly.

"Let's assume, arguendo," Douglas continued, "that they were in fact godly women. Even if so then they were godly women who couldn't write. They're contracting their minds, not stretching them. Godliness does not equate to talent in general and to writing talent in particular. The concepts are orthogonal."

Sherry added another thought in agreement. "Nor does godliness equate to authority and vice versa. The people up at the top can and do make mistakes, sometimes bad ones."

The session ended there. Maybe there was a little blue in the sky after all.

*December 4, 2002, in session*

Sherry's brown and gold conservative skirt and blouse reminded Douglas of earth tones, but Sherry herself was airy light, not heavy like the earth.

"Hello," he said.

Sherry's smile was friendly, "Hello again. How are you today?"

"Well, that's what we'll find out, isn't it?" Douglas responded with a smile of his own. "Let's pick up where we left off with that last letter I wrote Jacky, April 15, 1975, though I wasn't much of a writer back then."

"Go on," Sherry said.

The very old paper in Douglas's hands crackled until he found the right place. He read it out loud.

> *"'An individual abides by government rule, but in doing so he is denying his own ideals and his will, losing his freedom.'"*

"Writing about freedom was a response to feeling too restricted by the search for perfection," Douglas explained. "I was probably thinking of Janis Joplin singing "Me and Bobby McGee." 'Freedom's just another word for nothin' left to lose.' Nothing. I was gradually gaining the freedom of an adult, but it left me feeling empty. And you can't just decide not to become an adult. Peter Pan isn't for me."

"It's easy to think that the moral of Janis's life is 'Duh. Another dumb rock star ODs on heroin,'" Douglas added. "But it's not that simple. She created something new in her lifetime. I'm not sure how to put it." Douglas's words were leaving him again. "She opened a door no one else had seen, smiled, and walked through."

Douglas's life up to the early 1970s had been drenched in a purportedly normal but rigid conventionality within a highly religious church still protectively based in the 1950s. Discovering rock music from the late 1960s had added to his love of Bach organ music and Beethoven piano sonatas, not replaced it. The revelation convinced him there were alternatives. His church's view of music, if nothing else, was too narrow.

"So somewhere in the early '70s I found myself thinking: am I creating something new myself? Am I stretching out to new possibilities? Am I opening new doors? Am I helping people to expand their view and to see things differently? Does my church facilitate my desire to create or hinder it?

"This is the first time that my writing hints, even indirectly, that the answer to that last question is 'No.' And that happened because I looked into Leanne's eyes. How my relationship with the Church changed is intertwined with how my relationship with women changed. Lee was there both to watch and catalyze."

Douglas sighed then added, "I probably would have missed that if you hadn't pointed out those two themes a few sessions ago. So thanks!"

Sherry smiled. "You're welcome. We have time for another story if you keep it short."

"OK. The day after I got back from the Ramble Free Faire, April 16, 1975, my sister almost died in an auto accident. Truth be told, she really should have died."

"Go on," said Sherry. "I used to work in ER before becoming a therapist."

Douglas was in the school library prepping to tutor his college calculus students when Mrs. N stopped by and told him that Rose had just been in an auto accident. He looked up from his notes, said, "Thanks!" then made plans to tell his calculus students that he'd be out today. Rose got into lots of accidents as a kid, so he didn't think much of it at first.

He got lost on the way to the hospital and arrived during the first operation. It was at the reception desk when he first learned of the seriousness of the accident. Douglas had expected to hear a simple room number then he'd go in to see her with at worst a broken leg. He'd tease her a bit (what are little brothers for, anyway?) then drive back to help out with the rest of class.

Instead, the nurse glanced up and said, "Intensive Care. Immediate family and chaplains only." Well, that was still Douglas, so he found the elevator and punched the number for the right floor. He was getting nervous.

As luck would have it, the first person he saw was her doctor. The prognosis was bad. It'd been a head-on collision and Rose hit the steering wheel with no airbag. The immediate danger was that she'd die of heart failure, but her fractured trachea meant the doctors didn't know how to give anesthesia.

Eric, Rose's fiancé, showed up during the conversation and was more optimistic. Douglas wasn't so convinced, especially when the next person to show up with Pastor M, the lead pastor of Lands Baptist.

Pastor M wasn't called in except in near-death cases. This was one of them. Then Pastor M shocked Douglas by admitting that he'd anointed Rose with oil then performed the laying on of hands. That was much more Pentecostal than Baptist, but it made sense when he remembered the section of the Bible that described the behavior. Pastor M hadn't prayed for a miracle; he simply followed a biblical ritual.

But the whole affair started to feel surrealistic. He felt so emotionless, not realizing he was still in shock himself. 'Am I alive?' Douglas asked himself. 'If Rose died, would I care? Can I answer any question? Reality! What is Real?'

"Time's up!" Sherry called. Douglas startled then laughed. He'd been in shock over Rose's accident and now Sherry's notification was yet another shock. The situation felt ludicrous. But the session was still over, there'd be another session next week.

∽♪∾∽♪∾∽♪∾

*April 17, 1975, at home*

*Dear Jacky,*

Rose survived a second operation last night, but she sure does look messed up. She's on an I.V., an EKG, a tube down her nose, a tracheotomy, and an air pump through her tracheotomy. She's got 6 inches of steel in her arm, stitches in her face, a broken jaw, wired cheeks with steel plates, and a bandage on her thigh where they took a tendon graft for her arm. Her heart and lungs are still bruised. Otherwise, she's OK.

I mean she'll probably live. I think.

Is this really happening to me? It doesn't seem like it. Besides, I've been thinking a lot about reality, and now I have a chance myself to

experience alternate realities. Right now, I'm here in the library just writing, wishing I were at home instead waiting for the phone to ring with mom and dad at the other end, telling how me Rose is. What is real?
*Love,*
*Douglas Baign*

~~~⬦⬦⬦~~~

*December 11, 2002, in session*

He deliberately drove an alternate route to Sherry's office so that he could swing by the scene of the accident on Camino del Plata. The concrete barrier had been built courtesy of a lawsuit: *Rose Baign v. the City of Santa Brisa.* His sister had been speeding, but the city was declared half at fault because the road shoulders lacked the barrier. It's still a dangerous, hilly curve.

Rose's accident was still on Douglas's mind.

"My sister is one of the few people I trust." As he occasionally did, Douglas opened the session without preamble. "And Rose was in ICU for another week.

"That entire week was dreamlike, very peculiar. Friends, relatives or pastors would show up at the right time, right place without even knowing what was going on. People I hadn't seen in years showed up at the hospital to ask me, 'What's happening? I felt like I needed to come.'

"It was a religious experience, we literally willed Rose back to life. It was very surreal. But then a touch or a hug would come from nowhere and reach me.

"In the meantime, I just wandered through the hospital in a bemused haze."

"Hello," said Sherry. "It's good to see you, too." Douglas laughed.

"Sorry," he said. "It's just that I'm just now realizing that I didn't properly deal with my sister's . . . almost death, I guess you could call it. The incident was very upsetting to me. And hello."

"Hello," said Sherry again. She wanted to slow things down a bit. "I gather that you're still thinking about your sister's auto accident."

"Yes. But I didn't feel like I could talk to anyone about it, much less Leanne. I still had to be Mr. Spiritual, who wasn't affected by a sister trying very hard not to die—and succeeding, thank God. Asking Leanne for a date was on the outside of my walls. Worry about my sister was on the inside.

"Maybe it strikes you as obvious," Douglas added, "but to me it's a revelation. Rose was and, fortunately, still is one of the few people who can get behind my walls. And I almost lost her. Asking Leanne for a date was one way to fill the void. It was time for me to grow and change. Rose's accident and dating Leanne forced me to stretch.

"But it was a very dizzy week. Rose almost died twice more. But at the end of the week, my musical sister put a finger over her tracheotomy and sang.

"I knew at that moment she would live. Twenty-seven years later, Rose sings at weddings and directs her church choir, and every moment for her is in pain."

Sherry smiled. "It sounds like you love your sister very much."

"You betcha. Yes, oh yes. I love Rose dearly."

"Good. And you've connected Rose to Leanne."

"Yes."

"Do you want to talk about Rose more? Or Leanne? We've got plenty of time left over."

Douglas stared outside again. It was one of those lovely December days that Santa Brisa can get—warm with a gentle breeze. A perfect day, even in December, for the beach, which he avoided because the crowd noise made him feel hunted. The beach at night was an escape, quiet and cool.

"No," he finally said. "I don't want to talk about Rose or Leanne right now. The only thing that I can think of to add, at least for now, is that if Rose had been Jeff's sister, not mine, he probably would have dragged out his Bible and started preaching to her nurses."

The sarcasm was clear. But the pause had gotten Sherry and Douglas back onto the same page. "OK," said Sherry. "What do you want to talk about?"

"The order of events, just to get my head straight. Sometimes it's really confusing to even remember which maze I'm in." Douglas's last statement wasn't that serious, but he did find the process befuddling.

"All right," said Sherry. "Last I knew we were still talking about the events of April and May of 1975."

"Right. If I've got my timeline straight, these events occurred on consecutive weekends:

1.  "I attend the Ramble Free Faire on Sunday, April 13, 1975. Rose has her accident on Monday, April 14.
2.  "There's a church high school 50-mile bike ride on April 19.
3.  "Rose gets out of intensive care on April 20. I visited Rose every day that week.
4.  "I argued with PD on April 27. That's probably why I eventually left that church.
5.  "PD and the high school group leaves for the bike trip without me on May 4.

"I ran a race on Saturday, May 10, and asked Leanne out that Sunday, May 11, 1975.

"Those events were soon followed by two dates with Lee in late May, then I graduated from Hosanna High on June 16. I'm probably missing a few things. Anyway, there I am just about to start racing away from the Church and everything just explodes on me. Talk about mind-stretching—a very busy time frame."

"I dare say," Sherry responded. "If you're done with Rose," she continued, "did you want to talk about the first bike ride? That's the next event on that calendar."

"How much time do I have?"

Sherry glanced at the clock, "About 5 minutes."

Douglas nodded, "Yeah, I can keep it short.

"PD scheduled the church high school group for a 350-mile one-week bike ride, ending May 11. That's 50 miles a day, so PD made a preliminary 50-mile one-day bike ride in advance. You had to do the 50 miles in less than six hours to qualify for the longer ride. Made sense for a change.

"Remember, I'm the high school president so PD expected me to attend both bike trips and either be one of the best riders or to shepherd folks around, preferably both, I might add. Ever try to be the best in front while being the shepherd in the back? But never mind.

"I had no problem on the 50-mile. I placed third overall while spending the first 25 miles in the back of the pack encouraging folks along. But the 350-mile trip was over the same weekend as a big track meet, and my track coach was fairly insistent I attend. PD was insistent I go biking.

"That's what led to the argument with PD a week later."

"And that's a good place to stop," Sherry said. "We can pick up with the argument next week."

It had been a productive session. Douglas had dealt more with Rose's accident and sorted out an order of events. Off to work he went.

Douglas took the long route back home after work that day. Yup, he reassured himself. The concrete barrier on Camino del Plata was still there. Fortunately, so was Rose.

# Revising the Plan

*December 18, 2002, in session*

Douglas made sure to say, "Hello" to Sherry before he launched the next session. It was easier to talk now, but sometimes it was too easy. Knowing when to start can be as important as knowing when to stop.

"Can we change our planned topic?" he asked. "I was going to talk about arguing with PD, but that could take several sessions and it's getting close to Christmas."

"Sure. Why not?" Sherry was amenable to nearly anything. "You're in control."

"I wish," Douglas responded, "but it's getting better now."

"I agree. You're improving. What did you want to talk about today?"

"Junior high. It's a gap in my head anyway, plus it's probably short enough to fit into one session. Then we can start the new year talking about PD and I'll have as much time as I need."

"Makes sense," said Sherry. "Tell me about junior high." She glanced at her notes. "You were at Lincoln, correct?"

"Right." He shifted position and began the story.

"Anne was cleaning out the garage one day in 1999 or so and ran into my old junior high yearbook. We were curious about what was in it so glanced through it. Let's hear it for Lincoln! Remembering them helps me to see things differently."

Douglas's classmates' yearbook comments fell into four categories.

- "See you next year," or if they knew Douglas was attending Hosanna, "Good-bye."
- "I love/hate/am not sure about your puns in class," as most of Douglas's puns were very bad. But the consensus comment was Randy's, he who dated Leanne three years later, "Keep up your semi-funny jokes and be sure not to forget to tell me when to laugh." Even Douglas's bad jokes broke up the monotony.
- "You're a good actor."
- "You're a math wiz."

Douglas kept roughly three groups of friends in 1972.

- His peers at Lands Baptist, who saw each other about twice a week and were very conservative.
- The drama club at school (artsy and very liberal).
- The chess club at school (nerds, before nerds were 'in').

It wasn't until later that he saw this in context. There was an art/science split, a religious/secular split, and a conservative/liberal split, quite a diversity. Douglas didn't care. He just went from one to the other to the next because that's what he was interested in. His church, of course, saw it otherwise. Science was atheistic humanism. Art was corrupted and possibly demonic. He quoted from a letter to Jacky in response:

*The object of all psychotherapy is synthesis, my dearest Jacky. The object now is to synthesize and love all the parts of me once more again.*

"The older I got, the more I synthesized. By 9th grade, I wondered why the chess club wasn't as much fun as drama, then I'd go to church and wonder why they weren't as rigorous as the chess club. Then I'd practice my acting while puzzling over why the troupe just didn't seem to have the morals of the Church.

"What is actual synthesis in junior high or high school can be taken as rebellion, especially at Lands Baptist. It wasn't. It's just that I antagonized everyone equally simply by being myself." Douglas wasn't bitter about it. He just said it.

Folks often gravitate toward a specific field. Douglas gravitated towards integrating multiple fields. That was unusual, but the result was that, unless someone knew him well, he felt like he constantly disappointed specialists who tried to mentor him in their respective fields. A specialist, he thought, is someone who can custom-build a super-duper spark plug without knowing how to drive a car, or even what it's used for. What's the point?

He continued his story.

Douglas's memory of Hosanna High is of a beautiful dream. Three years of walking on air, a thriving desert full of color, bending, flashing. Just thinking of it brought back the girls in long dresses, the stone wall where he ate lunch and played chess, teachers who cared and helped. He ran cross-country through magical woods, then ran track during the heat of spring. Douglas knew all of his 63 classmates by name.

Douglas' school was special, it was beautiful, it was a miracle, and it was his. Hosanna High is an insanely fabulous memory.

But there was a small part of him that wondered: what if? Going there had been one of his earliest decisions. Douglas's mom and dad asked him if he really wanted to switch, they knew it meant a break in his educational continuum. Would he be OK with that?

Douglas talked with his friends at Lincoln. Karen Jefferson in the Bible Club thought he belonged in a public school where he could be a Christian witness. Being in a public school can be an advantage. Maybe Douglas had a better sense of his Christianity and perhaps more commitment to it. There was plenty of opportunity to trip out, even for a 9th grader. He was offered drugs, sex, alcohol, and Independent Baptist that he was, he just wasn't interested.

Douglas looked up from his memories.

"But heck, Sherry. I admit it. Rock-and-roll is dynamite! Rose played it behind mom's back (despite our church smashing as many rock LP's as they could buy, and no, I'm not kidding), and I somehow managed to listen to The Doors without losing my immortal soul. I liked The Doors. Still do, actually."

He felt like he was confessing a guilty sin to the priest, hoping for absolution. Sherry just nodded and asked him to continue.

His parents wanted him at Hosanna. Douglas thought about it some and told his parents, "Yes." He couldn't see much difference at the time, little did he know, and he wanted to please his mom and dad. Besides, he'd still see his church friends at Hosanna, so it didn't seem like much of a switch.

But it was.

Douglas lost part of his heart and gained another. He gained a spirit and lost a head. There was more of him at Lincoln than he realized at the time. Friends he knew, relationships he developed, names and faces he remembered and lost. Karen Jefferson, Saul Bardo, Ron Spear, Brenda Mudd, John Table, John County, Cheryl Mercedes, Margo Norringer, Jean Lorne, John Tramer, Thomas Vanderbuild, Julie Spark, Pedro Rodriquez—all of them are gone to him.

Maybe Douglas had a better sense of himself in junior high than in high school. He knew the things he liked and nourished them: puns, math, social studies, music and drama. He listened to J. S. Bach and Simon and Garfunkel with equal fervor and fell in love with Karen Carpenter. He collected coins and joined the chess club and got pretty good at it.

Douglas's awareness returned to Sherry's office. The ceiling and walls were still white, but he was secretly glad to see that the walls weren't padded and the door would open at his touch. There was a simple rose in a vase next to him and he smiled at how something so small gave him so much pleasure.

"I was painfully unprepared when I went to UCSB after graduating from Hosanna," he told Sherry. "It's 100 percent humanist!" I panted heavily to one of my friends. Well, that's a shock. So is most of the rest of this planet, but I was young and quite stunned to see the hedonism.

"And I had forgotten my lessons from Lincoln. You can live in this world and still be a Christian. Heck, Jesus did it for 33 years or thereabouts.

"If I had gone to Coolidge High instead of Hosanna High, what would I have gained and lost? I think Karen Jefferson at Coolidge might have been right. Maybe my Christian ministry was there."

*January 8, 2003, at home*

*Dear Jacky,*

Well, here I am again. What a Christmas! I dropped a mondo kidney stone over the holiday, which is a heck of a way to spend it. There I was, writhing on the bathroom floor screaming my head off while trying to make sure I got Anne the right Christmas present.

YAAAAAAA!

Should I have gotten her the purse or the dulcimer earrings?

YAAAAAAA!!!!

You can die from this. That kidney shut down and urine started backing up. Fortunately, I got on the priority list for 'shockwave' surgery (and I still waited a week on priority!) and after two more painful weeks of dribbling pieces I finally got rid of it all. Three freaking weeks on pain meds and on the bathroom floor.

Yeah, the perils of being 45. I threatened Anne that I'd superglue the last stone I passed, rather a large one, onto a 3x5 card, punch a hook through it and turn it into a Christmas tree ornament, "Christmas, 2002"

. . .

Oh, God, it hurt. Hear my prayer.

It hurts to talk about Leanne, too, you know, but I started thinking about it. Is talking to Sherry as painful as passing a kidney stone? And I decided that . . . yeah, it is.

But if I dealt with the kidney stone, then I can deal with Leanne. Actually, I have more control here than over the kidney stone. Hey, there are some advantages to being 45. Maybe I'm emotionally stronger.

Ah, well. Time for bed. And to be honest, sleep sounds good right about now.

I love you very much, Jacky. Thank you just for being here to listen to me.

*Love,*
*Douglas*

*January 9, 2003, in session*

A painful kidney stone meant a missed appointment but gave him more strength to talk to Sherry about painful events.

"Shall we get started?" Sherry checked her notes. "You were going to talk about the argument with PD."

Douglas gathered the courage to disagree, "I'm not sure that's the best thing to talk about."

"Why not?" Sherry was curious, not critical.

"Because I get stuck whenever I try to think about that argument. Besides, it was really only the culmination of a long series of events with my church, my old church. I mean, dating back at least to junior high. I just can't get rational enough to deal with the whole nine yards."

"You don't have to deal with the whole nine yards. Just pick one," Sherry pointed out.

"Yeah, yeah. I know," he growled. "But it keeps coming out that way. My head says one thing and my gut says another. I guess therapy is partly about moving thoughts from one place to the other."

"True," said Sherry, "so if you're not going to talk about arguing with PD, what are you going to talk about?"

"I thought about that while dribbling kidney stones—lots of time on my hands. The general question about arguing with PD is 'Why did I leave the Church?' At first that seemed like an easy question; just make a (long) list." Douglas dug out his notebook and pulled out the appropriate page. "It came out something like this."

- Repeating Bible stories. Repeating Bible stories. Repeating Bible stories. Learning that, 'Mary was a virgin when Jesus was born' again and again and again—29 times, even. I wonder: what is the max # of times that Mary can be a virgin? Focuses on PD.
- Mom and dad as art and science teachers, asking open-ended questions vs. close-ended Bible studies. See repeating Bible stories.
- Gothard's Basic Youth Conflicts. See close-ended. Taught authority-driven Christianity without compassion, which I couldn't accept when I kept asking questions, especially open-ended ones.
- Church more interested in defending their idea of the faith rather than helping individuals, but their faith isn't necessarily the Bible's. See also Basic Youth Conflicts.

"What's Basic Youth Conflicts?" asked Sherry. "And how does it relate to your mom and dad?"

Douglas didn't directly answer, "Yeah, they're all intertwined. It's like you have to grow up in the Church to understand it all, and I certainly wouldn't wish that on you."

He continued, "So I don't exactly know how it all relates to mom and dad. I do know the list doesn't give you the feel of it. It's bloodless. Events didn't happen one at a time, they splatted on top of me.

"So the question of why I left the Church is much more difficult to answer than I realized. There's this whole smoosh of emotions down in my gut. It feels like a tangled ball of string. And the ball's so big that it blocks the cooling ducts and fries my head in anger.

"I just can't seem to detach enough to talk, or at least, be detached enough to talk in therapy. Screaming I can do. The idiots!" Douglas's disgust was plain. "If I can't talk about the ending, then talking about the beginning and everything in between will take a ton of explaining."

Sherry smiled. "It's not exactly as if I'm doing anything else. That's what I'm here for."

"For which I'm eternally grateful, which reminds me. How is it that you can sit and listen to clients whine for six to eight hours a day anyway? That doesn't make any sense to me. Not that I'm complaining, mind you."

"How is that you can sit in front of a computer screen six to eight hours a day and take notes?" Sherry responded. "That doesn't make any sense to me either." She was unapologetic.

Douglas laughed. "Fair question. Well, if it's all the same to you, let's start with birth. Most important day of my life and I don't remember a thing about it," he joked. "But anyway, leaving the Church will make more sense if I talk about what it was that I left. It's quite the mess down there."

Therapy is like organizing the dirty kitchen in a restaurant. You don't have the slightest idea as to what's going on when you first gather the courage to step into your own crazed mind. It's messy and complete chaos. It's all you can do to recognize the order tickets and a stack of dishes needing to be washed.

Humor the analogy.

- Order tickets are what computer geeks call a FIFO queue. The First ticket In is the First ticket Out.
- The dishes are a LIFO stack, the Last dish placed In the stack is the First dish washed Out.

Sherry started her end of therapy by taking Douglas through a queue. "Tell me about the first girl you knew, tell me about the second."

Therapy on Douglas's end started not by understanding the significance of this girl or that, but by realizing that the queue was there to begin with. There was order where he thought there was chaos. There was an approach he could take to make things better.

Problems are like a LIFO stack of dirty dishes. You clank new problems on top of old ones and you can't deal with the grunge at the bottom until you wash the dish on top. The analogy isn't exact, but getting better gave him the energy to buy a new dishwasher and split the stack of problems into two. Any new dirty dishes went into the dishwater to be washed automatically. Douglas didn't have to pay too much attention to it.

That in turn gave him more time and energy to deal with the original yuck. But where to start? In one sense, it doesn't matter. Just pick a problem and deal with it like washing any old dirty dish. Stacks can be convenient that way because it's easy to grab something below the top. But in this case, Douglas had moved one problem, arguing with PD, only to discover a bunch more underneath; among them, the angst and sense of abandonment while growing up in a fundamentalist church.

It would take Douglas many sessions to discuss the grunge he found underneath when he picked up the emotional and psychological rock.

# More Training

*January 16, 2003*

Douglas' old church is insular.

1.  His mother (Annette Baign, née Schneider) was dedicated to the Lord (the church didn't have infant baptism) at Lands Baptist in May 1932, not that Douglas remembered that far back.
2.  Annette Schneider married Bill Baign at Lands Baptist in June 1951 at the age of 19. Bill was 18.
3.  Annette Baign's Memorial Service was at Lands Baptist in May 1987, an event that Douglas remembered all too well.

Between items #2 and #3, Annette Baign gave birth to Douglas in 1957. She was 25, Bill was 24. Pastor M held Douglas in his arms at church two weeks later and dedicated *him* to the Lord. Douglas still had the service of dedication memorial program.

> *Minister*: Recognizing the dignity and responsibility of parenthood and of your dependence upon divine help for strength and wisdom to faithfully discharge the duties of parents, do you now present your child Douglas Baign in dedication to God, seeking divine blessing and guidance for his life?
>
> *Parents:* We do.
>
> *Minister:* Having thus purposed in your hearts, do you in the presence of these witnesses solemnly covenant to strive, by precept and example, and using the many agencies of the church to train your child Douglas Baign in love toward God and in knowledge of His Son Jesus Christ our Lord
>
> *Parents:* We do.
>
> *Minister*: Having heard these vows and sacred assurances, as a minister of Christ, I joyously and with earnest prayer, commend your child Douglas Baign to the gracious keeping of God, our Heavenly Father. Tell him early of the covenant and the prayers made this day in his behalf.

Years later, his father told Douglas that he screamed his head off. Ah, well, such are babies. Douglas could just barely remember being a toddler in the church nursery, perhaps late in 1960, watching a newborn kid, Richard Masters, age 0, being brought in. He saw Richard nearly every Sunday after that for the next 18 years. They grew up together, became friends.

"Let's be honest," Douglas told Sherry that session, "I miss Richard and other friends and in fact part of me misses the whole church. Another part of me wonders why I'm not stark raving mad just from being there 19 years. Puke! My baby dedication was a covenant. Did everyone keep their bargain or would I have been better off if they hadn't?"

Douglas wasn't sure he wanted to know the answer.

*January 23, and 30, 2003*

"Years later, Pastor M tried selling a book on Amazon," Douglas continued the next week, "I kid you not. And here I am still screaming, not that I'm exactly in the arms of his warm embrace any more. But for the first 19 years of my life, I tried desperately to fit in. And ya know, no matter how hard she tried, mom could never comb down that last cowlick. Question: would I be the same person if she had?"

Sunday mornings when Douglas was a child were an event. The family would all deck out in their lower-middle-class best—a suit and tie, even at age five—then drive up Sunrise Street to church. Dad would park the car on Palm, mom would frantically run a comb through Douglas's hair (for the fifth time) and the family would walk a block or two to church, every Sunday. You could tell how much Lands Baptist grew by how far they had to walk to get there.

In the meantime, Douglas heard every Bible story there is by the time he was five. Multiple times.

Jumping ahead, dad became a deacon and ran the 9:00 a.m. Sunday service when he was 10. Then dad went to adult Sunday school at 10:30. Mom went wherever her husband went and Douglas's siblings Rose and John rotated between junior high or high school youth groups in one time slot with the main service in the other. That left Douglas repeating 5th- then 6th-grade Sunday school, as his parents thought he was too young to show up in the brand spanking new sanctuary. The church was still growing.

Douglas complained. There are, after all, only so many times you can learn that Mary was a virgin when Jesus was born and face it. When you're a 10-year-old boy, the *Apollo* program is a lot more interesting than 5th-grade Sunday school, twice.

So when Douglas was 11, in 1968, his parents promoted him to the church library for the second service under the threat of moving him back to 5th-grade Sunday school if he misbehaved. Not 6th, a dire threat, indeed.

But Douglas liked the church library, even if their budget limited the shelves to donations from the church octogenarians. Douglas got along well with the librarian, and after he had read all their 19th century Bible lit—Douglas is probably one of the only people around who's actually read *The History of Goody Two Shoes*—he soon asked for something a bit more sophisticated.

There wasn't much at the high school level, so the librarian fed him theology. Six months later Douglas worked his way through Dr. M's ThD thesis on the Book of Revelations. He was 11 years old. The book made a big impression on him. It was logical, very well-researched, organized and not too hard to read if you just kept at it and Douglas was a stubborn SOB. It ran in his family. At that point, Douglas wanted to be a brilliant theologian just like Dr. M when he grew up.

Seventh grade brought the obvious cognitive jump in Sunday school, plus Douglas finally got into the adult church service. Bonus! The junior high teachers sparked discussions from open-ended questions in Sunday school. Why did Elizabeth pledge her first-born son as a Nazarite but not her cousin Mary? Or was Jesus a Nazarite? And back into the library Douglas would go to dig out the arguments. It was wonderful!

It was also the beginning of the end. The first slide occurred when Lands Baptist shifted Sunday school guides. Dad may have been a deacon, but he was outvoted, his experience as a professional educator apparently being irrelevant to what and how kids should learn in church.

In the meantime, the eighth grade Douglas saw the material move from open- to close-ended questions. From questions like "Why is Mary's virginity important to Jesus?" Douglas now read "Mary was a v___n when Jesus was born."

Have you ever tried to discuss whether this meant "virgin," "vegan" or "Virginian"? And if Mary's virginity is important to Jesus—something they'd just taught him—then shouldn't it be important to him? How? No one discussed that.

Maybe the change came because it was 1970 and the Church felt threatened. But by what? Hippies? Hey, man, peace! Major threat, that. Maybe we should wage war to reduce the threat of peace, Douglas thought in 1972. No, wait. We're already doing that and it hasn't worked out so well. But isn't God bigger than the protestors and if not, then why am I a Christian?

Douglas had already started to ask questions and asking questions was dangerous. Asking questions was training to leave.

The Baign family went to the beach lots back then. John was 4½ years older than Douglas, prime hippie age. Douglas talked to any hippie who'd listen to a 13-year-old. Some did and some of them had something worthwhile to say. Didn't Jesus talk to the harlots and the tax collectors? So shouldn't we listen to the protestors?

No one in the Church answered him, except to say that, yes, we should bring the protestors into the fold, but that's not what Douglas meant. He wanted to bring the Church to them. But instead of listening (to a 13-year-old), Lands Baptist promoted a teacher to youth leader to teach the teens how to be "responsible Christians" in the '70s: Pastor Dan.

Douglas earliest memory of PD was when he called a reach-in foul on Douglas on the 8th-grade basketball court. Douglas's fingertips barely brushed the guy and PD blew the whistle then screamed at him with all the bedside manners of any friendly drill sergeant. "You stupid fool!" At a 13-year-old.

Douglas spent lots of time with PD over the next five years and his initial opinion didn't change much. Whether in basketball or the rough and tumble game of life, you scored points and stayed isolated by following PD's rules perfectly in the midst of mindless and unnecessary adversity. "Scream at a child, that way he shall go and he shall depart from it." Douglas can't play basketball worth a damn.

Douglas spent lots of time with PD because mom and dad were parent sponsors for PD's high school trips when John and Rose were in high school. He got dragged along, not that he minded at the time, mostly because 13-year-old kids didn't have to follow all the rules. Then the trips were fun!

The catch was that Douglas learned PD's methodology before he even hit high school, plus all the Bible stories. Fifteen years of church and Sunday school twice every week will do that to you. So when Douglas joined PD's youth group, he'd already sponged up most of what he was taught from his older sibs, only to go through it all over again. There comes a point where you have to ask: am I training for the right event?

PD was not very creative and not very bright. At first Douglas thought he just repeated the same lesson every three years, then Douglas realized PD was repeating the same lesson every *trip*. Follow the rules and you'll thrive. Follow the rules and you'll thrive. Follow the rules and you'll thrive.

Works great for robots, doesn't it? But Douglas wasn't a robot and he didn't thrive.

Douglas wanted more, more of his own spirit, more of his God. He thirsted to learn. Hosanna High let him learn as fast as he liked, which was pretty damn fast. But Douglas wanted the same thing in the spiritual world that he achieved in the material world. OK. I believe that Mary was a virgin when Jesus was born, he thought. Fine. What's next?

And back to the book of Matthew PD would go. Mary was a v___n when Jesus was born. Next week: Mary was a v___n when Jesus was born. "I'd cite the facts about the Virgin Mary again," Douglas told Sherry, "who was a v___n when Jesus was born, but you get the picture." Or maybe PD would move to the book of James and say the same thing. Follow the rules and you'll thrive. Beep! Follow the rules and you'll thrive. Beep!

But Douglas still wasn't a robot and he still didn't thrive.

By the end of January's therapy, Douglas had at least sorted out some basics about his ex-church. First, life at Lands Baptist went through roughly three stages, one per education level.

1.  Elementary Sunday school taught Douglas what he *can* do as a Christian—study theology. The church was extremely conservative, but genuinely nurturing.
2.  Junior high taught him what he *can't* do as a Christian: smoke, drink, dance, and go to the movies. "I haven't talked much about this yet," Douglas ruminated to Sherry, "but at Lands Baptist the legalism was there in spades. Ha! I couldn't play card games either." In junior high, the church was conservative and proscriptive.
3.  High school taught Douglas what he *must* do as a Christian, down to specific formulas in specific situations: dress this way, talk that way. By the time he was at Hosanna, Lands Baptist was conservative and prescriptive.

The older Douglas got, the more he was treated as a child.

Second, Douglas's bitterness lay more in PD's youth group than in Hosanna High, something that only hit him while working through the sessions. A few Hosanna Bible classes focused on books he didn't know much about, Micah, for example. Things did not always move as rapidly as he wanted, but things still moved.

Hosanna High served as a happier balance to the repetitive dullness of PD, even though PD taught there. As long as Douglas was at Hosanna, he was growing, learning, thriving intellectually and spiritually. But his graduation date was June 19, 1975. After that, he really didn't see a road ahead for spiritual growth.

*February 6, 2003, in session*

71

"I was trying to talk about my experiences in junior high with the Church," Douglas started, "but as soon as I began to do that, I remembered a ton of stories. I certainly didn't realize it at the time, but I may have been slowly separating from the Church even that far back. So . . . that's where I need to start."

"Seventh grade?" asked Sherry.

"Let's start with 8th grade when I was 13. Wow! That's not that long after I finished reading through Dr. M's thesis." Douglas was surprised. "I might have some of the dates a bit mixed up, after all, that was 30 plus years ago, but it won't make that much difference to the gestalt. At any rate, let's start with Jabber."

"Jabber?"

"Yeah," said Douglas. "His real name is Jasper but everyone called him Jabber. He talked a lot, too."

"All right. What about Jabber?"

"It's the L'Abri story all over again. Didn't realize that until just now, though I suppose I should really say that L'Abri is the 8th-grade Bible study with Jabber story all over again. Eighth grade came first."

It was a simple story. The adult teacher set the students in a half-circle in front of him (always a "him," of course) and read scripture. Then he asked each student what he or she thought the verses meant.

This time, Douglas was about a third of the way around the half-circle. Of course, the other 8th-graders claimed not to understand the verses at all, which seemed odd to him because the scripture was obvious. This wasn't one of Dr. M's careful analyses of obscure verses in Revelations. It was a cut-and-dried verse from one of Paul's epistles.

When the teacher asked Douglas what the verses meant, Douglas just explained them simply.

And nearly everyone, except Jabber and Douglas, started laughing, including the teacher. Howling is more like it. Douglas's face turned beet red and he tried to clarify what he meant, but it was no use. He was already humiliated and no one would listen. Douglas tried again but the teacher cut him off and moved to the next student.

And still no one had any clue and Douglas felt disgusted. 'Everyone is just waiting for the teacher to tell them what to think,' he thought. But finally, the teacher got around to asking Jabber what he thought.

Jabber repeated Douglas's explanation.

"Oooh!!" everyone exclaimed. "That's brilliant! Now I understand!"

Jabber protested, "That's really just what Douglas said," a comment that endeared Jabber to Douglas for a lifetime. But the comment had no effect on anyone else.

"No, not really," said one student. "It's so obvious once you say it."

Jabber continued to defend Douglas but again, no one listened. For the rest of junior high and high school, Jabber was labeled as popular and smart and Douglas was labeled as eccentric.

"Did you make friends with Jasper in high school?" Sherry asked.

"Unfortunately, no," Douglas lamented. "He and I were both at Hosanna High but Jasper was one class below me and we traveled in different circles. I wanted to become friends but we simply didn't see each other that often."

"That's a loss," Sherry agreed. "That was a short story so we have time for another, if you can make it quick."

"I think so," he confirmed. "This one also indirectly involves Jabber."

A year later, the 9th graders were taught to evangelize. The students were told to pretend to be giving a survey and to give blue 3x5 cards with different religious questions, like "Do you believe in hell?" and so on. One of them was "Do you know how to get to heaven?", which was used to segue into buttonholing someone with a religious tract. ("*The Four Spiritual Laws*. Yack!" Douglas commented out loud).

Douglas went along to do this once or twice. It was a Sunday school assignment, but it felt deceptive. The survey was simply a prop, and Douglas felt like he was lying when he told random strangers otherwise.

So Douglas collected the 3X5 cards to use them as an actual survey. He only knew enough statistics to realize the questions were badly designed, but when he tried to present his findings, such as they were, no one wanted to address the deception. Even Jabber looked uncomfortable. Douglas stumbled through a paragraph or two then wisely shut up and moved to the next topic.

"But I remembered," he told Sherry. "At first I was pulling away from everyone except Jabber. Now I was pulling away from him, too. I felt lonely and isolated, even though I was still in the group."

"And that's all the time we have," Sherry ended. "This was a good session. Same time next week?"

"Of course," Douglas responded. It had felt like a good session to him, too, but a small part of him felt cheated because he found himself wishing that Sherry would say more. He didn't always know if he was going the right direction.

# Scheduling the Date of the Race

*February 13 and 20, 2003, in session*

There's a misconception that therapy is emotional or traumatic. It can be, which is why there's always a box of Kleenex handy, but therapy is usually just drudge work. You have to spend lots of time tracking things, and in many sessions Sherry just helped Douglas put the facts in order. It was then that therapy became a cold and unglamorous slog through a muddy wash of confused facts and impressions.

Douglas was in the middle of the next slog. "I don't know where to start," he admitted. "My memory of 9th and 10th grade is pretty good when it comes to school, but I get confused when I think about my church. Everything is a hodgepodge."

"What's the first thing that comes to your head?" Sherry suggested.

"Putting together mom's stage over the summer. But that happened at school so it's probably irrelevant."

The rest of his time with Sherry that sessson was simply trying to find topics to talk about; nothing exciting there. But before they closed, Douglas realized that the problem wasn't too few subjects to address, but too many. He listed the topics to Sherry in no particular order then showed her the list.

- The Great Catacomb Service Fiasco
- Gothard's Basic Youth Conference (1-3 stories)
- Two stories about Rose
- Nate D. climbing on the outside of the bus (the Rad Red Rocket)

There wasn't enough time at the end of that session to address any of the stories, so Douglas began the next session by talking about Rose.

"Rose was raped at a church function when I was in 9th grade," he began.

It was one of the few times Sherry showed emotion, "Wow! She was what?"

"Raped. At a church function."

"At a church function," Sherry repeated flatly.

"Yeah. At a church function," Douglas confirmed.

The story was simple. Rose's high school Sunday school group was having a summer party at a friend's house. One of the boys in the group forced Rose into the nearest bathroom and raped her.

Sherry was curious. "What happened to him?"

Nothing. The perpetuator was not held to account. The church assumed the girl's behavior was the problem, which was laughable to anyone who knew Rose. Douglas was close to her back then and Rose told him about it soon after. The worst part of it, she said wasn't the boy, but that everyone just pretended like it never happened even though they heard the whole thing.

"Yeah. 'We're all one big happy Christian family who tolerates rape and blames the victim.'" Douglas added sarcastically.

Sherry was visibly upset. "Give me a minute to calm down," she asked. Douglas was certainly willing to do that. Sherry had waited for him to calm down any number of times. She put her head down in her hands, took a few deep breaths, then came back into the conversation as her usual composed self.

"How did you react?" she asked.

"*Moi*? Oh, I volunteered to track the bastard down (Rose provided the name) and to arrange a creative accident, with any number of possible injuries attached."

"It's a good thing you didn't try," Sherry said dryly. "You were what, 15? He was probably three years older than you and lots bigger."

"Oh yeah," Douglas agreed, "not that it would have made any difference." He shrugged. "I knew the risk, but I can be a very sneaky and stubborn SOB. There are all sorts of ways to annoy folks from a distance and I'm good at that kind of stuff. Besides, it looks undignified for an 18-year-old senior to beat up a freshman."

Douglas was clearly unrepentant, and he briefly empathized with his ancient Baign Scottish ancestors. The rape hadn't just been an attack on Rose, but an attack on his family. Something that the Baign family valued very much, not Rose's virginity, but Rose herself, who had been treated as an object. Clan honor was at stake.

"Rose talked me out of it," Douglas' mind returned. "She wanted to forget the whole thing." He was silent for a moment, then he added, "Sometimes I wonder if a victim failing to speak up is as bad as the group not speaking up. But it's different when you're the victim."

"Correct," Sherry confirmed. "It's an entirely different situation. Still, it's better for a victim to speak up, which your sister didn't do."

"Nope. She didn't." Douglas tried to calm himself. "My point, though, is how the incident impacted me, not her." He took another breath then continued. "Rose was leaving high school, I was coming in.

I could have attended the same party myself. But I went into that group wanting to change things. I knew a huge impact was unrealistic, but I still wanted to make it a little bit better for Rose."

"You love your sister very much," Sherry repeated.

"Yeah, I do. Though back when we were young, she sometimes took advantage of it. Rose admitted once that I was easy to manipulate." He shrugged, "Maybe so. But that doesn't change the fact that I love Rose."

Douglas paused asked, "Do we have time for another story?"

Sherry checked the clock, "Yes." Douglas noted there was no provision to keep it short, but didn't want to push his luck either.

"This one's about Rose, too. Everyone in our family has some musical talent, but Rose got a triple dose. She picked up Anne's bodrain (that's a Celtic drum) a few years ago on her last visit here and started playing this incredible stuff, not just rhythms, but music: ringing, pounding, shifting—playing every part of the instrument and then some.

"So I listened for a few minutes and finally got curious, 'Hey, sis,' I asked, 'Didn't know you played the bodrain. When did you start learning it?'

"So she thinks about it for a second and says, 'About two minutes ago.'"

Douglas smacked his forehead, "As if I'd ever get a quarter of that."

There was no doubt Rose was talented. About a year after her rape, Lands Baptist hired a new music director ("Let's call him Dr. A," Douglas said) and decided to cut an album of religious music. Dr. A. wanted a poster child for the LP, so he used a standardized music test to vet church musicians for their talent.

Rose tested off the charts, the highest score Dr. A. had ever seen. But then Dr. A decided he couldn't use Rose because she "didn't represent church values." Then he picked the cute daughter of a church leader.

"People will do that," Sherry commented.

Douglas was not persuaded, "Yeah, but if they're going to do it, then why bother with a standardized test? Why not just pick the cute girl to begin with and save the trouble? Never mind. That's a rhetorical question.

"My main point is this: apparently my sister was pretty enough to rape but not pretty enough to represent church values. Rose is talented. But then again, talent didn't seem to be a church value."

The sarcasm was obvious. Again, Douglas's empathies were with his Baign clan paternal ancestors. Turning down Rose for the role, or at least, turning her down when she was more than qualified, wasn't just an insult to Rose but an insult to the Baigns. Douglas's family had been at Lands Baptist for more than 40 years by then, pouring time and money into church institutions. In what way did the most musical person in the church from a stalwart family in the church not represent church values for church music?

'Was I born 1000 years too late because I'm a Baign Scottish tribesman?' Douglas wondered, 'Or 1000 years too early because of my ideas about politics and religion?'

*February 27, 2003, in session*

Douglas was impatient to start the next session, so he was annoyed when Sherry asked him to do some breathing exercises before starting. Still, he saw the wisdom in it; he'd gotten wound up last session. So he went through the process, then began by talking about Rose and the album cut by Lands Baptist.

"They called the album *In His Lands,* for heaven's sake," Douglas complained. "Not that Lands Baptist was narcissistic or anything." His sarcasm closed on bitterness. "But that's not what I want to talk about."

"So what do you want to talk about?" Sherry was resolutely pinning him to a topic.

"The album notes."

"The album notes?" Sherry couldn't see what they'd have to do with anything, but Douglas was equally resolute in taking the topic in an unexpected direction.

"Yeah. The album notes on the back cover. I brought them with me." Douglas slid out an old-fashioned 33 1/3 LP and read from the album notes.

"Blah, blah, yadda yadda yadda. Here we are. Dr. A. quote: 'has a great sense of the type of music that reaches the heart while communicating the truths of God's Word to the mind. Without this tricky balance, music will either unduly inflame the emotions or deaden the brain.' That's a direct quote from Dr. M., the head pastor."

Sherry was curious, "OK. But what does that have to do with anything?"

"Balance. The key word is 'balance.'"

There was a surprising amount to discuss before Douglas could even talk about how balance applied to Rose, much less himself. The short version was Douglas found himself agreeing with Dr. M. that balance was important while disagreeing over what items were balanced and where balance was reached.

Douglas believed that the balance wasn't between heart and mind, but between the larger categories of chaos and order. The difference was important because for Douglas chaos and order were simply features of the universe God created. They were just . . . there.

But by now Douglas had read enough of Dr. M's books to realize Dr. M. saw 'heart' and 'mind' as spiritual entities. To "inflame the emotions or deaden the brain" gave Satan the opportunity to invade and possess the 'heart' or 'mind.'

Where the balance occurred was equally important. For Douglas, his Celtic ancestors came to the forefront. So what if "inflamed" dancing led to temporary madness or even . . . sex (gasp!)? Sex was human. The prohibition against "inflamed emotions" reminded Douglas of the joke about why Southern Baptist spouses never made love standing up. After all, if they were caught someone might think they were dancing.

Douglas believed the imbalance point, the point where music became dangerous, was when music controlled people rather than people controlling the music. Douglas's Schneider ancestors came from near Strasbourg. And during Strasbourg's Dancing Plague of 1518, some of his distant ancestors or their friends literally danced themselves to death. Historians still don't know why.

Dancing into sex was one thing, dancing to death was another. The balance point wasn't determined by the influence of music towards "inflaming" or "deadening," but by control. Besides, he thought grimly, if I want music to deaden my brain all I have to do is listen to that album.

Which wasn't quite true, because Rose was on it.

"Remember," Douglas remarked, "the Church forbade worshipping God with guitars. Rose is a guitarist and pianist and every other instrumentalist, too. So she goes to Dr. A and demonstrates what she can do on the guitar, which, of course, is quite a bit. Then she asks if she can strum away on the album.

"And Dr. A. says . . . no, she can't play the guitar on the album because it would 'upset the balance.' Eventually, Rose persuades Dr. A to let Rose and her friend Brenda play the guitar, but only if they play basic chords. No picking, sliding, thumping and so on that might disturb how Dr. A 'balanced' the music.

"So the good news is that Rose and Brenda break an important barrier. They were the first two people to play a guitar in that sanctuary. If you listen to the LP carefully, you can hear the guitar and that's my favorite cut on the album. The bad news is that the album has pictures of every single musical contributor, including the choir, except for Rose and Brenda.

"Rose decided Lands Baptist was just too much trouble soon after and left the church to attend another. She was 18 and mom and dad agreed with her choice, which was a good thing, because that's where she met her husband, but that's another story. Rose's car accident was about a year after that."

"But how does this impact you? It's an interesting story, but why are you telling it?" Sherry had a good point.

Douglas looked at the ceiling. The connections seemed obvious in his head, but he still had trouble moving thoughts from his head to his tongue. Math was easy. Religious concepts and emotions were hard.

"Two reasons," he explained. "First, because this story is the Church in a nutshell. It paints the situation I wanted to change, if only a little. Rose's rapist came and went. He entered and left the group just before and after the rape. He was an external problem, but this was an internal problem I wanted to fix."

Sherry nodded. "That makes sense."

"More importantly," Douglas continued, "that's when I began distrusting my church. I didn't have the vocabulary or a clear theology, but even back then I could see that Lands Baptist was going in one direction while I was going in another. I was 14 years old and already leaving the Fundamentalist Church."

"I might have left, too, to go to Rose's church," Douglas added, "if I hadn't wanted to help my church. I'm a runner, and in the race away from my church, this was the wrong starting time."

The realization left Douglas exhausted and upset, and he leaned his head back to stare at the ceiling. Sherry just let him sit and rest and didn't interrupt until it was time to close the session.

# Pre-Race Jitters

*March 6, 2003, in session*

"We've been talking about your old church a lot lately," Sherry began the session. "Is it time to get back to talking about Leanne or sex?"

Douglas thought about it, "Probably not," he concluded reluctantly. "Sex is still such a tangle that I don't know how to deal with it. On the other hand, I'm progressing on the Church front and that's easier for me to understand. No reason to stop now. So let's keep going with the Church and untangle that snarl first."

"All right," said Sherry, checking her notes. "Is there anything else about the album you wanted to say?"

"Yeah, one more thing. Another quote from the album notes says 'The music heard here is second only to an actual visit to Lands Baptist.'" Douglas had the album in front of him.

"So?" Sherry was unimpressed.

"So you go to them. They don't come to you. And if you go they'll give you the privilege of listening to them glorify God for you. You won't get much chance to glorify God yourself."

"Ah," then Sherry paused. "Is that really the way an evangelical service is arranged?" she asked. "I wouldn't really know myself, but I thought you sing hymns. So that's audience participation, isn't it?"

"Barely. You could only sing approved hymns, with the most recent ones written before World War II. Thirty years after that catastrophe, my ex-church was still singing them. I thought culture had maybe changed a bit by the '60s. I wanted to sing something reflecting human experience *now*."

"I can see how that might be a problem," Sherry commented.

"Yeah, it was stagnation city. Plus they're the ones who define God for you, not you yourself."

Douglas looked at the flower near his hand. There wasn't a whole lot to look at in Sherry's office. Just the flower, white ceiling tiles, a picture or two, desk, desk chair, spare chair, sofa, end table, and a box of tissue. He liked the pictures, but sometimes he wished the office were more interesting to make it easier for his mind to drift. But he wasn't there to let his mind drift, so he let himself smile at the flower, ran his fingers through his hair, sighed and moved forward.

"Talking about Evangelicals who define God for you is a good segue to talking about Gothard."

He stuck out his tongue at the name. "Besides, he'll come into play when I talk about dating Leanne, so you need to know about him now. There's a lot to say about that bastard, so let's get started. A holy hell that he is, I might as well get it over with. Puke!"

Not as well-known now, Bill Gothard and the Institute for Basic Youth Conflicts (IBYC) was a major Fundamentalist force in the 1970s and '80s, drawing up to 20,000 folks for a single session. Douglas's involvement pre-dated the rush. His older brother John had helped vet the seminar for the church and determine its doctrinal soundness.

John thought the material converted vague spirituality into practical discipleship but noted that Gothard was, in fact, the only person on the planet who was more conservative than Dr. M. For example, Gothard believed that the Bible should be taught only to men and Lands Baptist let women sit and learn from Dr. M's sermons.

The policy on women should have been a red flag. It wasn't.

Douglas wanted to attend the next seminar but at first, both dad and John thought he was too young—7th grade. They changed their mind when John realized he'd seen a few young boys at the conference (no girls, of course).

So in 8th grade Douglas attended the annual one-week conference for the first time. The commute from Santa Brisa was a bit far, but John liked refreshing his memory along the way.

"What's the big deal, dad?" Douglas asked on the way home on the second night of the conference.

"What do you mean, Douglas?"

"What's the big fuss about? People treat Gothard like he's the second coming of Christ," Douglas exaggerated, "and it's just a bunch of rules we already know: how short to keep your hair, when to apologize, how to apologize what clothes to wear, et cetera, et cetera ad infinitum." Mom had just taught him the Latin.

Dad thought it over some, "It's the principles, not the rules."

"I don't see that, dad. Gothard yaks all the time about rules, not principles. Like you don't date girls, you court them, then there's a bunch of rules on how to court. And you have to follow the rules or else."

"Maybe it'll make more sense to you by the Saturday session when he wraps it all up," dad suggested.

But that didn't happen either. John said it made more sense to him the second time he attended so maybe it'd be that way for Douglas, too.

"And that's a good place to stop," Sherry interrupted.

Douglas, blinked, refocused and then came out of it. "OK," he readily agreed. "Besides, there's only so much talking about that SOB that I can tolerate." Those weren't happy memories to revisit.

*March 13, 2003, in session*

It was March blue outside and Douglas smiled, his convertible open to the sunlight. A recent brush fire had passed. But today the burned bushes burst into Scottish green, another simple day in paradise.

"All right," asked Sherry, "how old were you when you first attended the Gothard conference?"

"Eighth grade. Hmmm. Eighth grade." Douglas mused to Sherry. "Come to think of it, I was either still in speech therapy at the time or just ending it, so it's no wonder that I didn't feel listened to. My words were still blurred."

"That makes sense," Sherry remarked "But you didn't finish the story last session, so let's continue."

One year later the entire family was back in Long Beach, Gothard somehow getting a revelation that women could learn his gospel. "Or maybe he just saw more money in it," Douglas suggested to Sherry. She nodded.

Having mom and Rose there was a welcome bonus, but IBYC still didn't make any sense to Douglas —same presentation, same principles, same rules. The lecture series repeated almost exactly and it was legalism: "strict conformity to the letter of the law rather than its spirit," to quote the Princeton WordNet.

Douglas interrupted his narrative before he'd barely started. "Damn, this pisses me off!" he exclaimed. "And here I thought Christianity was about actually loving God, not the law, silly boy that I am. Galatians 5:17. 'For all the law is fulfilled in one word, even in this: Thou shalt love thy neighbor as thyself.'" Douglas rattled it off from memory again. "But perish the thought that I actually read the Bible, not Gothard."

He took a breath, trying not to think of how red his face must be. "Damn," Douglas said again, "I've barely scratched the surface and the only things that come to mind border on vengeance, not sarcasm."

"Do you control your feelings," asked Sherry, "or do your feelings control you? That's what it boils down to. Are you going to let the tail wag the dog or not?"

Douglas paused to let that sink in. It was times like this where he realized Sherry was worth every penny. "My heart was wounded," he said finally.

"Agreed," Sherry said. "It hurts and it should hurt. It's not something you want to happen. But it *did* happen and you can't control that. But does hanging onto the pain buy you anything you want? Do you want to keep the pain or do you want to move on to something else?"

He thought it over. "Vengeance sounds sweet," he finally said.

"Yes, it does," Sherry answered. "But would you be happy if you got it?"

"Probably not," Douglas said dryly.

"So do you want vengeance or do you want to be happy?"

"Yeah. That's the question, isn't it?" He chewed on it then shrugged. "Given that I'm clinically depressed, I dunno if I'll ever be 'happy' happy. But I'll take the next best thing. I don't like hurting people."

Sherry smiled, "Then you need to tell me the rest of the story. What is it about Gothard and the IBYC conferences that gets you so riled up?"

Douglas took a quick breath then let the air out slowly, trying to get unriled. *Un, deux, trois, quatre, cinq, six, sept, huit, neuf, dix,* he thought. It's supposed to take 20 minutes for anger toxins to drain out of the system. Counting to 10 in French won't do it, but it's all I've got right now. I just don't have time for this.

Of course, I don't have time for Gothard either, his inner voice added, but he's one of the anger hormones poisoning my system. So guess what: I have to continue the story for my sake, not his. And . . . here we go again.

He took another breath, went through another calming exercise, shifted position, then kept going.

"That gets into theology," he said, "which rapidly becomes a sticky wicket. Theology is a big topic. So hmmm. How to summarize: what are the reasons close to my heart why I don't like Gothard?" he asked rhetorically.

"Those are probably the reasons you need to deal with the most," Sherry commented, "not theology."

"Yes and no," Douglas responded. "Theology, at least in the sense of seeking God, is also close to my heart." He thought for a moment.

"The simplest thing to say is that Gothard thought everything is a nail." He finally continued.

Sherry raised an eyebrow.

"It's an engineering cliché. If you're a hammer, everything you see is a nail, so you pound it. That's fine if the object really is a nail or something close to it, but rotten if it isn't. If it's glass and you pound it then it breaks. You need to see engineering bugs from multiple points of view, not just the hammer's."

"You don't want to try to jam a square peg into a round hole," Sherry rephrased.

"Yeah. How else can you solve the problem? I can't seem to be rational about my 9th grade experience with Gothard, so let's jump to 10th-grade Bible class."

In 1972, his parents had asked Douglas to attend Hosanna Christian High. The school still met at the old sanctuary near El Camino Real and it felt like home.

Digression: one class met in the basement with an open window at the ground level. Douglas bet a friend that he could give him a 10-second head start and beat him into class. The friend laughed and ran around the corner. Douglas waited 10 seconds, slid through the window and got into his seat before his friend did. He-he-he. Douglas knew all the shortcuts, all the little cubbyholes, and everywhere to hide.

But he couldn't hide from his classes, and guess who taught Bible. Pastor Dan, who decided that the best way to feed his hungry 10th-grade flock was to fill them with the great vision of Bill Gothard, for the entire semester with 20 hours of material from IBYC.

"Sounds like PD simply didn't want to bother with prepping lessons." Sherry said.

Douglas started steaming. "Yea. I hadn't thought about that but yea.

"For me at the time it was simply a third time through the entire material, sloowwly, just to get the magnitude of all that mature wisdom." Douglas was trying to stay in control, but his voice leaked sarcasm. "Ooooh! Excitement! I got the chance to listen to Gothard's distorted version of the Bible for weeks!

"It was really starting to feel like punishment, tripled. Or maybe a Kafka novel, my brain gradually turning into a cockroach from a lack of thinking, cognitive process being forbidden in favor of correct dogma." Douglas finally stopped the rant.

The problem wasn't just the repetition or the difficulty of stretching roughly 20 hours of material over a 15-week semester, but that PD knew that Douglas had already attended the Gothard course. PD expected Douglas to tutor other students.

"That sounds reasonable," Sherry commented.

"It would be," he responded, "if I were a nail or a round peg, but I'm neither one."

The problem appeared to be threefold.

First, Douglas's speech impediment had (through no fault of his own) limited his chances to develop social skills. He gained a few of those skills later, but he was still 15 years old at the time.

Second, Douglas had never been a round peg since before his mom unsuccessfully tried to comb back his cowlick. He'd studied theology at age 11 then steadily drifted away from his peers.

Third, and possibly most important, Douglas thought Gothard was full of it, both fecal matter and ego. What was he supposed to do? Tutor folks on how to disobey the teacher who taught that you were always supposed to obey the teacher?

There was a section, for instance, on women being submissive to men, especially to their husbands. In turn, men were to protect and guard their spouse.

A fat lot of good that had done Rose. No one had protected her, and the church had simply looked the other way. And why would he want a woman to be submissive to him in the first place? (Douglas had a hard time visualizing Rose as submissive, but did get a laugh out of it.)

It wasn't just gender roles, though he thought that was the worst of it. Gothard's so-called "principles" (Douglas's middle fingers framed air quotes) formed a matrix of round holes, which was fine if you had round pegs but ungodly if you didn't.

Sherry shook her head. "I'm not sure I follow what this has to do with you."

It seemed obvious to Douglas, but he'd grown up with it. How to explain in 25 words or less?

"It's all about pointers," he finally decided. "Do you try to get to God or does God come to you? In Christianity, God came to us in the form of Jesus then Jesus taught us to love, that we may bring God to other people in the form of love."

Sherry nodded. "OK. That I can follow. Go on."

"By contrast, Gothard is all about rules. God doesn't come to you, you try to get to God. The rules formed a matrix of round holes. PD was a true believer in Gothard's principles," Douglas finished, "so he considered it holy when Christians turned themselves into round pegs. Square pegs were not part of God's will. And I'm a square peg. Or triangular. Whatever.

"Church Sunday school, then 10th grade Bible class involved the constant screeching realization that I'm a square peg being hammered into a round hole, hatred in the name of Christian love."

"And that's all we have time for," said Sherry.

Douglas felt aggravated, she stopped the session just as he was starting to figure this out. But it was still time to go. And overall, it'd been another session that left Douglas feeling exhausted, yet stronger. A good brushfire, he knew, simply prepared the ground for greater growth.

*March 27, 2003, in session*

"I really seriously do not want to talk about Gothard this session." Douglas opened the main part of the next session feeling stubborn.

Sherry smiled and consulted her notes. "You don't have to. The other items you tagged back in February were the Great Catacomb Service Fiasco and a story about Nate D climbing on the outside of the bus. I'm curious: what's a catacomb service?"

"You know what a catacomb is?" Douglas asked.

"I think so. It's where early Christians in Rome buried their dead." Sherry's background included nominal exposure to Roman Catholicism.

"Right, though it could be anywhere and it's not always relating to a burial. It's just any religious event underground," Douglas explained. "The ones in Rome, started as burial grounds, were probably shelters during persecutions then later on they were expanded to include worship chapels. There's lots of interesting artwork down there." He sounded pedantic, but mostly he was just on autopilot, trying to get to the main topic.

Sherry dipped her head in agreement, "And sometimes people today replicate a service in the catacombs?"

"Right. A Catacomb Service," Douglas' hands capitalized the phrase "is a high-fidelity reenactment."

The youth leaders went to some length to create the proper mystic environment. Mr. and Mrs. K's house had a convenient cave nearby, participants were told not to bring Bibles or hymnals (there weren't any in 250 AD and literacy was rare). The service was held at midnight and you needed to know the secret message to enter. And you were sworn to never ever breathe a word of anything about the service to anyone.

To top things off, the leaders fashioned togas and prearranged a persecution. Douglas had helped design the show (he'd heard of catacomb services before) and was in on the secret. His job was to be the Roman centurion: show up late in faux armor and sword, bust up the meeting, and drag away a few other kids who were also in on it. Looked great to him—a chance to play the bad guy.

"Sounds like good planning," Sherry commented. "How old were you?"

"Ninth grade, I think. Uh . . . it happened towards the end of the school year, so I was 14."

"All the parents had to be notified this was going to take place."

"Yeah. They all had to sign and return a consent form."

"And if you called this a fiasco, something went wrong."

"Yeah. You could say that." Douglas' face indicated that calling it a fiasco might be putting it mildly.

It was the last time he'd seen his grandfather. Grandpa Schneider had terminal cancer and it was the first time Douglas was exposed to death. His family made the long trip from Sunset Boulevard out to Santa Roselyn to give him a hug and say good-bye.

There'd been some family estrangement between his mom and her father. "I'll have to tell you about that later, Sherry." But Douglas's own relationship with grandpa had always been filled with kindness. Grandpa was one of the few people who believed in him.

They got home late that night, nearly 11 o'clock, and at first Douglas was worried that he'd have trouble sneaking out to make the catacomb service at midnight. But then he realized it was late enough that he didn't have to sneak out at all. Just leave and walk to Mrs. K's house. He'd get there in plenty of time.

He thought about parting through the back door, but that went straight past his parents' bedroom, and the shortcut through the canyon at midnight didn't sound attractive. So Douglas dropped through the front door, which was right by his own room anyway. Just pretend to go to bed and keep going out the other door.

It took him directly past Rose and Eric, her fiancé, making out in his car and Douglas hadn't expected them to be there. He wasn't sure they saw him or not but the only thing he could do was keep going. Both Douglas and his youth leaders took a vow of silence seriously and he had given his word.

It was a perfect night for a catacomb service. The sky was overcast and gloomy, almost gothic. The air felt foggy and dark, the dankness rolling in slowly. No moonbeams stretched through the gloom, no starlight shivers, just the ever-present damp of foreboding.

A car pulled up behind him just as he reached the Palm Street bridge. It was Rose and Eric. ("What is it about bridges anyway?" Douglas complained.)

"What are you doing?" called Rose.

"I can't tell you," Douglas said. He sensed that this would end badly, no matter what he did, but maybe he could salvage honor by keeping his vows. He kept walking.

But you can't outrun or out-walk a car. Eric simply pulled the car forward.

"Get in the car now," he said emphatically. Douglas kept walking.

"You're running away from home," Rose added. "Do as Eric says."

"Do I look like I'm running away from home?" Douglas wasn't carrying anything at all, just his wallet, some spare change, and a house key.

"Maybe. What are you doing?" she asked.

"I can't tell you."

The pattern continued until Rose and Eric finally forced Douglas into the car. His only grace was that he still hadn't broken his vow and that he was sure mom and dad would clear everything up soon. That was enough to at least keep Rose and Eric civil during the short trip back.

His parents were less than pleased at waking up. Eric and Rose explained the situation and dad turned to Douglas to ask. "Well?"

Douglas tried to figure out how to defend himself without breaking his vow. "Come on, dad. Mom got the memo from Mrs. K and she signed off on it."

"What memo?" his mom asked.

Douglas turned white. The next 20 minutes were a blur of parents screaming, accusing him of disobedience, disrespect, unfaithfulness, deception. Rose and Eric chimed in, asking him how he could do such a hateful thing to betray the family. Douglas wanted to cry, but was too upset to even know how. He'd simply been doing what was asked of him.

Douglas realized he would have to break his vow to explain. He asked Rose and Eric to leave so he wouldn't break his vow to more people, but they were adamant about staying and his mom and dad backed them up. If the family was disgraced, everyone wanted to know about it. Douglas could only be grateful that his brother John was a missionary in Europe by then.

"There's a catacomb service tonight, mom."

"You're lying. I would have been told about it."

"No, mom. Please believe me. There's a catacomb service tonight."

"I don't believe you. You're lying," his mom said. No one believed him at all. It was simply not possible for them to have not heard about it. "Mrs. K would have just walked up to me at work and told me." They were both teachers at Hosanna High.

"No, mom. Please, please believe me," Douglas was begging. He couldn't believe this was happening. Mom would see Mrs. K soon anyway and he knew that Mrs. K would back him up. But that didn't prevent what would happen now.

He had trouble keeping his composure. Eventually, the fact that he'd had nothing with him fit Douglas's contention that he wasn't running way. And finally, finally, finally, mom and dad agreed to drive him to the catacomb service. If Douglas were lying, it would be obvious and the consequences would be dire.

Mrs. K, of course, was there as scheduled and other cars were clearly pulling up to drop off children. Douglas got out to walk over to Mrs. K. She was his only protection. His mom and dad looked stunned.

"Can you give me a minute with Mrs. K?" his dad asked.

"Sure dad," Douglas stepped away, knowing that Mrs. K would back his story. She did. His mom was crabby, sleepy, and confused about why she hadn't been told, but Mrs. K said that she'd dropped off the consent form in Annette's school mailbox. His mom wasn't sure whether or not to believe her.

"There's time for you to still join in, Douglas," Mrs. K encouraged him kindly. But it was too late. Douglas's insides were broken and didn't think he could play his part. The family drove back home in silence and the catacomb service he had helped plan went on without him.

The catacomb service had been on a Friday night. Douglas's mom found the consent papers in her school mailbox Monday morning. She hadn't checked her mail on Friday.

"You didn't feel like you could ask your parents for a ride?" Sherry asked.

"No. I would have been interrupting them."

"Interrupting them from what? You were that low on their list of priorities?"

Douglas sighed, "Yeah, that's what it feels like."

They closed the session and said good-bye.

*March 30, 2003, at home*

*Dear Jacky,*

Things were going along well enough with Sherry so I tried getting off the meds a bit more than a week ago.

That was a Really Bad Idea. A few days later I drove to work, got out of the car, and started to walk smack into the middle of the street. Whoa! Like most companies, we're quite close to a busy thoroughfare and traffic is everywhere. What was I doing stepping off the sidewalk?

I got into my office and right away got the urge again to go find a bridge and jump. No particular reason, Just Do It. Nike. The goddess of defeet. I didn't get a lick of work done that day. I spent my entire energy just stopping the urge to walk into the middle of the street or find a bridge nearby (there is one, too).

Fortunately, I had a few pills left over and got back onto my meds the same day. It takes awhile to catch up but I'm feeling better now. If I hadn't gotten back onto the meds, I might very well be dead. It was awful there for a while.

*Eppur si muove.* I have to take care of myself because the world won't wait for me and it's not vested in my sanity. The reality of the situation is that I must *always* take my meds. That means that I have to keep seeing Sherry and keep writing you, Jacky, because emotional healing is the only way I know to gain strength.

Aargh. I think I'd rather pass another kidney stone . . .

89

Douglas Baign

Thanks for listening, Jacky! I love you!
*Douglas*

# The Referee Raises the Starting Gun

*April 3, 2003, in session*

"How do you feel about the fiasco at the catacomb service, Douglas?" Sherry asked. It was very much an appropriate question.

There'd been trace amounts of rain on the way to the session, and Douglas had pulled over to put up the top of his convertible. His hair was damp now, but no real harm had been done.

"Confused, guilty, angry, distrusted, not listened to, offended. Lots of things. It's that ball of string in my head I mentioned earlier. The emotions are all tangled up and the snarl makes it difficult to process."

"You felt guilty?" Sherry decided to pull at just one thread.

"Yeah. I was supposed to be there for my classmates and I wasn't. And I wasn't supposed to break my vow of silence and I did."

"Could you have done anything different?" Sherry asked.

Douglas thought about it, "Probably not. Maybe play my part but I don't think I could have done that."

"Then there's no reason to feel guilty."

He pondered that for a moment, trying to let it sink into his heart.

"That's hard to do. It all feels so very weird to me. My church asked me to be trustworthy and honest and those things make sense to me. Then when I'm 14 and trying to do just exactly that, be trustworthy, and honest, no one believes it. No one believes in me."

"Then you have to believe in yourself," Sherry responded.

Douglas nodded, "Yeah." He sat there for a second, working it through. Then he continued, "Can we back up a second? I wanted to list a few other feelings I had about the catacomb service."

"Did you hear me say that you have to believe in yourself?"

"Yeah. I'm still trying to get myself to believe it down deep."

"OK. It takes time, I know, so go ahead with your other feelings."

"I also felt isolated, singled out. I'm just sitting there, minding my own business, doing precisely what I'm supposed to be doing, then mom and dad scream at me. Or as in the case in 8th grade with Jabber, folks laugh at me. It's hurtful. Why do these things happen to me?"

Another rhetorical question; he seemed to be full of them these days but soon added another.

"Or more precisely, why do these things keep happening to me? I mean, L'Abri is basically the same story. Answer a serious question in 8th grade, then get laughed at. Do what I'm asked to do in 9th grade, then get screamed at. Answer a serious question at L'Abri, then get mocked for my response. Why ask something if you don't want an answer? Why do these things keep happening to me?"

Douglas paused. "Wait. I've just said the same thing multiple times."

Sherry smiled, "That's OK. The job of a therapist is often repetitive listening. Repeating yourself lets the stories sink in to the point where they stop controlling you and you control them."

Whatever the reason, Douglas didn't feel "these things kept happening to him" because he painted a target on his back. For that to be the case, he would have had to have started back in elementary school or sooner. And that didn't make sense. What had happened to him as a child that made him a victim?

In any case, the question wasn't how it started but what to do about it now, to begin believing in himself, taking care of himself, trusting himself. That would be a good start and possibly a good finish. But no one would do the work for him and the world won't wait for you. He'd have to do the work himself.

"I'm going to need to think about this," Douglas said finally. "So I may need to get back to talking about this again sometime. He felt slightly deflated. "I think that completes talking about junior high." he added. It was a milestone.

Sherry nodded. "OK," she responded. "Where to next? We've got some time left."

"The story of Nate D climbing on the outside of the bus," he decided.

The trip to Big Bear, where Douglas first met Leanne, demanded two busses, one for each gender. The boys relaxed in the Rad Red Rocket, which enhanced its reputation first by throttling the rear gas pump, then by fire-working fluids as the front gas pump crumbled. Apparently, the decision to install two gas pumps to ease the strain on the elderly bus had doubled the accident rate.

PD just kept driving while Douglas, Kevin and PD implored God to let the poor bus limp up the hill to the next gas station. Douglas left his eyes open as the bus swayed and to his surprise, Nate. D clambered out the window while the bus was moving. The constant stoppage had gotten to him, too. Then instead of edging back in, Nate wormed up to the top luggage rack to hold court like some Buddha rocking on an elephant.

But once up there, Nate didn't know how to safely get back into the bus. Nate had broken the rules, and what's more, Nate's dad was the associate pastor of Lands Baptist.

Oops.

Douglas didn't care. Compared to his sister being raped, this was small potatoes. More like tiny. But then the second fuel pump began leaking gas into the engine and the Rad Red Rocket lurched into the next town. God had graciously answered their prayers, Nate's position became obvious, and PD blew a gasket.

The colors in PD's face spanned the rainbow as he ran through his litany of threats. The most significant threat left Nate abandoned in that town, with just enough money to call his dad and ask for pickup. Nate would be entirely removed from the trip.

It seemed all so petty to Douglas. Ignore a rape and read the riot act for the benign impulse of a bored teenager. Besides, if PD carried through on his threat, he'd be annoying a senior pastor.

But how to convince PD? Douglas knew he had the status to at least protest to PD, but he also knew that he only had one shot and anything he said had to be biblically based. Common sense didn't apply.

His mind ran through his inventory of Bible verses and he finally hit upon the obvious: Matthew 5:7, from the Sermon on the Mount. "Blessed are the merciful, for they shall receive mercy." Romans 6:14 also came to mind: "For sin shall not have dominion over you: for ye are not under the law, but under grace."

PD eventually came to Kevin and Douglas and asked for their opinion: was abandoning Nate in the middle of nowhere justice?

Kevin said definitely. Douglas agreed that it certainly was and managed to keep a straight face while doing it. But justice wasn't the point, he added. If the Old Testament stressed justice, the New Testament relied on mercy. Douglas cited both verses (word-for-word by memory from the King James) and suggested, why not just let it blow over? It wasn't that big a problem and annoying Nate's dad for Nate's misbehavior probably wasn't justice for the assistant pastor.

"Hmm. I hadn't thought about justice for Nate's father," said PD.

It still took PD a few minutes to calm down, but he finally called Nate over to announce his fate. Nate approached with trepidation, but PD managed to grind out Nate's fate between gritting teeth: "Mercy."

Douglas gradually emerged from storytelling mode. "It was probably the one time I actually made a difference when I was the church high school president. Such as it was." It felt discouraging. "Though I suppose it may have made a lot of difference to Nate," he added.

"Probably so," Sherry commented. "And I can see the hypocrisy, but why else are you telling the story?"

"It's an intermediate step towards splitting with my church, especially with PD," said Douglas. "I used to think of my leaving the Church as a sharp drop-off. Going through these stories helps me to understand that it was a much more gradual slope, starting from 6th grade. This was yet another straw on the camel's back. It was just so petty."

"Another reason," he continued, "is that with Nate my basis for disagreeing with PD was something PD could accept. Cite scripture.

"That was much more problematic in our last argument when PD was sure he had scripture on his side. My position was that he was misreading scripture. Or possibly even that scripture didn't apply. But you can't prove scripture doesn't apply by using scripture, and PD wouldn't accept anything else."

"I can see that you're passionate about it," Sherry said. "Let's explore why next week."

Again, Douglas was glad the session was over. The memories were painful and he didn't like getting into them. At the same time, he knew that he needed to do just exactly that if he was going to heal.

*April 10, 2003, in session*

If therapy is repetitive listening for the therapist, it's repetitive talking for the client. It takes time for healing to sink into your heart, not your head. And one way to get there is to look at the same thing from different angles and viewpoints.

Douglas ran through Gothard's theology with Sherry again and again and again. In the '70s, the young Douglas knew he disagreed with Gothard, but didn't have the intellectual vocabulary or emotional strength to clearly express why. To say nothing of his speech impediment.

Therapy in the 2000s not only let him express *that* he was angry with Gothard. It gave him the strength to cope with his anger and to use his intelligence to learn *why* he was angry. It built a firm bridge between his self then and now, a scaffolding that let him deal with other issues.

"A few weeks back," Douglas started the main body of the next session, "I said that Gothard's principles created a matrix of round holes. I wanted to say more but we ran out of time."

"Right."

"Pardon me if we get into theology, but it's relevant to why I left."

Sherry smiled. "It's your session," was all she said.

"OK," Douglas got a dogged look. "Theology should always start with the facts. I went to the website for the Institute for Basic Life Principles, IBYC's changed their name since the '70s, to dig out a short summary of their basic seminar, which I took four times. They believe that:

> *Conflicts often indicate that we are living by our natural inclinations, which are opposite to the ways of God. The goal of this seminar is to explain God's way of life and provide further training and resources for those who are committed to God's best.*

"Which is a barf statement I could rant on for hours. We don't have hours and I don't want to spend a zillion sessions barfing, so let me cut this down. I have two objections to this paragraph:

"First, 'natural inclinations' can't mean that eating, drinking or sex are opposite to the ways of God, because then your religion deserves a Darwin Award. If your religion tells you to stop eating or having sex then your religion kills itself, thus doing social evolution a favor by removing its stupid memes from the meme pool."

Douglas continued, "For example, the Shakers actually stopped having sex and the group died out. The Peoples Temple is another example of a religion that earns a Darwin Award, albeit for different reasons."

"Interesting," Sherry commented. "How does that relate to Gothard?"

"The notion of 'natural inclinations,'" Douglas explained, "can't take the usual definition you or I mean, like it's natural to eat and drink, so the only other definition that makes sense is Platonic forms: 'the natural universe' instead of 'the spiritual universe.'

"So first, you're dividing creation into a spiritual universe and a material or natural universe. The Bible may support that contention. Genesis 1:1. "In the beginning God created the heavens and the earth." Well, that took a long time to find in the Bible, to be sure.

"But second, you're saying that the natural universe is so corrupted that normal behavior in it is sin. And I don't think that's biblical. It's gnostic or maybe Neoplatonic. In any case, it's not Christian. The Bible says that the natural universe, if there is one, is *cursed*, but not evil."

Douglas hadn't gotten very far and was already wound up. But he continued, "In the Gothard view, all or part of the natural world is bad. But if you follow their rules and listen to the muse, then you can elevate yourself above the corrupted natural world just like one of those pole sitters.

"Except now you call the muse Jesus, not Aoidē. And the only thing that's changed in the 1,600 years since Simeon the Stylite is the type of pedestal on which to place yourself."

"Simeon the Stylite?" Sherry asked.

"Yeah. *Stylite* in Greek means 'column'; probably the first pole sitter. Simeon was worried about getting away from the vile world so got away from the vile world—60 feet up on a pole for 30 years. Simeon conflated gnosticism with Christianity."

Douglas showed Sherry a 6th century depiction of Simeon, which expressed Simeon's philosophy perfectly. The natural world was coming to get you, just like a serpent. But if you elevated yourself above it - literally - then you could be divinely inspired and see the higher reality.

In short, Simeon the Stylite admitted that you get into heaven by the Grace of God (the Christian position). But he also thought that we need to protect ourselves from the evils of the natural world for as long as we're still here (the Gnostic position).

Douglas stopped, took a deep breath and tried to steady himself. "Anyway, I could go on that point alone, the point on Simeon's head, I mean, for hours and we don't have time."

Sherry encouraged him. "You're doing well to stay calm."

"Calm?"

She smiled, "Relatively. You said you had two objections and you've only covered one."

"The start of the second sentence. 'The goal of this seminar is to explain God's way of life . . . '"

Sherry encouraged him, "Go on."

"I didn't know God had a 'way of life,'" Douglas wound up his annoyance meter again, despite himself. "There are too many different types of saints in the Bible for any one particular 'way of life' to be defined as God's." This time he just used his index finger for the air quotes.

His mind took a typical hop. "Compare Simeon's view of 'God's way of life' to the Buddhist view."

*Before enlightenment: chopping wood, carrying water.*
*After enlightenment: chopping wood, carrying water.*

In the Eastern view, the mindset changes but not the tasks, only your emotional outlook differs when you become enlightened. ("How, I wouldn't know, not being a Zen Buddhist," Douglas commented to Sherry). The mindset is in charge of the tasks.

Simeon the Stylite reverses the process. Your tasks change after you convert (you climb the pillar of Rules). And so does your mindset because now you see the higher reality. Or at least, you think you do. In any case, the tasks are in charge of your mindset.

In other words, Simeon thought leading God's "way of life" would let him see the "ways of God." If you fill all the round holes in Gothard's matrix with your round behavior pegs, then you'll have the perfect dogma that lets you understand God.

"What PD, the Church, and DotHead all assume," Douglas finished, "is that you'll be happy and holy if you follow the rules. Conversely, if you're not happy then you didn't follow them so you're not holy." Follow the rules and you'll thrive.

Douglas left Lands Baptist because he followed the rules and *didn't* thrive. Their "fundamental" premise is false. Some folks argued that he didn't follow the right rules, which usually just gave them more rules with which to browbeat him, but changing your rule set doesn't help you become a better Christian either because Christianity isn't defined by rules in the first place.

"God is love, God is light. God is faithful day and night," Douglas sang at Bible camp.

If one takes those verses seriously (stolen from I John 1), then one must believe in God, not the rules. The two must be kept distinct. Otherwise, what does one do when God tells you to break the rules? When a hungry Peter (Acts 10) saw a big heavenly sheet full of "four-footed creatures and reptiles and birds of the air."

*Then he heard a voice saying, "Get up, Peter; kill and eat." But Peter said, "By no means, Lord; for I have never eaten anything that is profane or unclean." The voice said to him again, a second time, "What God has made clean you must not call profane."*

"Me God. You Peter. You live in My universe and if I want to change My mind, then that's My problem. YHWH thinks that maybe He can handle it." Telling God how to act always struck Douglas as rather odd.

Sin occurs, says Isaiah 14:14, not when we disobey rules but when we say, "I will ascend above the heights of the clouds; I will be like the Most High."

*Eppur si muove.* Earth moves whether we like it or not. For us to tell God that we'll set the constraints instead, thank you very much, is to move God aside and that's where sin begins. God's not moveable.

Humans, however, are. At one time, Douglas went from realizing it was legalism to thinking he'd try it. He was a kid who wanted to please mom and dad, to say nothing of his entire church.

He took a deep breath. "So I trusted God Uttered. I mean, Gothard." Douglas ended. "Or at least I did at one point in high school. And now there are times when I believe that I don't need to talk to you at all, Sherry. I need to talk to a de-programmer so that I can finally get out of that bastard's cult. Or rather, to get Gothard's cult out of me."

It was nearly the end of the session and Douglas looked up to grin. "You got any margaritas around here?" He wasn't serious. "I'm pretty wound up."

Sherry grinned back. "Nope. That'd be illegal and unethical." She glanced at the clock. "We still have a minute or two. Did you want to say something else?"

Douglas contemplated the matter, "One reason why I analyzed things so carefully now is so that I can get in contact with who I was then. Some of these ideas were rattling around my head as a kid and I didn't know how to get them out. Now I do. It's a matter of being true to oneself.

"The way I read theology is exactly the same as Galileo. Theology moves around God. God does not move around theology. Jesus said, 'Follow me.' He didn't say, 'Follow the rules.' We are more important than the rules and we are the ones who make the choice."

*April 17, 2003, in session*

Driving to Sherry's calmed him, which was a good thing because Douglas knew he'd talk about Gothard yet again. Aargh. Now that he'd waited 33 years to start talking about him, the problem was how to stop.

The only thing that came to mind was something Anne had once told him: the gospels focus on "It came to pass that" such and such happened. Not: "It came to stay." If something is properly addressed, it tends to move on. Conversely, if something isn't properly addressed then it becomes a demon and stays. It was time, past time, to properly address Gothard, not the ball. Douglas thought "Hello, ball!" as he imagined his arms wildly swinging like those in Art Carney or W. C. Fields comedy golf routines.

"Hello!" he smiled at Sherry as he walked in. He'd almost said, "Hello, ball," a thought that made him giggle. It was one of the few days where his smile was actually genuine. On the meds, Douglas was no longer suicidal, but most days were still a struggle through the grey. It was nice to catch a break.

"Hello," Sherry replied. "You're looking well."

"Oh, I'm not too bad today. Thank God for the meds! Shall we proceed?"

"Certainly. Let me ask: how did Gothard impact your day-to-day life?"

Douglas thought about it a second. "Here's what actually happened to me, soon after I became president of PD's high school group."

Douglas felt committed to God, but Gothard's seminars upset him, even if he couldn't exactly identify why (then). Something about them just didn't feel right. So when PD asked him to attend IBYC again (trip #4) to "encourage the faith" of his high school president, Douglas told him that attending the seminars made him too angry to think. Maybe he should avoid it.

He hit the double bind. PD responded that anger was a sign of rebellion against God, which certainly proved he needed to attend, didn't it? Wasn't Douglas committed to God's best?

"Yes, this happened to me, damn it!" Douglas exploded. "Though I do seem to recall YAHWEH screaming a few times, say at Sodom and Gomorrah. Ka-Boom! Nuke it till the salt bounces! And of course, I wouldn't dare mention Jesus whipping the temple moneychangers as an example of God getting angry. I mean, that might actually require me to believe that Jesus was God!

"So . . . was Jesus pissing off God? No, I've got it. Jesus suffered from teenage angst. The Son of God rebels against His Parent.

"Righteous anger is anger," he summarized. "Maybe you're angry because something bad happened. You should at least give an angry person the benefit of the doubt, and church leaders are human, too. They commit mistakes.

"But it's the double bind. If I don't attend, then I'm not committed to God. And if I *do* attend, then I commit to their interpretation of God while discovering nothing about how to grow in God for myself. *They* gain control while they pretend to tell *me* how to gain control.

"Aargh!"

Douglas didn't wait for Sherry to tell him to calm down. He went through another calming exercise, let himself sink deeper into the couch and deliberately stayed quiet for a minute.

In retrospect, Douglas didn't get why Gothard was teaching him 'biblical principles' and not his church. Didn't they know him better than IBYC? When Douglas was 17, Gothard was *loco* to think he was *parentis*.

On the other hand, given his experience with PD, Douglas wasn't so sure that his own church would do a good job of it either.

Douglas looked toward he foyer of his church from the courtyard one day and realized Lands Baptist had changed. The church was growing from Dr. M's radio ministry, and new members dressed differently. Being a new Christian became a fashion statement and their approach to Christianity wasn't the same.

Douglas's church wasn't really there for him and that left Gothard. Then the more Gothard oozed into the Church, the more Douglas saw its disintegration. There was a pattern to it.

1.  IBYC changed the linguistic terrain of the battle by redefining *natural* to mean the platonic ideal. Then his old church bought into the separation of spiritual and natural worlds. (Never let a deceiver set the terms of a discussion. By definition, their terms are deceptive.)
2.  Lands Baptist took the corollary that the "natural" world is evil. This is easy for Christians to accept because they believe in original sin. But there's a difference between "cursed" and "evil."
3.  Point out that it takes divine inspiration from the muse to see the spiritual world.
4.  Then nominate yourself as the muse, because you were wise enough to point out phases 1-3.

It's a formula used successfully by Gothard, Jim Bakker and other televangelists. If you can convince folks that you're wise because you're wise enough to recognize your own wisdom, then ask them to send money now.

"It wouldn't work for me, though." Douglas added. "Must be a sign I'm not wise."

Douglas growled once more at televangelists before getting back on track, "Let me summarize so I can get on with it. Without even bothering to get into specific IBYC issues, I object to Gothard's entire premise because I believe that," he said, lifting a finger for each point:

- "Humans were originally created sinless. Thus, humans have a natural inclination to serve God, not oppose Him (or Her). Sin isn't natural.
- "Christianity revolves around mercy, not law. *Eppur si muove.* The Earth moves, not the Sun.
- "You work out 'God's way of life' for yourself, not them."

"Those three points in IBYC's single, small paragraph remind me of the Army MRE 'Meal, Ready-to-Eat.' Three lies for the price of one!"

Sherry looked puzzled for a moment then groaned. "Go on."

He grinned then continued. "Clearly, I didn't have this all worked out when I was 17. But I had pieces of it. The first time I sparred with PD, I gave in. I went to Gothard yet again. The second time, near the end of May of 1975, I didn't. I mean, I didn't give in to PD."

"And as far as I'm concerned, that's when I mentally left my church. Even if I stopped in from time to time after that."

"Two weeks later, I asked Leanne out on a date. In one sense, that's where the story begins."

# And they're off!

Douglas didn't leave the Church all at once. It came mile after mile of many small decisions and a few big ones. That left Douglas approaching his upcoming session with Sherry with a sense of dread. He knew that today he would dig up old fears and angers and hate. The fear was compounded by an April gloom, the sky already overcast so early. It was also the time of year when his mother had died, so long ago.

The day was not starting off well. On the other hand, he told himself, it's scarcely begun and there's no rule that requires a day to end as it started. He held that thought as he drifted past the hills of the nature preserve.

"Hello," he started. Sherry was wearing pants again. He liked her tall and elegant look: graceful and pretty without being obnoxiously sexual.

"Hello," she responded. "How are you today?"

"Gloomy. Mom died this time of year, so many moons ago, and it's always difficult."

"Did you want to talk about your mother?" Sherry asked.

"Not really. Or at least not today. I'm more or less geared up to talk about my last argument with PD about Gothard. And I want to get that over with so I can stop talking about those bastards."

"OK. Shall we get started?"

Douglas's argument with PD focused on what Gothard called "the chain of command," derived from a story in Matthew. Douglas wanted to set the context correctly so he dragged out the Bible he'd brought to the session and read the parable from Matthew, chapter eight:

> *5 As he entered Caper'na-um, a centurion came forward to him, beseeching him*
> *6 and saying, "Lord, my servant is lying paralyzed at home, in terrible distress."*
> *7 And he said to him, "I will come and heal him."*

*8 But the centurion answered him, "Lord, I am not worthy to have you come under my roof; but only say the word, and my servant will be healed.*
*9 For I am a man under authority, with soldiers under me; and I say to one, 'Go,' and he goes, and to another, 'Come,' and he comes, and to my slave, 'Do this,' and he does it."*
*10 When Jesus heard him, he marveled, and said to those who followed him, "Truly, I say to you, not even in Israel have I found such faith."*

"Gothard uses that story to bolster the idea of a chain of command because creating rules doesn't make sense unless you can justify your own authority for imposing them. PD used the same model. I disagreed and that's the source of the argument.

"After that everything cascades. It's all about matryoshka dolls.

"Once we get past the story of the centurion, then
"I can discuss Gothard's chain of command so
"I can discuss the double bind Gothard so
"I can mention how PD treated Gothard so
"I can finish talking about Gothard so
"I can go back to talking about Leanne so
"I can pop the stack back to sex so
"I can return to connecting Leanne and Deirdre to L'Abri so
"I can figure out what L'Abri has to do with my wanting to commit suicide 15 years later.

"And hallelujah! Now we're back at the main topic!" Douglas rolled his eyeballs in frustration, his hands bouncing down a level each time he closed a matryoshka doll.

The mainstream Church sees the story of Jesus and the centurion as a parable about the nature and results of faith. The centurion comes, the centurion goes. Jesus remarks on his faith in verse 10 and heals the servant. That's all.

Gothard doesn't disagree, but shifts the focus to verse 9, not faith. Gothard thinks that, "For I am a man under authority . . ." justifies a chain of command. Everyone's under God's chain of command. It's all part of God's plan. Soldiers submit to centurions, centurions submit to tribunes, children submit to their parents, women submit to men, your father submits to the boss and so on.

It means a place for everyone and everyone in their place. If you disobey, said Gothard, then you step out of the chain of command and

God can't protect you from the consequences. It's God's will that you Obey.

Douglas saw this as dishonest, because Gothard used the verses to bolster his own authority. Creating a chain of command then placing yourself at the top of it, is self-serving.

"Or to simplify things" Douglas pointed out, "see Pope. And I don't mean Alexander. Why Goat Turd, I mean Gothard, didn't just become a Catholic is beyond me, but never mind. Oh, wait. I've got it! Catholics can't elect themselves Pope. You're vetted through the College of Cardinals."

"Which is probably a good thing, too," Sherry commented. "And where does PD tie into this?"

"Off track again?"

"Just a little"

"Hang on and I'll tell you in just a sec. Let me finish this thought, please."

Sherry waved a hand gracefully, "All right."

"There's any number of reasons, and I can cite Bible verses to any bozo stupid enough to insist on them, to disagree with how Sot Head – I mean, Gothard – warped a story about faith into a story about obedience. And I'm annoyed enough now that maybe I should write them down tonight. Get it out of my system.

"But what I noticed back in high school was the ethical impossibility Christians reached even *assuming* the centurion's story was about the chain of command, which I don't think it is, but never mind.

"So back to PD. The story's simple enough but I'm still struggling with the consequences. "Remember back in December I told you about the short bike trip that was required before the longer 300-mile trip?"

Sherry flipped back through her notes, "Right."

PD explicitly expected Douglas to go on the 300-mile bicycle road trip. But Mr. H, Douglas's track coach, wanted him to attend a track meet on one of the same weekends. Douglas couldn't do both. What happens when two different chains of command, assuming that such a thing exists, order you to do opposite things?

Gothard recognized that humans were subject to multiple chains of command: church, parents, boss, teachers, track coach, and so on. But neither he nor the Bible had a formula to handle conflicts between them, possibly because that situation never arose when you lived in an empire. You did what the emperor told you to do and responsibility chains between you and him were well-defined.

We live in a representative republic with its complex web of interlocking hierarchies.

"So I asked PD," said Douglas. "'How do you resolve the conflict?' We went back and forth on this awhile and finally I pinned him down to a single response: he said, 'Who do you think is your spiritual mentor?' Determine your muse and follow it. I'm sure he thought I'd say it was he.

"Then I flashed on it. It was my choice and what if I said that my muse was Timothy Leary? Yes, I really thought of Timothy Leary.

"But would my church really buy him as my choice of muse?

"Of course not. But that point didn't really matter because here was my ticket out of the dilemma! If I must pick a muse to follow, then I pick myself. I became the muse *because I had to pick my muse.* The power to choose requires the power to make choices for yourself. And once you make choices for yourself, then you never need someone making choices for you. Never! There is no muse!"

Douglas stopped to wipe away tears. It's difficult to describe how he felt at that moment: elated, angry, lonely, betrayed, confused, sorrow. But of all the emotions spinning through him, perhaps the most important was grief.

"Realizing that became a . . . a . . ." he struggled to express the complex net of emotions.

"The straw that broke the camel's back," Sherry suggested.

Douglas thought about that one, "Yeah. Or maybe . . . what's that game you play with all the blocks stacked and you try to remove a block without it falling over? Jenga. That's it.

"The beliefs I'd been given as a child were like theological Jenga blocks. The events that happened to me, the ideas I developed in junior high or high school meant I'd been removing blocks here and there, bit by bit, piece by piece, all along. But the overall theological structure still held together. Then I removed the 'chain of command' block and the entire theological tower crashed down.

"If I was the muse then everything that Gothard and my church was telling me fell apart, because I was responsible for my own salvation. Not PD, not Gothard, not my parents, but me.

"And if the Church was wrong about the chain of command, then what else were they wrong about? I had no criteria to even take a guess and maybe that's why I ended up at L'Abri."

He wiped another tear from his eye and sat back in the sofa.

"Can you tell me how you feel about it?" Sherry asked gently.

Douglas looked startled. "Well, angry of course. Confused. But back in 1975 I wasn't really angry. I was sad." He searched for the right word or phrase, "Grieving. Everything I knew was wrong." He winced. "It was like the death of my mom, which happened years ago. I felt like I'd just lost everything that was valuable to me, and there was nothing left. Like ashes in my mouth."

He took a deep breath, "But that didn't matter. I still had to be honest with myself and honest to my beliefs. So I told PD that my track coach was my spiritual mentor. He might have been, too, not PD, not that it really mattered. None of it. I was a runner for Jesus not a centurion, not even a lowly legionnaire.

"Then I walked out on PD. If there was a single moment in time in which I left my old church that was it. The difference was not only because I interpreted scripture in a way that my church did not but more importantly, because I interpreted scripture for myself in the first place. I decided to think for myself.

"Two weeks later, I ran a race; then the next day I asked Leanne for a date. I wouldn't have been there at all if I'd picked PD as my muse. Leaving the Church is the egg. Dating Leanne is the chicken. And my confusion over Gothard is near the beginning and end of that relationship."

Talking exhausted him and once Douglas ended he just sat there with a dull look on his face. Sherry let him sit a bit then asked. "We still have a minute or two left in session. Did you want to say anything else?"

He thought about, then nodded, "Yeah. It's important to know that I didn't walk away from PD to run away from God. I walked away to try to *find* God. I didn't exactly know who God might be, but I realized that at least as far as I was concerned, PD didn't have Him."

"Or Her," Douglas added automatically.

Sherry nodded, "Yes. That seems clear. Shall we talk about Leanne next week?"

Douglas looked up briefly, "Yeah. I guess so." It was hard for him to admit, but it was time, past time, to put Gothard behind him and to move on to his next mistake.

He sighed and got up to leave the session.

"Thank you for listening to me, Sherry. That's not something I felt PD did with me."

She smiled. "You're welcome, Douglas. I'll see you next week."

Douglas wasn't tempted to linger. The sooner he stopped thinking about PD and Gothard, the better. And today he was grateful to be driving a convertible. The openness let him savor the freedom he'd never seen in high school.

*April 25, 2003, at home*

*Dear Jacky,*

I got pretty wound up talking about PD and GoatHerd in session today, Jacky. I guess it beats having all that . . . vomit . . . churn around inside you, but it's still painful. I suppose one could say that the best thing to do is to just leave Gothard behind me, but the emotions are still churning. Writing them down helps me cope.

What qualifies Gothard or PD "to provide further training and resources" rather than someone else? Why is he the muse? Because he's read the Bible more than I have?

I've always been curious about that. Take Romeo and Juliet: "Romeo, Romeo. Wherefore are thou 'Romeo'?" So if I read the whole play and memorize Juliet's speeches word-for-word in the Elizabethan English—then am I now a better marriage and family counselor than Sherry?

The Capulets were dysfunctional. And they explain everything there is to know about dysfunctional families, right? Besides, dysfunctional families are a good place to look for wisdom on how to be a functional family, right?

Never mind. If we go down this tangent we'll end up discussing who is more divinely inspired: de Vere (who made his name holey to avoid the Queen's cannon) or the Synod of Hippo (who made a canon holy and crowned it King). But that's waaay too much digression, James.

Having been there, the chain of command felt like chains. And was about as effective as whipping me with chains, too. But let me un-forge on, Judas that I am, and break those links!

Here's Psalms 82:6.

*"I say, 'You are gods, sons of the Most High, all of you . . . '"*

Of course, that's not YAHWEH saying that we're gods, just the psalmist. But then again, Jesus quotes this verse in the gospel of John (10: 31-38). Which means that now I can say
```
(that you can say
 (that I said
  (that the scholars say
   (that the editors who compiled John said
    (that the author of John said
     (that John said
      (that Jesus said
       (that the Psalm's author said
        (that he
         (that psalmist) said))))))))))
```
that we are gods.

Maybe I should just drag out my old LISP computer programming skills and do this all up right. But I digress. Between Jesus and the psalmist, the Bible really does say that humans are gods. Christians being humans, Christians are gods. The Bible also says that Christians are servants. The Bible says that Christians are soldiers. And the Bible says that Christians are runners, farmers, and the children of God.

I can just see it now. If we take this all literally, then we've got modern Roman centurions running around in the Breastplate of Righteousness trying to serve everyone for Jesus, but only if you're for them, not against them, while they farm the financial soil and build altars to themselves. And their kids.

Yup. Sounds like Lands Baptist to me.

But perhaps we're better off if we take parts of the Bible as analogy. For every verse that PD can find saying that I'm a soldier under the chain of command, I can find one that says I'm a god giving them.

Let's stay in the New Testament. "Everyone who hopes in Jesus purifies himself as Jesus is pure," says St. John. If we are in Jesus and Jesus is in God, then we are as pure as God is pure. The Bible accepts no other type of purity. Everyone in Jesus is pure!

And if I'm pure then I don't need a muse because I *am* the muse. This is something you must repeat to yourself until it becomes your mantra. You are responsible for your own salvation. Work it out "with fear and trembling."

Thanks for listening, Jacky. I'm very tired now and need to rest.
*Love,*
*Douglas Baign, Runner*

P.S.

I was hoping to be asleep by now, but I'm obviously still quite worked up. And there's nothing to be done about it but to write you some more, Jacky, and hope to put the topic to bed, with me to follow.

The argument with PD became a tipping point, the dominoes flashing out in the multiple directions of my life. But don't get the impression that I had my beliefs neatly worked out by the time of the argument. I didn't. But I did know that choosing myself as the muse would ultimately mean leaving the church.

I felt devasted, the pieces of my beliefs strewn around at random. It took years for me to put something back together, only to have things broken again at L'Abri.

I attended Lands Baptist from time-to-time for those two or three years, but the more I put together my values, the more I saw the falseness. I became alienated from my own church, my own second family. Then there finally came a moment when I walked away from Lands Baptist so I could keep my belief in God.

Leaving the church was painful, a divorce. These were people I knew well. Some of them were friends my own age that I'd literally known since babyhood. But noone had answers to my questions, and talking to them was like walking on fire. I couldn't stay too long without being burned.

I didn't set foot inside that sanctuary until my Mother died. I've not been inside since then.

Sigh. I'm not sure of this, Jacky, but maybe I'm done talking about Gothard. He's an evil deceiver as far as I'm concerned, but you know? He's gone and I made the right choice to leave him, then I made the right choice to leave my church. God talks to me just as much as He talks to Gothard or PD.

You can leave now, Gothard. Go away. I don't regret leaving you and even answering that question is silly. What I regret is touching Leanne with my anger while leaving you. True. I had to work out the errors in your theology, even back in high school. But hurting a person that I cherished is far, far worse than disappointing a spiritual mentor that I didn't.

Good-bye and good riddance.

# Leanne

# Asking Out Leanne

*April 26, 2003, at home*

*Dear Jacky,*

Leanne and I corresponded (by letter; no email or text messaging back in the 1970s) before and after we dated. I'll cite some of those messages when I chat with Sherry about that relationship. Aargh.

I did so many things right at the beginning of this romance. Writing letters was one of them. Non-romantic letters between a single boy and girl may sound odd, but it worked really well for us.

I did so many things wrong in the middle of that relationship, Jacky, and near the end. Then I did a few things right again afterwards, not very many, but a few.

My first letter to you from that time frame is May 9, 1975. I ran a race the 10th. Lee was there, but I was in race mode and I asked her out on May 11th. I continued to write you extensively over the summer.

It's very easy to make fun of those 1975 letters, Jacky. I get so fulsome at times, like holding hands with Leanne at Starfall was the end of the world or something. Gack.

But I took too long to respect my own feelings. *Que pasó, pasó!* What happened, happened. I experienced the hurts and pains that I felt, and it doesn't do me any good to deny or make fun of them. I loved Leanne deeply, felt deeply, hurt deeply. The tears and wonders I felt, the stuttering smiles of a young man are part of me. I am him. He is me. If I am to love myself now, then I am to cherish who I was.

It's not that the feelings are part of my emotional landscape that I need to deal with it. I *am* the hills and waters, the pain and joy and the ever-so-tender brush of my hand against hers. They are part of me and I let them into myself.

*With much love,*

*Douglas Baign, Runner*

Douglas Baign

*May 9, 1975, at home*

*Dear Jacky,*

Leanne wrote me recently about breaking up with Randy. Perhaps you do not realize the extent of our correspondence. I've been able to get to know her as a friend and to be honest with her.

So I asked Leanne why a girl flirts. She commented that a girl did it (1) to see if the boy liked her (2) to experiment if she liked the boy and (3) to show the boy that she liked him.

So here we are able to talk about the interaction between boys and girls quite openly, and that's heavy dogging, believe me! We both agreed that it was best to talk next, not write so now I have a "date" with her on Sunday to discuss X (herself!) and she knows it's her! So now we are able to talk about whether or not we like each other. This is, of course, a very interesting position.

I'm a bit worried about it. But why? Our relationship 'approaches' my ideal case but I don't feel much about it. I seem to be just a machine telling her my ideas and collecting hers. I'm scared I'll lose myself. Her last letter quotes a poem about people wearing masks and she asks if it reminds me of myself.

I've got to be human. But I don't feel romantic toward her right now. I don't feel anything about her at all. But I must feel. It is imperative to learning anything. I have to learn to be hurt. Perhaps that's why God put me a vulnerable place. To hurt me so I feel more and think less.

*Love,*

*Douglas*

*April 27, 2003, at home*

*Dear Jacky,*

"I'm a bit worried about it," I say.

"Worried"—my eye! For as much as I wanted Leanne inside my life, I was terrified of her getting there. I was afraid of women before Leanne, though I'm not sure why. Again, this is one of those perfectly obvious things that you're not able to see while mentally imbalanced.

Looking back at it, my Sherry sessions seem so normal. But I still cut myself or yell at myself or destroy things I've created. I feel better in that I don't want to commit suicide, but I'm still prone to flash anger and self-destruction, just not as much. Sometimes I'll still cross-dress and play with Barbie dolls. I'm not completely sane.

Of course, the psych types might say that cross-dressing and playing with dolls isn't really a problem and for all I know, maybe it isn't, for someone else. All I know is that for me it's a problem now because I don't control the cross-dressing. It controls me and I'm not on good terms with my own behavior.

I'll let the shrinks worry about the theory. My responsibility is to at least get to the point where I cross-dress and play with Barbie dolls because I want to, not have to. Or to stop doing it because I don't want to anymore. And neither is now the case. I still hurt myself when I cross-dress. This is not only dangerous; it's embarrassing to talk about.

So the only thing I can do is talk to Sherry anyway, to cut a window from inside my tower. Maybe there's a better way to do this out there somewhere, but have you ever tried to work out the best approach to mental health while you're still mentally ill? Try it sometime. No, on second thought, don't. I don't wish that illness on folks.

In the meantime, I gotta keep going the way that I'm going. I gotta do the same stuff over and over and over until I get it right. I gotta tell Sherry and you about Leanne, tell you about sex, tell you about my fears, tell you about my church over and over and over.

Oy vey! It's almost 1:00 a.m. and I'm still not ready for bed. The words are coming to me now and I don't want to quit. But then again, sleep sounds nice, too. Even when the words come, I still need to take a break. And sometimes, neither words nor rest come easily.

Thank you so much for listening to me, Jacky, and encouraging me along. Thank you!

*With much love,*

*Douglas*

P.S. I'm not sure how to approach my next meeting with Sherry. It's as hard to talk about Lee as to talk about PD and Gothard, not because I'm very angry but because I'm very sad.

Wow! This part of therapy really has me going through the emotional wringer.

*May 11, 1975, high school*

After the 50-mile bike warm-up, plus 2 miles racing on foot the day before, the 5 miles biking to Patrick Henry High felt like a very short ride. He could have borrowed dad's car, but the sweat channeled his chattering nervousness into his 10-speed.

Leanne was there already on her own bicycle (it'd only been a mile for her), but she hadn't waited long. They greeted each other with warm smiles.

"Hello!" she said.

"Hi, Lee!" Douglas said brightly. The pun amused him, as that's how he thought of her.

The conversation started off typically (for them), going over her problems in chemistry, gossiping about her ex-boyfriend, and discussing the theory of romantic relationships. But Douglas knew he'd have to talk about girls A, B, C, and eventually girl X.

Leanne kept hinting at it, so after a few minutes, Douglas gathered what little courage he had and decided to discuss romantic practice, not theory.

"Y-y-you know how it's hard for me to t-talk to girls about romance without constantly qualifying everything." A bit of Douglas's old stutter came back when he was nervous.

"Randy mentioned it, yes," Leanne looked inscrutable.

"L-let me preface my remarks with three comments.

"First, I'll t-try to be straightforward without hedging, at least until later, if necessary.

"Second, I wasn't the one who came up with the idea that I might like girl X. Randy did.

"Th-third, I'm currently not hung up on any one girl."

He took a deep breath. "But girl X is you."

Leanne just nodded, "I thought it might be."

But Douglas hadn't actually asked Leanne out, just that, yes, he was thinking about it. It's easy to mock his roundabout approach, but it took all of his courage to even get that far.

The next part of the conversation was odd, with both parties slowly taking in each other's feelings and impressions on both sides. Douglas had never really quite felt anything like it and it was a fascinating situation to be in. It was difficult to be utterly honest with a girl who wasn't already committed, but in a way, it was exhilarating. He enjoyed himself.

"Randy suggested that you may like me as well," Douglas continued.

"He did, hmm?" Leanne still looked blank to him.

"I mean, it's OK if you don't," Douglas hastened to say, "as I'm not tied down to any one girl myself."

"How do you really feel about me?" Leanne asked.

Gulp! A critical point. Douglas had hoped she would give him more information, but her question put him on the spot. He felt the mood change and decided to go with it.

"U-uh. Well, you already know that I'm not hung up on you, because I said I'm not hung up on any girl right now. There are several girls I'm attracted to right now," which was a true statement at the time.

"That's logical," Leanne actually used his own terms rather than 'That makes sense.'

"On the other hand, I can't say that I dislike you. I'm . . . in a sense st-stuck in the m-middle, maybe leaning a bit toward liking you."

She just looked at him and the conversation hung for 15 seconds or so. Douglas didn't know how he looked to her, but he felt pale. He usually tried to be logical and clear around Leanne, but in this case he was feeling very scared! He wasn't used to someone being able to read him as well as he read them.

He continued, "Umm, yes, I do like you to some extent."

"Randy said that you told him that you didn't."

"Th-that was true at the time, one month ago. We've run into each other several times since. And you're pretty and friendly, but there are other girls, too." Douglas was trying to protect himself a bit while still being honest.

Leanne nodded sagely but didn't respond.

"OK," then Douglas decided to turn the tables. There was an element of fencing about it. Leanne may have gotten the better of it, but Douglas knew the object was friendship, not winning an Olympic gold medal.

"How do you feel about me?" he asked. "It's OK if you don't feel romantic toward me. There are other boys out there, too." She'd been blank throughout so he was guessing that she didn't like him.

It seemed harder for her to show feelings than Douglas, but his guess made him genuinely unprepared for how she handled the rest of the conversation.

"I have mixed emotions, too," she said. "When Randy asked me who else I might want to date I told him a half-truth. I said I was thinking of Bernie but I didn't tell him the other half." Douglas was looking at her with disbelief.

"I've been looking for other boys to date," she added "and you're a convenient person—you and Bernie. I dated Bernie once and I don't think anything will come of it, so that eliminates half of my problem."

"The other half is you," Leanne finished.

"I could shoot Randy," Douglas said wryly.

She already knew what he was thinking, "Yes, you asked him not to ask me who I wanted to date."

"Yup. I thought it'd be rude."

"Perhaps. Randy also told me a few other things about you."

"Thrills," but Douglas didn't say more. Let's hope Randy just told her that I usually move slowly with girls, he thought.

Leanne hadn't actually admitted to liking him, so he asked her point-blank, "Do you like me?"

"I can't say either way," she evaded. "It seems illogical to like Randy's best friend, Bernie, and you, too. But you're . . . convenient."

"Rah. I had hoped to get you to commit either way so there would be less strain between us." Douglas realized that was the wrong thing to say.

"But I won't make you do that until you really want to." She relaxed immediately, but Douglas wasn't one for pressuring women anyway.

The conversation continued its absurdity. Leanne said she had two tests for him before she could commit to a date. Douglas immediately thought of the 12th-century romances in which gallant knights had to undergo trials to win the maiden's hand. But he also thought he should listen first, maybe she meant something different.

"Here's the first test," Leanne said. "You may have already failed it. You told me once that it took you about four months and a lot of thought to like one girl, and I doubt that you've met this minimum."

"How long have we known each other?" Douglas asked.

She counted out the months, "Oh yeah, a bit longer than four months." Of course, Douglas had counted the months himself before making that comment to her back when she was still dating Randy. Score one for me! he thought. Ha!

"The second test is what you think should be done about it," Leanne continued. "My dad won't let me say everything I mean." She was 16 at the time.

Douglas was curious about what exactly she meant. Ask her out on a date, duh, entered his mind. But she wouldn't have phrased things so oddly if there wasn't more than just that. Maybe her dad is conservative enough that he won't let her ask me out or maybe I'm supposed to talk to him first. What a pain!

"So . . . I should ask you out for a date? Please do note that I haven't actually asked you out yet." He wanted to play it safe.

"Close," was all Leanne said.

"For fun? Not a serious date?"

"Closer."

He couldn't figure out what else she might be talking about, so he let the conversation drift while the back of his head pondered the problem. Eventually they worked their way back to Douglas's fear of dating, even double dating.

"Even in a situation like I mentioned to you at the track meet yesterday?" Leanne asked. Then she mumbled something under her breath about her dad not letting her say more.

Oh yeah, Douglas thought. He had actually chatted with her at the track meet but hadn't paid that much attention because he was focusing on the race. But her reference back to that conversation let him catch her train of thought.

If Douglas had said he would never double-date, he would've failed the second test. But he had said that it was difficult, not impossible.

"Oh," Douglas said casually. "You mean the situation you talked about with ice skating?"

"Almost," she said.

"Roller skating?"

"Yes, that's it." They'd chatted about Bernie and Margo wanting to double-date while roller skating. Douglas's distracted reaction at the race was "Hope they find another couple!" Then he went back to visualizing his quarter-mile split times: 70, 72, 72 . . . *I really don't want to do a 69 just yet.*

Douglas turned his mind back to the present. "Well, I won't learn anything about double-dating until I actually double-date, so I'd be willing to give it a try."

"Good," Leanne nodded sagely.

By now he had the outline. Her dad wouldn't let Leanne ask him to double-date with her, Bernie, and Margo. Douglas had to ask her.

"Oh, I see." Douglas commented, "You want me to ask you to double-date with Bernie and Margo." He was careful not to actually ask her.

Leanne clapped her hands and said, "Yeah! That's smart, Douglas!"

Come to find out, Leanne even had a date in mind—May 30. Douglas had to say no to that plan as he was acting in his mom's play on that date. That allowed Douglas to ask her out on a double-date on June 6th, assuming all parties (especially her parents) agreed to it. That was a month away but it was a busy time of year.

Leanne enjoyed the rest of the conversation, but Douglas felt jittery and agitated. He decided that if he were to date and trust Leanne a bit, then it'd be OK to admit his fear. So for the last 10 minutes of the conversation, Douglas just explained his mixed emotions. Leanne responded well to that!

What impressed Douglas later was Leanne's fine control over what was said. He couldn't pin her down and she never committed herself. On the other hand, he didn't feel like it was a time for commitment anyway. Both of them had used masks, but both of them were gradually removing them to show care and respect underneath.

He didn't press the issue. *I'll have opportunities to take the initiative later,* he thought. *Plus, we haven't yet talked about some things she's committed to answering. Right now, I'm not worried about it.*

They rode their bikes together part way back home and this time Douglas didn't show his fear. But he was with a girl on a bicycle mini-date and the girl might like him. And it was the first time he'd had a relationship with a girl that might even have a chance to continue.

The thought was terrifying. And he didn't know why.

*May 1 and 8, 2003, in session*

Sherry explored his story. "You acted in your mother's play? I thought you were at Hosanna High."

"So was mom," Douglas responded, "where she taught art and drama. Hosanna High is a private school and they didn't have a problem back in 1975 with having a kid in a parent's class. Mom and I mostly got along well. It was a good experience.

"Though I did have to argue her out of giving me an 'A' in her class once," Douglas reflected.

"Come again?"

"Mom wasn't sure I should get an 'A' or a 'B' in drama at the end of the first semester. So at first she gave me a 'B' thinking that people would see an 'A' as favoritism, then she gave me an 'A' anyway. But I could tell she didn't feel comfortable with it, so I argued her back into giving me a 'B.'"

"Wow," was all Sherry said.

"Yeah. It fractionally reduced my GPA, though I wouldn't have been valedictorian anyway. Still, I can't help but wonder between that and other things . . ." Douglas shrugged. "Anyway, I made sure to work harder next semester and she gave me an 'A' that time around."

"OK. Back to asking out Leanne," Sherry asked. "When did you come up with the idea?"

"I don't know," he thought about it a bit more. "My mind is like a corporate boardroom with different characters in conflict, trying to discuss and compromise a direction for who I am.

"Leanne had mentioned the double-date idea the day before at the track meet, and I thought she was crazy. Why was she talking about the theory of romance now? I had a race to run. But another member of my board wanted to date her the moment I saw her with Randy. A third board member froze on Rachel.

"The board took a vote one day, ignored Leanne, then ran a race. We voted again a day later and decided to experiment and not worry about it. I took a risk. And I didn't try that hard to score fencing points."

Sherry smiled and took a note, "OK. Next question, you said you were frightened by the end of that conversation? It seems like you would be excited instead. What was frightening?"

Douglas looked frustrated, "I dunno. I know that wanting to commit suicide a few years ago when I first starting seeing you had something to do with sex and fear, but I didn't know why. All I can say is that this is close to when I first felt that fear.

"But that all seems so academic. When I first asked out Leanne, truth be told, I was in the middle of a whirlwind. Sex, fear, confusion, annoyance at her father—I felt both weird and in a trancelike state of grace. I'm not sure how to show the tension. It wasn't a game. I was shaking and afraid."

"We can explore why as we go along," Sherry suggested.

"Yeah," Douglas confirmed. "Maybe I should have chatted about Lee right after talking to you about L'Abri, but that didn't make sense to me without talking about arguing with PD first and that got me sidetracked onto Gothard. And here I am six months later. Oh rah!" Douglas was annoyed with himself.

"Sometimes therapy brings the unexpected," said Sherry. "Diverting into Gothard helped me understand the religious context of your relationship with women during this time frame. Of course, it also gives me general insight into your religious background. The time isn't wasted."

Douglas felt glad for acceptance, "That's good to hear."

The next time Douglas saw Leanne was on another PD river trip. The conversation was so long and involved that they got so engrossed during lunch in El Centro that PD almost gave them up for lost and left without them. Douglas had been watching the time on a clock nearby (they were supposed to be back on the bus at 1:00 p.m.) and the clock turned out to be an hour slow. Nonetheless, Douglas and Leanne had to ask forgiveness from the group to get back onto the bus, as they would have been late anyway.

Sherry just shook her head at that one, but didn't say anything, so Douglas continued.

That night, Leanne and Douglas sat down next to each other near the river (within view of the camp, of course, without touching). The cool wind off the wandering water made it easier to talk.

"Are you sure you want to talk with me, Leanne?" Douglas asked.

She nodded her head, "There's nothing in the world that I want to do at the moment other than listen to you talk."

"I don't see why," he wondered, "but don't bother explaining. I'll just have to accept it."

"Good," Leanne said. "You're not expendable."

"Such a compliment," he responded tongue-in-cheek.

"It is one," she grinned.

"Are you sure you want to get to know me better? I might be dangerous."

She nodded again, "I'm willing to take that risk."

Their conversation flowed into a pleasant meander about their feelings, what to do, their motives, relationships in general, theirs in particular, "boy" and "girlfriend," taking the pressure off, "safety valves" for any "physical contact" between them, and general gossip.

Sexual behavior is an issue in a fundamentalist environment. Neither one of them felt comfortable with heavy petting, but where were the lines? Leanne was comfortable with kissing, but Douglas was not. One of his principles was never to kiss a girl before they married. ("I decided that was silly later on when I dated Deirdre, but never mind," he commented to Sherry.)

They'd been talking for an hour and still hadn't touched each other.

"I've got a lot of principles," Douglas said. "Kissing is just one of them. Another is that I'm not sure when to touch you. I'll have to trust your judgment."

"I know," Leanne said, "that's one reason I like you. Your principles are part of you and I'm willing to accept them and you."

Leanne waited for him and respected his boundaries, for which Douglas was grateful. When he asked her to stop flirting, she did so. When she knew he was hiding, she didn't pressure him. She asked him only to be honest and to trust their friendship. They talked honestly before, during and after they dated and generally kept the trust.

"I had almost decided no girl would do that," Douglas responded.

"I have. So obviously some girls will."

Douglas wisely decided not to argue with that logic. Logic, he thought wryly, is a very powerful force within a romantic relationship.

"Are you sure you're willing to do that?" he asked out loud.

"Yes."

The thought made him shiver, not from the cold, but from the thought of a girl liking him. He shook and trembled from the reality.

Then Leanne swept locks of hair from Douglas's eyes. Her touch scared him. They had touched before while she was dating Randy, but this was the first time they touched when they both knew they liked each other. He was upset about it and felt a sudden urge to fling himself into the river. But, he thought, this is what happens when you like a girl.

She touched him again a bit later, softly and briefly, on the arm. This time Douglas felt calm and at peace. Douglas knew that Leanne understood how he felt and accepted it.

"Back up a second," Sherry interrupted.

"Yes?"

Sherry queried him. "You said you were upset about being touched by a girl. The first time she touched you?"

"Yes."

"And scared?"

"Yup. Let me quote from the end of that letter."

"Go ahead."

*"I don't believe I'm ruining Leanne by touching her. As she said, I'm in control and she's been a lot more careful since I warned her that it's dangerous for me. So we aren't violating anything."*

"Did you really think that touching a girl ruins her?" Sherry asked.

"In 1975? Yeah, I did. Leanne gradually helped me see otherwise, but I'll have to tell you that story as we move along," Douglas grinned, "albeit slowly."

"What about her ruining you? You were upset by being sexually touched by a girl. Can you talk more about that?" Sherry felt like there was more there to discuss, but couldn't identify what it was.

"No, I can't really talk more about that. And I mean *can't*. Not 'don't want to.'" Douglas was puzzled too.

"OK," Sherry side-stepped. "Maybe we'll find out more about that later on. Were you done with this story? We're almost out of time."

"Almost. Over the course of time, Leanne dropped enough hints for me to realize that she wanted me to ask her to the Hosanna High junior/senior banquet.

"Remember, her dad won't let her ask me out, plus we're living in a fundamentalist environment. I had to figure out if that's what she really meant, ask her if that was what she meant, qualifying that I hadn't actually asked her yet, then think about it for a day before I finally asked her.

"The prom or the equivalent is a big deal in Christian Schools, too, maybe more so because of the religious overtones."

Douglas rolled his eyeballs. Sherry smiled back, took a note, and the session ended. The sessions were still grueling, but they both felt he was making progress.

# The First Date—the Junior/Senior Banquet

*June 3, 1975, the banquet*

Douglas arrived to pick Leanne up right on time, then pinned on her corsage. He was so nervous that he wanted to leave for the banquet right away, but her dad took pictures, embarrassing him tremendously. He kept thinking that he was too much like Randy, just another beau in a long line of them.

He stayed nervous all the way to the banquet. Then it took him awhile to stop watching everybody else, thinking they'd be surprised to see him with a date. Fortunately, they were too preoccupied with their own dates to pay any attention to him and he finally loosened up enough to talk.

And talk. And talk.

"Am I talking too much?" he said after blabbing for 15 minutes, while waiting for dinner to be served.

She smiled, "Not at all. Your eyes are sparkling." The thought washed him in happiness.

"How about you?" he asked, "Are you enjoying yourself?"

"Oh, yes!" she said, "Very much so. I'm much more comfortable with you than with any other boy, and I like to hear you talk."

He laughed. "I'm not thinking enough to organize what I say. But then everyone seems to agree that I think too much anyway. Hmmm. I seem to recall you said something like that once . . ."

It was her turn to laugh, "I did, didn't I? Well, you do. And I want you to feel free around me. Free and unafraid, not thinking all the time."

A better word than "thinking" is "restricted." Restrained. Bound by Gothard or the conventions of his church, bound by his self-imposed principles. Douglas was afraid to be himself for fear of losing himself. Just because he no longer believed in Gothard didn't mean that he could drop the shackles right away.

The first time they touched was at their official picture. The convention was for the man to put his arm around her waist then touch her right hand with his left, encircling her. Leanne was comfortable,

Douglas nervous. But the picture didn't take long and required little effort.

Her hand felt so soft in his.

He couldn't remember much afterwards of what he said during dinner, but did recall asking if she got anything out of the relationship. He couldn't help but wonder. Was he really valuable to her? Leanne couldn't answer and promptly turned the question back on him. What did he get from dating her?

"You really do let me be myself," he said. "I enjoy everything we do together and enjoy just being around you. So much so that I'll have to be careful with the one thing that expresses feeling well." He meant touching her, as he didn't want to lose control or to spoil her.

Several times while eating he just stopped and stared out into space, grinning his head off. There he was with a beautiful, beautiful girl. And he liked her. And she liked him! Miracles still occurred.

He'd shake his head "no" then watch her out of the corner of his eyes only to see her nod her head "yes." He was happier then than he ever remembered being.

The second time they touched occurred when he crossed his legs at the table and she smacked him with her elbow. He just giggled, uncrossed his legs, and finished eating.

They went to Darrell's Ice Cream for dessert. "Are you still enjoying yourself?" he asked. He was worried that this wasn't real.

"Oh, I'm quite happy! I can't explain why," she said. Then she paused before continuing. "One thing I can say is that I never felt this special with Randy except when he held my hand. But you haven't touched me at all, really, and I feel just as happy, just as special." It pleased him.

"I'm happy, too," he responded. "Though I can't understand how I can be in this situation. I never thought I deserved it."

She laughed. "Well, you are in this situation, obviously."

"I'm going to stop what I'm doing and just look at you," was all he responded. Looking at her was far better than staring into space. There was an air of mystery about it.

He talked later about his poor race the day before, feeling frustrated with his performance. Leanne reached out and touched his arm to show that she knew how he felt and sympathized. He felt much more at peace after that. Quiet, unworried, accepted.

It was the third time they touched that night and the last. Soon after that, he dropped her off at her house just before midnight, said, "Goodnight!" then walked away.

Walking on air beats good race times any day.

Douglas Baign

*June 4, 1975, Leanne's Letter*
*Help me!*
*No . . . I have to answer alone.*
*How did it come about?*
*Nothing like this has ever*
    *happened before.*
*Is it right, are we in His will?*
*I never thought it could happen to me.*
*I feel peaceful, no cares.*
*Does he really like me?*
    *Wonder.*
*I wasn't too excited at first.*
*He's just a friend, I enjoy his company.*
*But I looked forward to it,*
*Maybe a little apprehensive.*
*He was nice, acting as usual.*
*I was having fun watching*
    *him have fun.*
*I became myself.*
*Relaxing and enjoying the night.*
*Then it changed.*
    *Completely.*
*I knew what was going to happen*
    *But couldn't stop it.*
*Leanne*

⌾⌾⌾⌾⌾⌾

*May 15, 2003, in session*

"Wow!" Douglas remarked. "Telling you that story brought it all back to me. I can still smell Leanne's perfume from nearly 28 some odd years ago. Glorious!"

Sherry smiled, perhaps thinking of her own husband. "But you were still afraid of sexual behavior with Leanne. Even holding her hand."

"Yeah," he said. "I wrote Jacky later that night." He flipped pages to the appropriate place.

*You may wonder how I feel toward Leanne sexually. I must admit that I have evil thoughts once in a while. But 98 percent of the time, I'm not bothered. Leanne is beautiful, but I'm not just attracted to her by her sexuality.*

126

"You thought sex was evil?" Sherry probed.

"Yes," Douglas admitted. "I was terrified of touching Leanne – and of her touching me—absolute panic! And I never told her that. I couldn't! I'm not even sure I knew it at the time.

"98 percent of the time I didn't feel dominated by sexual thoughts. I certainly thought Lee was awesome, but . . . I dunno how to explain it. Leanne made everything around her awesome, too. I was so in love with Leanne that sex wasn't really why I dated her. It was her.

"Does that make sense?"

"Yes, it does," Sherry confirmed. "But go back one step. Why did you panic over being sexual?"

Douglas thought it over, "Partly because of my religious upbringing. They were so hung up on it. But that doesn't seem to be the only reason. And . . . I can't tell you more than that."

Sherry didn't push. She simply added it to her notes, "OK. Let's let that thought bounce around in the back of your head while we move to the next topic. How did religion play into your relationship?"

He nodded. "I was out of Gut Turd by then—I mean, Gothard—but some of Gothard was still in me. PD and the Church had drilled two things into my head. Men are made as creators and leaders. Women were made to be helpmates and responders."

"You don't think that sounds medieval?" Sherry commented.

"Well, yeah," Douglas was embarrassed. "I do. Of course, I had plenty of company at Lands Baptist. I really thought this way for a while. Maybe it's biblical, maybe it isn't. But it didn't work for me that way. And I'm angry that I have to confess it, angry that I'm still trying to cope—angry, angry, angry.

"Part of me disagreed with it all, but trying to come up with something else while handling a relationship plus reorganizing my religious beliefs was just too rough.

"Bottom line. For heaven's sake, I was 17. So by now it's probably also a good time to forgive myself for being 17. Rather hard to prevent, you know. That is, if you want to keep living."

Sherry laughed at that one, "Yes, it is hard to prevent. Let's close on that note, shall we? We can continue chatting about Leanne next session."

Douglas left the session feeling comradely towards Sherry. They were both on the same side. He walked back to his car whistling a happy tune. "I owe, I owe, so off to work I go."

It was funny to him because he'd paid for his convertible in full up front, using stock options. His only debt was on the mortgage.

# The Second Date—Roller Skating

*June 7, 1975, dating*

Everyone got to Leanne's house a bit late for their double date, but Douglas and Lee jumped into Bernie's car as soon as he arrived and the couples headed down to the skating rink. Leanne skated well but it took Douglas awhile to get used to the skates.

"I'm afraid of what will happen in a year from now," Douglas commented. "Your Dad got orders to stay in Santa Brisa but you'll be at JECU and I'll still be at UCSB."

"Don't worry about it, Douglas," Leanne suggested. "It's a year away. Enjoy the time now." Douglas decided that was sound advice.

"How are Margo and Bernie doing?" he asked instead. He'd seen enough of their relationship to know that it was spotty.

Leanne thought they were fine for now, " . . . but when they start looking for a mate they'll have to find someone who can make them be honest."

Douglas laughed. "You do know what you just said about us." They were honest in their relationship. Leanne hadn't realized what she'd implied, but she figured it out on her own. They were friends who cared for each other. The announcer eventually called for couples skating. Couples must hold hands. Leanne wanted to go out but had to work hard to persuade Douglas. He finally got up the nerve to get into the arena then said, "Now I'm supposed to hold your hand." They did and started skating.

Douglas couldn't keep his mind on anything, wasn't concerned about anything at all. It was a strange sensation. Several times, he just stopped talking and stared. He couldn't believe that he could be so privileged to be that happy. They were not just friends building each other up, but were giving to each other help and peace. He felt more integrated.

"It's rather odd, you know," he remarked a bit later.

"What is?"

Douglas tried to put his thoughts into words. "I figured that our feelings would start from heart or mind. But it's not. It's our hands, warm not just from touching, but from sex and spirit."

Later on, he couldn't remember the actual words he said as he reached out to touch her without the announcer's prompt. All he remembered is that he took his left hand and with his three longest fingers, barely touched the top of her right hand. They talked while their fingers brushed.

Douglas told Leanne he was unconcerned about their future, though it held destruction, because he had the present with her now. But sometimes he felt the destruction, the old sin nature in him, and didn't care because he could fight to subdue it.

"You're beautiful to me," he said as they walked to the church nearby. "Not just physically, although that would still be a true statement," he hastened to add. "But that I can see you as a person. You're unafraid of showing yourself and want to stand on your beliefs." They walked in and found a place to sit down near each other.

"You've helped me so much, even in your letters before we started dating." Towards the end of his little speech, he thanked her for being herself, for all the help she had given him.

"Thank you, Douglas," she said heartfelt. Then she thanked him for being himself, and stared into each other's eyes. They accepted each other and were complete. It was beautiful and he knew he'd never forget it.

He almost cried later from happiness. Leanne was also overwhelmed and said she'd not forget it either. How can this be mine? he asked himself. Why do I deserve this? The memory is so unbelievable. Each second is so precious, worth more to me than anything else in the world. I would willingly give up anything for it. He had been giving and was blessed by it.

They held hands all the way home, her eyes shining. They didn't say much but just looked at each other. Their time was being. They were. Feelings that are part of a couple can't be described to the outside. They were, they are.

When the couples got back to Leanne's home, she got out of Bernie's car. Douglas got out on the same side, touched her hand briefly, said, "I'd better go now."

Then he walked over to his own car and left.

∽✐✐∽✐✐∽✐✐

*May 22, 2003, in session*

"Aargh," Douglas started the next session with his standard minor curse. "There's just so many things to talk about, even in that one story. Sex and the Church, Leanne the girl, Leanne the woman, my family, her family, theology and so on. I'm feeling battered by too many topics."

Sherry tried to simplify the matter. "You don't have to talk about them all. Just pick one."

"Yeah, that's the problem," Douglas replied. "I want to get at the gestalt and I can only talk about it one topic at a time. There's simply not enough bandwidth. I'm stuck looking at just one thing."

Or to put it another way, if therapy is about putting yourself together, then by definition you start disconnected. There's a lot of stitching to do—and you don't even know how to sew.

Which in turn means therapy can take forever and that fact alone makes it frustrating. Right around the time you think you're done talking about a topic (like arguing with PD) something else comes along (like Leanne) or you realize that there's more worms under the rock of an old topic.

It's all you can do to just plod along one thread at a time, unweaving then reweaving an entire tapestry.

After more than two years in therapy, he felt like he was still in the same place. Why did he want to commit suicide? The meds helped a lot. So did therapy. But he still had some particularly bad days. And Douglas was still afraid that without discovering the root of the problem, he'd find a bridge somewhere then jump.

This session just thrashed round and round. No, Douglas couldn't remember. No, his mom wasn't the problem. No, his dad had mostly been out of the picture. No, he still couldn't talk about it.

"That could be a sign of a preverbal trauma, Douglas." Sherry was at least providing some diagnosis.

Douglas' eyebrows rose. "What do you mean by that?"

"Something may have happened to you before speech therapy and probably before you could talk at all. That something is damaging you now."

"Great. Just great. How do I get at it if I don't know what it is?"

Sherry was adamant. "Keep coming here. Keep trying. Talk to your other family members."

"Yeah, that's about the size of it," he growled, missing the last half of her message. "Don't stop believin'. Some 'Journey' through therapy, huh? Just keep coming here and you're back in the same place. Hooray for the Red Queen's race. But yeah, you're right."

"You've made good progress, Douglas. Keep going." Sherry was sympathetic.

"Yeah," he growled again. The session ended in frustration, but there was nothing to do but to keep trying.

*May 22, 2003, at home*

*My dear Jacky-Jack,,*

Bleh. It's time to back off from trying to deal with all this. Fahgettaboutit. There's too much going on. I've been in a lot of tough sessions with Sherry lately and it's time to do something fun. So . . . let's talk about astronomy. I like astronomy, just like Michael Gordon in Potok's *The Promise* and for much the same reasons. Galaxies can't hurt you. You can probe them, but they're safe and very interesting.

If ever I study astronomy seriously, I'd probably specialize in cosmology and that means quasars. This particular one is (oh) 14 billion light years out and sheds light through a gas cloud. The gas cloud acts like a prism and that means you can do a spectrograph of the materials in the quasar.

Compare that to a spectrograph of the same materials here on Earth and guess what. It's different and physics says they shouldn't be; similar materials yield similar spectrographs. If the results hold up, then one of our assumptions about three basic values in physics must be wrong.

- The charge on an electron
- Planck's constant
- The speed of light

Perhaps the laws of physics change depending on where you are in the universe—the quasar or on Earth. Or maybe physics changes as the universe gets older.

I used to dream about these things when I was a child. Who are we in this big universe of ours? Why are we here? Is there someone else out there with us?

I love looking at the sky and the stars. I love seeing nebulae. The swirls and colors eddy and flow. It's so much fun to see what a beautiful place this is, to dance in the numbers and the colors, where every place you go just radiates with surprises. I want to go to the quasar, or at least to *Ursa Major,* and then stand there (on a planet near *Ursa Major*) to look farther still. I want to see the end of time.

Sigh! Instead, it's time to go to bed here on terra sometimes firma. That's California for you. Maybe I'll be lucky and not sleep well and have to get up and look at the sky. Bummer.

Or maybe I'll sleep very well and dream of the stars and the clouds, the baby emeralds crackling and dancing with each other to give birth.

To make a star, to make a planet, to make a cradle for people to live in and to wonder.

I wonder.

Good night, my dearest Jacky. Sleep well.

*D.*

*P.S.* I woke up that night and got up to look at the sky, and gray clouds covered every star. Ah, well. I didn't sleep well the rest of the night.

*Eppur si muove.* The Earth and the universe still moves with or without our consent.

# Reality Bites

# Early June 2003

*June 1, 2003, at home*

*Dear Jacky,*

A week ago, I lamented that therapy could take forever, partly because just about the time you've licked one thing something else comes along.

Ouch! Talk about premonitions. A lot has happened in the past week or so, and now there's so many things going on that it's hard to talk about anything at all. My mind is flush with too many other worries. Talk about overload. I had to cancel last week's Sherry appointment to give me time to deal with it all.

Let's start from the beginning.

The fecal matter hit the AMD at work just the other day. First, some co-workers yelled at me for doing exactly what they asked me to do. Then I was snowed with email. Ugh. Then I babysat an engineer through some simple doc issues (sorry, Jacky, but that's really dull) then found out one of my co-workers has metastasized brain cancer.

To make a bad day worse, my wife Anne and I had a stressful marital counseling session with Dr. H on Tuesday then got home only to find out dad had to get an emergency triple–bypass heart surgery ASAP on Friday. Wow!

The docs said surgery went well on Saturday, but Sunday night my tooth inlay fell out. I had emergency dental work on Monday, where they discovered more problems, and I was back in again on Tuesday.

I really hate dentists! There you are with your mouth jammed full of rubber and fingernails when the guy rams a needle through your cheek, sticks his wrists down your tonsils and asks, "How you doing?"

Just fine, doc. My dad's got a bad ticker, my friend has brain cancer, my career's a shit, people are yelling at me for doing what they asked me to do, my wife and I are tearing at each other, my mouth feels like kindergarten glue, and I thought you were supposed to use a scraper on my teeth, not your nose hairs. Thanks for asking.

Anyway, things started getting better as soon as dad got out of the hospital yesterday. My boss gave me a kind word at work, my co-worker's cancer is treatable, Anne and I made progress at today's session (we can be civil to each other) and I could actually taste my tea this morning. No more kindergarten glue.

Hallelujah! Thank you, Jesus! And I'm at least half-serious about this. I'm grateful that things are calming down at least enough for me to write you here.

I'm still snowed with email and I can't really keep up all that correspondence going very well. Everyone is talking about the war, but sometimes I get the feeling that they don't understand the subtleties.

We all polarize it somewhat, but there's this Goldilocks feel to it. One friend thinks that the U.S. is tooooo liberal. Another thinks that the U.S. is tooooo conservative. And (now that we've insisted on fighting a war we don't need) I think the U.S. is juuuuuust right.

But I'm having trouble getting either side to see the balance points. IMHO, we need to reject our current political polarities and start all over again. The most American thing we can do is to reinvent ourselves.

Screw the conservatives. Screw the liberals. The first decision any government must make is how to stay alive long enough to make the second decision. First, we survive. Then we change things we see wrong.

Let us never forget the evil we have done. Let us sorrow and correct it. But let us also celebrate what we believe is right and good, that we may bring joy.

Thanks for listening, Jacky! Hopefully it's back to Sherry soon to talk about Leanne.

*Love,*
*Douglas*

*June 5 2003, in session*

"How's your father doing?" Sherry asked.

"Better," Douglas responded. "He's out of the hospital now and the doc said he's good for another few years, plus things are calmer at work. Thanks for asking."

"Do you want to talk more about the past weekend?" Sherry asked.

"Not really," he responded. "I'm just glad it's over and done with and I survived it. Time to move on to the next topic."

"Which is . . ." Sherry prompted.

"I wanted to talk more about how my romance with Leanne started," he explained after a moment, "so let's start there."

It would take two sessions for Douglas to go through the stories.

# Leanne, Part II

# June 1975, Dreaming

*June 14, 1975, dating*

He had dinner with Leanne's family that night. Douglas was nervous about it, especially since Leanne's dad was a commander in the Air Force, but the dinner went well. The fact that Douglas's uncle was currently a lieutenant in the Navy (and Douglas's dad had served, too) helped. The military connection made for a small bond.

Her mother was interested in music and that was yet another. Also at the table was Leanne's sister Jolene, younger by only a year. The family felt a little like the Baigns.

Douglas and Leanne wandered into the garden after dinner. There was still a bit of light left to enjoy the green then they looked east into the valley as the sun dimmed in a reverse sunset. Leanne's house lay on one edge directly above the valley and the view was breathtaking.

The evening cooled and they sat down on a bench under a trellis. Douglas found himself wanting to hold her hand again, but had his doubts. Was it OK to touch her? Was he presumptuous to ask? So he just sat and talked, getting reactions and trying to gauge her interest. He avoided the issue a thousand times.

His approach was so indirect that 20 minutes later they both knew what he was talking about. And he still couldn't bring himself to hold her hand or even to ask. Yet he respected and cared for her so much that his desire gradually exceeded his terror. Still, he had to try twice before he could even get started.

"Is it all right for me to ask you if . . ." he said, leaving his question unasked.

"Oh, yes," she said.

He swallowed and finally asked. "Is it all right for me to ask you if I can hold your hand?"

"Oh, yes. Please do."

*The Beatles* song rang irreverently through his head as he asked, "May I hold your hand?"

"Please do," she repeated.

He calmed as soon as he touched her. It wasn't the brilliance like at the Starfall date while roller skating. It was quietness and peace. He knew

139

someone cared, that he was important. Someone wanted him to be happy, wanted to help. Their feelings were the only thing in the world that mattered, because they were the world. We share a bond, he thought. And that fellowship is an unconquerable power, final resistance, and ultimate authority.

Later, he felt small and very childish. Leanne held his hand in both of hers, almost protecting it. It was almost as if Leanne was afraid of losing him. It was fierce.

'*Nothing can surpass the mystery of stillness,*' he thought, quoting e. e. cummings in his head. The convulsed orange square of moon was bright above them by now and the words felt appropriate.

"How can you be so calm?" he asked.

"I'm only calm on the outside," she responded. "I think I feel the same as you - trembling and afraid." He didn't know why they should feel frightened, but it still made sense to him. They were so small, because their feelings were so great.

"Douglas," said Leanne, "You have a tremendous capacity for feeling, more so than a lot of other people. To tremble, to be scared, to feel frightened but not lonely; all these are feelings. Let yourself feel them."

"I'll try," he said. "It is something for me to learn. What about you?"

"To learn? I'm learning trust, I think." Leanne reflected on it some, the starlight glittering in her eyes. "To believe in them for yourself, to follow them, to allow yourself to become part of them, and to allow them to make things that reflect on you."

"You didn't feel that way with Randy?"

"Oh, no!" she exclaimed, but didn't elaborate.

They sat silently for a few minutes, just being. Then Douglas thought of something. "Leanne, can you do me a favor, *por favor*?"

"If I can," she said.

"I know you like me. That's obvious."

She grinned.

"But I like details. Do you think you could write me more about how you feel about me?"

Leanne was startled for a second. "Write?" Then she thought about it. "Well, maybe that makes sense. We wrote each other before."

"Yeah."

"And I was just saying that I'm learning to trust you."

"Yup."

"OK. I'll give it a try."

There was little enough to say after that. They held hands a bit longer, looked out over the sparkles of the valley below once more, then drifted back inside.

*June 16, 1975, Douglas's high school graduation speech*

When I first came to Hosanna High, the thing that impressed me the most was the care that teachers had for their students. I found that I was important and that what was myself was accepted as valid, even if I were wrong at times. Teachers encouraged me to be myself and to stand up for what I believed. Rightness, they said, did not always depend on whether or not I was correct in my beliefs, but rather on whether or not I was willing to believe in them and in myself and willing to be corrected when I was wrong.

I'm still learning this, but this has been my greatest lesson at Hosanna High. Once I as an individual deny my own beliefs for the purpose of social acceptance, I would cease to become an individual and become a number, conforming to the world in purpose, accommodating the world's thoughts, and complying with them in my actions. I would be then no longer an individual, for I would have become divisible.

Now that my past at Hosanna High is over, my future lies ahead. I don't know what I am going to do, nor where I am to go, but then, I'm not expected to. But I do know that God is with me. He will guide me through my life and I will follow him.
*Douglas*

*June 22, 1975, high school*

Douglas wrote his graduation speech on the 16th, graduated the 19th, then went to Grad Night a few days later at Disneyland. He had wanted to ask Leanne along but the party was for seniors only. Once Douglas reflected on it, he thought it would be a good idea. It gave him a chance to say good-bye to friends he'd rarely, if ever, see again. His class had been a close-knit group.

The party itself was relaxed and enjoyable. Without a date, Douglas did feel like he was stuck wandering around Disneyland with the class dweeb, but he also spent time with good friends.

The trip back was a bit harder, as most couples on the bus were very obviously enjoying each other. School restrictions no longer applied. Douglas's best friend Matt draped himself over Rachel, so Douglas ended up second-guessing himself. Was he being too restrictive in only holding hands with Leanne?

Too much thinking, he told himself. All I know is that I'm afraid to touch Leanne more, but want to. Another voice in his mind told him that it was OK to feel, to care for Leanne, to see her as sexual. Despite the future, despite what it may hold. If I let myself experience her, Douglas thought, it will be right and I can let God worry about the future.

But there were so many voices in his head and the noise of the group confused him.

Oh, I hope I can do this, said one voice. By God's power may it be! I hope that I can hold Leanne's hand rightly, so that I don't need to do anything else. The important thing is to be natural! Don't think too much, it's bad for you.

Too much thinking. If I can stop thinking about myself, if I can somehow follow my beliefs and destiny, if I can believe in myself, if I can follow God, allow Him to lead, then follow my sense of right all the time and feed it by God's word, walking day by day, then who I am will come out.

But I still don't know. Should I touch Leanne more than I do now or not?

*June 23, 1975, letter to Leanne*

*My Dear Leanne,*

I can't speak when I put my arm around you. I was limited by speech.

It was fantastic. I found that we were very much closer than ever before. We created beauty, a higher form of it. It was seeing all that is real and alive. My goal of seeing all meaning was very nigh. I could see truth and honesty and trust. We had it in ourselves. We created, formulated all that is right and true, at least in a certain area. We saw, we perceived, we understood and beheld together in a way impossible otherwise. We stood as we are to stand, as individuals with meaning and with a message to call unto the lands that they should feel life and truly live as we are alive unto each other.

Leanne, a new day has dawned and the sun it is bright. You are that sun. You have given me life, given me warmth and, above all, bequeathed unto me myself. Every time I touch you, you've responded, caring for me myself, for reasons I cannot fathom. Even though I sometimes pain you, you still shine for me. Shedding your light and gladness upon me, as golden tears of joy, shivering their happiness on diamond shells of wonder, lying on the beach of awe.

I plunge into the ocean, drinking in its splendor. In its icy depths, I am unafraid, for you have given me strength. Although I tremble, I tremble in beauty and in fear-inspired joy. The seas become alive to me, something that has never happened to me before. Their swells surround me, but you are wholly there to comfort me and to give me peace within.

Oh, Leanne, I thank you from the bottom of my heart. You have given me your trust and I will not break it. You have given me life, truth and myself.

Thank you, for you are my light, reflecting the light of God.

*Douglas Baign*

142

*June 26, 1975, Leanne's letter to Douglas*

Douglas,

Ok, I'm ready. Let's see—an animal (animals are easier than anything to describe). Um . . . I've got it!

Have you ever held a kitten in your arms? One that's purring with his eyes closed and a semi-smile (?) on his face. He's beautiful—imagine this if you can. You've found this hungry, lost, lonely kitten so you pick him up. His yellow and white-striped coat is silky smooth but his bushy tail has a few burrs in it. You pet him as you're sitting on some stairs and he's licking your hand, purring away. Finally, he goes to sleep in the crook of your arm with his head right next to your body inside your elbow. He's peacefully sleeping, there is something possibly resembling a smile where his mouth should be, and his motor has not yet turned off. He's perfectly happy; he's right where he wants to be.

What impresses me about that kitten is that he has what he wants, no more and no less. He knows he's not alone in this great big cruel world. Someone cares enough to keep him comfortable and be there when he's hurting. He's loved and cared for. He's right there, in your arms, without a care in the world—just happy!

Now I have to identify—oh, let's see. OK, here goes try one. Like the cat I was peaceful, yet excited or happy. I'm using general terms again! Oh well, the best suggestion I can give is that you go back to the previous paragraph and everywhere I say something about the cat, put me in. I just reread it with "Douglas" in instead and it works. I just hope that it gives you at least some idea of the way I feel.

Oh, well, see ya later,
Leanne.

# Late June 2003—Of gods and goddesses

*June 19, 2003, in session*

"Your stories during this time frame," Sherry commented, "focus on two things: God and Leanne."

"'*Un dieu dans le ciel et une déesse sur la terre,*'" Douglas quoted, "as the French might say in the Middle Ages. 'A god in heaven and a goddess on earth.'"

Sherry nodded, "Exactly. But why was sex such a *bête noire?*" she asked. "Sex is supposed to be fun between lovers, a joy."

"Sometimes it was," Douglas commented. "Most of the time, even. I can't explain it all, but I remember fearing touching Leanne would hurt her. That I'd 'damage the goddess,' so to speak."

"If a woman likes her partner, it's not damage," Sherry pointed out.

He thought about it. "Yeah, that makes sense. But I felt the way I felt and I can't explain it better."

"And you can't talk about it more than that," Sherry confirmed.

"Yeah," Douglas didn't like it either.

Sherry hesitated, "OK. We're not making any progress with 'the goddess on Earth' so let's get back to 'a god in heaven.' I thought you'd given up on Gothard."

"I had. But that doesn't mean I'd given up on God," he explained. "In 1975, I thought that Rothead's interpretation of the Bible was abo, absolutely crackers. But that doesn't mean I rejected the Bible, just Gothard's—and my church's—interpretation of it"

"Abo?"

"Absolutely way out there, like aborigines in the outback."

"Ah," Sherry exclaimed. "So what were your religious beliefs at the time? And how does that fit into your relationship with Leanne?"

Douglas curled his feet up under him while he sorted through his memory.

"I was thinking through three things about religion:" he said finally, "the relationship between an individual and society, the relationship between an individual and God and the relationship between God and physics.

"What I mentioned earlier about Janis Joplin—'Freedom's just another word for nothin' left to lose'—describes the first category." He flipped through the pages until he found the reference again.

> *"An individual abides by government rule, but in doing so he is denying his own ideals and his will, losing his freedom."*

"When I wrote that, I was feeling alienated from my society, the Church. Which, I should add, is very, very dangerous within a fundamentalist culture. They might lovingly scream at you for being an apostate.

"My graduation speech takes the idea a step further, setting it inside a context familiar to my church.

> *"Once I as an individual deny my own beliefs for the purpose of social acceptance, I cease to become an individual and become a number, conforming to the world in purpose, accommodating the world's thoughts, and complying with them in my actions. I am no longer an individual, for I have become divisible."*

"That's close enough to what St. Paul said in Romans," as usual, Douglas quoted from memory.

> *12:2 And be not conformed to this world: but be ye transformed by the renewing of your mind, that ye may prove what is that good, and acceptable, and perfect, will of God.*

" . . . that anyone at my church who heard that probably thought nothing of it. Just another nice young man applying scripture to his life. 'Good boy.' Makes me feel like a dog, but never mind.

"But I gave that speech in front of several hundred people knowing that the principle of non-conformity or of civil disobedience applied not just to 'the world' but to 'the Church.' I was telling my church point blank that I would only be satisfied with acceptance by God, not them. Not only was I willing to stand up to 'the world,' but that I could and would stand up to them too. And no one got it."

"Sneaky," Sherry said.

"Yup. I ended the speech with 'God will guide me through my life and I will follow him.' And what I meant was 'Dude, God's gonna guide me, not you and certainly not PD. *Sayonara.* I'm outta here.'"

145

Douglas held his head in his hands for a moment. "That all seemed such a lie when I tore myself apart after L'Abri. But in the long run, my own words came back to heal."

"How much of what you're saying now did you mean then?" Sherry asked.

Douglas felt antsy and shifted his position on the couch. "Most of it," he said. "I remember standing up in front of everyone while thinking, 'This applies to you too.'

"The problem," he continued, "is I didn't completely admit that to myself. It was too dangerous."

"What were you worried about?"

"Disapproval. I had the intellectual wherewithal to come up with the position, but not the emotional maturity to sustain it. I was 17 years old."

"You didn't think your parents supported you enough for you to have the emotional security by then?"

"Frankly, no. I don't. It goes back to the catacomb service. I felt like just an afterthought to them. They were both too busy with their own agendas to see me. Aargh."

"What were they involved in?" Sherry asked.

"School. A zillion hours a week. Mom taught five different classes—Art 1 and 2, Drama 1 and 2, and English—plus taught Ceramics after school then worked as a producer in the local Drama troupe on the weekends.

"Dad didn't do any voluntary teaching, but he helped mom any time he had the chance. He wanted to spend as much time as he could with her."

He paused.

"You know? It's funny now that I think about it, but after I turned 12 or so, when mom started teaching, they both pretty much neglected me." He didn't like thinking ill of his parents, but the abandonment was painful.

"That hurts," he said. "Still hurts, I mean."

"It should," was all Sherry said.

"It's also one reason why Leanne was important. She accepted me. I didn't expect her to take the place of mom and dad," Douglas added, "but I was so grateful for her support."

Sherry added to her copious notes, then glanced through what she'd already written down, "You said you were thinking three things about religion. The third was the relationship between God and physics. Can you talk more about that?"

"That I can," Douglas confirmed. "But at that time, I didn't have enough background to make my ideas coherent. I can read you what I wrote Jacky," Douglas gestured towards his own notes, "but the letters don't make much sense. For example,"

> *I personally believe that our minds, although independent, exist only in God's mind as an expression of His consciousness. No, I don't really know what I'm talking about.*

"I think I was saying the universe only exists when we observe it. God observed us and here we are. Or as Moses or whoever wrote Genesis once said, 'And the LORD God formed man of the dust of the ground, and breathed into his nostrils the breath of life, and man became a living soul.' But beyond saying that, my ideas are too spotty to mention."

The mind wanders like the wind when running a race, which, of course, is one reason you do it. But you won't run the right split times if your mind races too much instead of you.

So there comes a time when you have to let go of the rhythms you form in the middle of the race and get back to its genesis. You're trying to beat your opponents. In this case, that meant Douglas needed to let go of physics and beat back to Leanne and PD. Heaven and Earth. Or the *Genesis* beat in their album *Wind & Wuthering*.

"All right," Sherry confirmed. "We'll leave at that. Let's continue this thought next week."

He stood up, stretched, and said good-bye. He felt much more optimistic about his progress, but it was time for Doug to go.

*June 26, 2003, in session*

In times of struggle, we often pray to our gods, "Lord, grant me patience. Right now!"

Impatience still often gets the best of us. Douglas, frustrated that therapy was so slow, screwed up and caused delays when he tried to move forward too fast. But when he slowed down, he made mistakes anyway, said the wrong thing, or focused on the wrong task. Did he really want to forgive himself?

His former speech impediment once served as a ready excuse. His tongue got in the way of itself; his brain seemed mis-wired.

But consider: wanting to kill oneself does not occur to most people who make mistakes. To quell that impulse, his strategy, haphazard at times, was to keep plugging away, one small step at a time.

"For now," he said when beginning to tell Sherry about his view of God that summer of 1975, "the next small step for (a) man is foot washing."

Douglas's new on-and-off again church recently sent a group of folks to India to be foot washers. Literally foot washers. They came back the other day and the church held a service in their honor. Behold the foot washers! They washed the foot of the local beggar king! It was such an uplifting experience to serve so humbly!

"So . . . if you wanted to be so humble," he asked Sherry, "then . . . why are you bragging about it?"

Enter Summer Servants, stage left (a phrase we've used since at least Edward de Vere). Summer Servants was the top of Lands Baptist's youth pecking order, playing the same part then as the foot washers do now.

"They were the group of older teens who were so spiritually advanced that they were proud to humbly serve you."

Summer Servants applicants were vetted by PD and reported directly to him rather than routing through the normal power structure. Douglas hadn't been invited, but it was clear that he could apply with a strong chance of being accepted.

"So long as I didn't mind staying in the same spiritual rut," he commented, "that is, and I was ready to move on. 'Commit new mistakes,' as they say."

One summer servant was Daniel. At the time, Lands Baptist was making an effort to link to other churches. Daniel was actually a charismatic Pentecostal. Naturally, the Church didn't trust him and during the summer of 1975, Daniel lived in a trailer on the Baign property so that Lands Baptist could monitor him properly. PD trusted Douglas's dad.

"Dad is now a backsliding Methodist," Douglas added in an aside to Sherry. "He shifted religions and churches once he married Gwen. Wanted to stay with her. Such a bummer now that he's happy instead being one of the frozen chosen."

But having a stranger around the house was an unwelcome change, no matter how godly Douglas was supposed to be about it. The shifting schools and religious views were stressful and he felt abandoned by his church and parents. His friends at school had scattered. He was new to the church college group and didn't fit in. His mom was involved in local theatre. His dad taught summer school.

It's one thing to kick the bird out of the nest, it's another to break their wings then throw them out. Douglas still needed a support structure and everything vanished faster than a Penn and Teller act.

"What I had," he said, "was Leanne and she was smart, pretty and loyal. Gosh, how I loved her!"

"Let's stick with your religious views for the moment," Sherry suggested. "That's where we're making progress. How did you feel about God that summer?"

"Like a deer in the headlights," he responded. "So many choices, so many gates in front of me, and God has only one theology, one master plan for my life, or so I'd been taught and still believed. I was so desperate to please, so desperate to follow God, that I created my own emptiness. How much will God hate me if I pick the wrong gate?"

"Isn't theology the work of humans," Sherry asked. "How can there be only one theology?"

Douglas thought about it. "You have to remember I was still 17 and still mostly fundamentalist. So sure. There were lots of theologies. But most of them were wrong because they weren't based on interpreting the Bible literally.

"That meant there was a very narrow range over which true theology could exist. From the fundamentalist viewpoint, which I was gradually losing, it's almost as if theology was a gift God gave to some folks whose job it was to make it clear that the Fundamentalist interpretation of the Bible was obviously correct. Because it was, wasn't it?"

Sherry kept her emotions well-hidden. "How literal is literal," she asked. "All the animals entered the Ark two-by-two?"

"Oh no, of course not," he responded.

This time Sherry looked startled. "I thought you said Lands Baptist took the Bible literally."

"Of course. So only the *unclean* animals went up the Ark two-by-two. The *clean* animals went up seven-by-seven."

"Ah. And creation took seven days?"

"Well, six, starting around 6 p.m. on October 22, 4004 BC. God rested on Sunday. I can't remember how Bishop Usher came up with October 22, but just for fun I repeated his work and if you take the Bible literally, you can in fact place the creation in 4004 BC."

Sherry shook her head. "OK. That's literal, all right. How did this impact you?"

Douglas took a breath. "Whatever reality is, whatever the Cosmos is, there is only *one* of them that we live in. All the people I knew kept telling me that there is only one God, one theology, one way to salvation and much more importantly, God only had one will for my life, up to and possibly including who I was supposed to marry. It was a form of predestination."

"Sounds quite demanding."

"Yeah. Work it out. If I marry the wrong person, then God's will for my life is now only second best. And God's will for my wife is only second best because *she's* marrying the wrong person. Which in turn means that the man God originally wanted *her* to marry is now marrying the wrong person. And the woman that God wanted *me* to marry in the first place is now *also* doing the wrong thing, and so on, *ad infinitum.*

"But the Church theology held that there's only ONE gate God wants me to take at any one point in time with lots of simultaneous false 'second-best,' 'deceitful,' or 'sinful' gates. All the folks I knew said that they knew exactly what gate God wanted me to take. And everyone contradicted each other."

It had already dawned on Douglas that he needed a new theology, but there was something odd about the way his friends and mentors set up the decision tree. PD knew he was right and believed X. Daniel knew he was right and believed the opposite. Matt knew they were both wrong. But did anyone talk to Douglas?

Something about God's sovereignty came to mind. Presumably, God can actually determine which theology He really believes in.

So how was it that PD, Matt, and Daniel knew God's thoughts so thoroughly? Who gave them God's phone number?

Let's keep it simple. Why didn't God just tell Douglas? Wasn't he just as holy as they were?

Douglas summarized the issue, "Bong! I made a theological choice right then and there. Let other folks worry about the details. *My* concern is simply following God.

"So when Daniel sat down to convert me, I felt angry. 'God,' I was thinking, 'not another thing I have to do to please God. Where is everyone who's supposed to help me out with this?' I wanted to just rip my guts out and throw them at Daniel. 'Here, now you've got all of me. Go away.'"

Douglas hoped that Leanne could at least help him talk this out. God, when can I talk with her again? he thought back then. I need to talk. I need acceptance. I need to just hear Your Voice, God, hear her voice.

The fact he was willing to share his doubts was important. He was deeply in love with Leanne.

# July 1975, Embracing the Spirit

*July 13, 1975, a musical with Leanne*

They went to a musical that night at Starfall school. Douglas liked being with Leanne but became depressed halfway through the program and couldn't identify why.

At the end of the show, the audience was asked to look at the cross in the dark and to examine themselves. Douglas had been holding hands with Leanne during the whole service, but when they stood, he had a strange sensation. As they looked at the cross, both of them before God in their hearts, he found himself standing together with Leanne in their spirits. She was supporting him, he her. God wanted them together for that moment.

They took a walk afterwards, while he told her his emotions.

"I don't know why I felt sad," he told Leanne.

"Can you describe the feeling better?" she asked.

"Empty," he said. "Down."

"When did that happen?"

"Towards the middle, then almost to the end."

"During a musical about Paul and Barnabas?" Leanne's voice was questioning, not attacking or incredulous.

"Yeah." It was one of his verbal ticks even then.

They walked down Starfall Drive towards Cardiff Street. Douglas thought it was funny to see familiar names so far east from where he lived, but some of the nearby streets shot west for miles. The fog pulled at him, a familiar grey. But it's hard to be depressed with a beautiful woman by one's side.

He reached over and lightly touched Leanne's hand. "This means so much to me," he said, "just a touch—to know you're beside me."

They walked another block or so in silence, a wisp of dampness nearby. Then he turned to her.

"I love you, Leanne," It was the first time he'd used that word.

"I love you, Dougie." He wasn't offended by the nickname.

"I love you so much I want to kiss you." That was a big deal for him. Her eyes answered him, she thought that was a very good idea.

"But I told mom and dad that I wouldn't kiss anyone until we were engaged." Her eyes answered him; she thought that was a very bad idea.

"So . . . don't let me kiss you." From anyone else, that may have been a strange request. But for him, it felt normal. Douglas loved her so much that he didn't want to kiss her.

She sighed. "I don't like that idea, but OK."

Later on, they drove back to her house, sat on her back porch and talked for hours, his arm around her. They simply sat and were alive to the world. He had started out feeling poorly, but it had changed to joy.

"You've told me a lot about your feelings, Dougie," Leanne said a few minutes before he had to leave. "But I've not had enough chance to tell you mine."

"You're right," he confirmed. "Go on."

"I'll have to show you."

He laughed. "That's an open-ended subject. Are you willing to let me decide if that's a good idea?"

"Of course."

Douglas prayed about it, then felt it was unfair to tell her how he felt, but not to let her do the same.

"OK," he said. "Show me."

Douglas found himself in a warm embrace, her head against his shoulder. They were nearly the same height, and her hair caressed his neck. They parted.

"Why are you trembling, Doug?" she asked.

"I don't know. That's never happened to me before."

"Well, let me stop it," she embraced him again, and yet he felt no temptation to kiss her. He trembled again, harder. It took a third embrace to stop him trembling.

He gave her his brightest smile when they finally pulled away, said good-bye and left.

*July 15, 1975, letter to Douglas from Leanne*

*Douglas,*

*I've been avoiding doing this all day because I don't know what to say! I got up at 11:00, washed my hair, discussed college with my parents. They started discussing how and when I should study for the SAT, so I came into my room and found a book to read. Now, I can't put it off anymore because I'm ready and dinner won't be ready for half an hour.*

*How did I feel Thursday nite? I felt warm and protected, cared for in every sense of the word. You care what I'm thinking, what I'm feeling, what I'm saying.*

*One thing wrong with that last paragraph: It was how I personally was feeling; you want to know how I was feeling in relation to you.*

*I was rereading my journal and found something from Sunday, July 6, you might be interested in. I'd been debating with myself whether or not you still liked me since you hadn't called. I rededicated my life to Christ Wednesday nite up at camp and knew that to be totally His, I had to be willing to give up things close to me. I had to be willing to have you taken away from me. Douglas, from now on I'll quote that entry.*

> *I've just reread Dougie's letter. It's so beautiful. Through me God is helping him, showing him things everyone needs to learn at one time in their life. I'm just the privileged person who gets to help him learn. He's so sensitive and he feels so much.*

*(I don't know why I'm writing this to myself, Douglas, I want you to read it so I'll continue as to you personally.) The way you phrase things, comparing them to objects I know! I love it, there is so much meaning there, meaning I am only now beginning to see. God is working through me and because I'm willing to be used, He's blessing me. As I've said before, I've learned and gained so much from knowing you. You know, reading your letter, I was almost ready to cry! I'm useful, I'm helping someone I care for! I don't know how some people can be selfish, going into a relationship with someone only for what they can get out of it. I get so much more by wanting to help the other person!*

*I wrote a lot in my journal about last nite. I'm not sure I can say too much more. One of the ways to express feelings is by a kiss, and there have been several times when I have very much wanted you to kiss me, but I didn't say anything. I didn't want to rush you or to endanger our relationship.*

*Two of those times stick out in my mind. If you don't want to know, skip down to the next paragraph.*

*The first time was in Bernie's car coming home from Starfall and roller skating. You were so close to me, yet you weren't even holding my hand. Thinking back on that night I get the same desires. I had just experienced something new and exciting. I had realized that I liked you and wanted to express my feelings. The second time was that Monday afternoon in the park. I was there in your arms, so close to you, liking you so much, and wanting to express myself. I wanted you to tell me, by kissing me, that you liked me. It was so special, so super-fantastic! Last nite, I had the same feeling after you told me not to let you kiss me. I had to fight down my selfish desires and abide by your wishes. With God's help, I was able to do that.*

*There are two basically different parts to my personality. There's the serious side, which you've already seen, and the playful side, which*

*I don't think you have seen yet. I would like to reach out and play with your hair, to untie your shoelaces and tie them back funny, maybe even take them out of your shoes. I want to laugh at you and with you when you do something funny.*

*Imagine the beach. It's almost deserted and you're chasing me up the beach in shallow water and all of a sudden you trip or catch me and we both fall. Just goofing around like a couple playful puppies. Or how about swimming in our pool. I could splash you and you'd come after me to get back at me.*

*Maybe my imagination has been working overtime. Maybe things like that only happen in the movies. But I would like to go out and laugh and just have a plain good time. Am I wrong in wanting this from you? Maybe you just aren't the playful type, but I am. I enjoy living and getting the most out of it as I can!*

*All my friends and the things I do with them make life even better. Douglas, you've made life even realer to me, showing me a purpose for living. I have shown you what it is really like to be alive—pow! Fulfillment!*

*Love always,*
*Leanne (XO)*

# When Fantasy Becomes Reality

# Of Identities and Kisses

*July 3, 2003, in session*

Douglas had mixed feelings about fireworks. The patterns were pretty, but he hated noise and crowds.

He'd watched a fireworks show once at Disneyland and almost had a seizure. Lights flashing, water splashing and wriggling, people dancing, gyrating, grinding against him. Screams of pleasure, bubbles popping, oohs and ahhs. The sensory overload unhinged his brain and he felt it falling apart. It was all he could do to staple his mind back together long enough to get through the 10 minutes it took for the Disney show to end.

Nights and stars were another matter altogether. A bit of music, a light kiss of perfume on the cool and distant air, a soft voice gentle to the ears and it was more magic than Uncle Walt could ever provide. Douglas had met him once.

That was the Christian musical at Starfall that night back in 1975, the magic and the man. And there was something wrong with it.

"Where are you, Doug?" Sherry's voice. "It's time to start the session."

He shook himself free of the cobwebs. "I'm back at Starfall, holding hands, embracing Leanne. And . . . not kissing her," he felt like cursing himself. But that wouldn't move his sanity forward either.

Sherry smiled. "It's a place where you talked to both the God in heaven and the goddess on the earth."

"Yeah." He still had a habit of saying that. "Twenty-eight years later I think I know what's wrong."

"Go ahead."

"Compare the musical at Starfall to the Bramble Free fair for a moment."

"Bramble Free," Sherry repeated, flipping through her notes. "Ah. Here we are. You talked about that back in November."

Doug nodded. "Right. That was the fair we attended back when I was High School president."

"Go on."

"OK. Between the two events – Bramble and Starfall, before and after I graduated – I started to see Christianity in a different light. Or at least, I saw the Church differently."

Douglas paused again, the touch of Leanne still upon him.

"So what was the difference between the two?" Sherry asked.

"I questioned God at Bramble," he responded, "because the church fair was supposed to be fun, but without the crowds or swirl, it wasn't. Was I to pretend spirituality in a church that lacked feeling? There wasn't any flavor when I stopped to taste the salt.

"By contrast, the Starfall musical was wonderful! Even 28 years later, I still cherish that night with my Leanne. The chords, the sense and smell of Leanne, the flowing notes and colors gave that evening a beauty, a texture. E'en now, I'm in the shadows with the movements pouring through me, barely touching Lee, her spirit whirling 'round me. There was a shiver to it, a music made to move you.

"And I'm wondering, exactly like at Bramble Free, why am I not so moved? Why do I feel so empty? What's wrong with me that I don't believe the holiness? Why do I feel the same as I did at Bramble?"

"Why did you?" Douglas nodded to confirm Sherry's question. It was the right one to ask.

"I wasn't going anywhere because the music wasn't going anywhere. It was a spiritual dead end. Happiness, say some philosophers, consists of three parts: pleasure, pride, and purpose. The pleasure was there because the music was good and I was with Leeann. But the only pride was the narcissism of being the Chosen Ones.

"The worst of it was that there was no purpose. There was no call 'Let's attack this problem next!' There was no outreach, no challenge, and 'without a vision the people will perish.' Instead, the gospel song repeated, looping back onto itself. It was a Möbius strip. There was only one side to it and I had already heard and believed. Now, I wanted to grow. What was the next step?

"And there wasn't one. There was no future – it was all about the beliefs of the past. "The musical just put me back into 8th grade and told me to believe. But why? How many times must I learn that Mary was a virgin when Jesus was born? I asked again that night, although not in so many words.

"But it's a good question. Silly man-boy that I was, I wanted to move forward. I wanted to advance. Become mature. I wanted to find more God.

"And the words to the music never once helped me to grow. Somewhere between Bramble Free and Starfall, *I* became the muse. *I* was to be the leader, even by their standards. And the music moved me backwards, not forwards."

Douglas paused and thought about it, "Maybe I lost Leanne right there or maybe not. I dunno. But in any case, I failed to see the danger. I was traveling farther and farther from the Church while drawing closer and closer to Leanne. I loved Leanne with all my heart and she was still in the Church."

"Could you talk to Leanne about it?" Sherry asked.

"Some," he responded. "We chatted more about it at Starfall than I mentioned. But it was all head games. The musical could be improved this way or that.

"I'd already left my church in my heart and my head hadn't caught up yet. It was just too scary. Leaving the Church meant leaving my home, leaving friends, leaving my beliefs. Maybe it meant leaving Leanne. Maybe it meant being shunned.

"My head had the same problem in reverse. Come fall, I was going to UCSB while Leanne stayed at Hosanna High. Trust me. These are radically different schools and even then I saw this put stress on our relationship.

"I could show Leanne my heart about UCSB but not my head. And I could show Leanne my head about the Church, but not my heart.

"Lee probably didn't see this all because I couldn't communicate it that well. I was torn between my love, my church, my head, and my heart then centrifuged in different directions. The forces ripped us apart."

Douglas grabbed a tissue, crying. Sherry sat not moving, just to let him cry. He sobbed quietly for a bit, dabbing at his eyes.

After he began to regain his composure, Sherry again spoke.

"You certainly communicated with her on some level. And from what I can tell, Leanne loved you and loved you truly. So why was there such a taboo about kissing? Women can like physical contact just as much as men, to say nothing of the emotional content."

"I dunno," he responded. "I can't talk about it," by now it was a familiar refrain. "There had to be a line for me somewhere, not to make love with her. But I think I picked the wrong line, both for me and for her."

"Did you ever kiss her at all?" Sherry asked. "At her wedding, perhaps? It would have been a positive for her to remember."

"That's a long story," he exhaled slowly. "I'll have to tell you next session."

Sherry agreed. "We're at the end of the session and it's been a rough one. Same time next week?"

Douglas looked up with a crooked smile. "I don't have any choice." Then he stood up to leave.

## Meeting Walt

Douglas had met Walt Disney when Uncle Walt was conducting the train. He recognized the face and at the age of seven or eight had enough nerve to just ask.

"Are you Walt Disney?"

"Why do you ask that?" Walt gave a question for a question.

Douglas was shameless, "Because you're the only employee in the park who isn't wearing a name tag. And only Walt Disney could get away with that."

Disney laughed. "Is that so?" But the next time Doug saw him later that day, still driving the train, he was wearing a name tag. It said "WALT."

Douglas's mind wandered through that story as he slowly walked back to his car.

Disney had affirmed his identity. He was "WALT." By contrast, Douglas had wanted to snuff out his own.

Why had he wanted to kill himself? He understood that he was depressed and lacked self-esteem, but why? But what was behind it—what was the cause? Two years plus into therapy and he still didn't know.

*July 10, 2003, in session*

The week crawled by with the usual idiocy at work. Sometimes work was interesting, most of the time it drove Douglas crazy, or perhaps, crazier. His weekly sessions with Sherry provided a much-needed break, but still hurt.

"This is painful," Douglas said to start the next session. "I don't really want to do this."

Sherry understood, "I know. What keeps you going through these sessions?"

"Therapy is less painful than suicide," he said bluntly. "And these sessions give me the strength to deal with the craziness at work.

"Which doesn't mean this doesn't hurt. The sessions have me living these experiences again, so of course I can see the end of my romance with Lee (What a fortuneteller I am!) and its pain.

"I don't want to hurt anymore. I don't want to break up with Leanne again. I don't want to hear Deirdre's words again. I don't want to feel the chaos in my heart again. Sometimes I don't even want to be here again. I don't want to live through those experiences again."

He took a breath, then continued.

"I chose to love Leanne, but I did not choose our breakup. I chose to go to L'Abri, but I did not choose their callousness. I didn't choose Deirdre's betrayal either—or my own to myself, whatever—but that's what happened. Breakups happen, betrayal happens, callousness happens, shit happens.

"But that doesn't change the pain of it. When you're betrayed—by your church, by L'Abri, by your girl or by yourself, you hurt."

"And yet you're here." Sherry decided that there was a time and place for Captain Obvious.

"Yeah. Been there, done that. I tried to suppress the pain then ended up on a bridge looking down and waiting to jump. Ya, know? Not a good idea-r," Douglas affected his boss's Boston accent.

"So . . . maybe it's time to try something different. Touching the pain again may not be pleasant but I'm not anxious to die. If there's one thing I have in common with the self of 28 or so years ago, it's the desire to grow and change. To see myself, my God, and my universe as it really is."

Sherry smiled faintly, "Good. Shall we continue with the next topic? You were going to talk about whether or not you kissed Leanne."

"Yeah. But it's out of order from other events in that relationship, so I'll have to give you the back story."

"Leanne and I were close, even after we broke up, taking walks together just to talk. When she started dating (then eventually marrying) Ken, Leanne and I were so close that at first Ken thought we were still dating. The three of us hung out at JECU, Leanne and I together, and me between Ken and Leanne.

"He finally came up to us one day a few months later," explained Douglas, "when Leanne and I were standing a half-inch apart and asked us point blank. Were we dating each other? He'd noticed we never held hands.

"'No,' I said, 'we weren't. Or at least, not anymore.' So Ken asked if either of us minded if he just butted in between us.

"I looked at Leanne and could see it in her eyes, she wanted him. So I just stepped aside and you can guess the story from there. Ken and Leanne are still together, and Ken stands between me and Leanne.

"And that's the way it should be. What I regret is not that they married, but that I lost my friendship with Leanne (and Ken) because I was stupid and rude, again."

Douglas stopped to grab a tissue, just in case.

"No," he said, "I never kissed Leanne, not even once. A kiss was just too holy. Leanne kissed me on the cheek more than once as she didn't have my barriers against sex, but I never kissed her. Two years later, I kissed Deirdre (although maybe I shouldn't have); she then taught me how to kiss and to kiss well.

"But I never kissed Leanne."

"Not even a peck at her wedding?" Sherry asked.

"Not even a peck at her wedding," Douglas confirmed. "I can't remember much of it partly because it was during the confused and insane muddle in the years after L'Abri. But Leanne's wedding was just too painful.

"I'd had my chance with Leanne and I screwed up. I screamed at Leanne when we broke up, I yelled at Leanne, and I treated her badly while dating her even before that. And I loved her deeply while I screamed at her. I hurt her, I hurt her, I hurt her and all the while I loved her. I loved Leanne so dearly.

"Damn." There was never enough tissue to remove the pain. He wept again, angry with himself, then angry with himself that he was angry with himself. He let the tears flow for a bit, then took a deep breath.

"But of course, it wasn't enough to be an idiot while dating her. I had to be a moron at her wedding a few years later, too. When I walked through the reception line, I managed to shake Ken's hand, but I couldn't bring myself to kiss Leanne and wish her future well. Every mistake I'd made flashed in front of me, every pain I'd caused her, every scream and every word in anger.

"A kiss was a commitment forever and I'd been such a dickhead. So I could never commit my life to her. Why would I dump a jerk, namely me, onto someone I would love for the rest of her life? I could best show Leanne my love, I thought, if I destroyed a threat to her, if I destroyed myself.

"I couldn't kiss her. It just tore me up so much inside.

"Part of my memory goes blank at that point, but I think I was extremely rude, started crying, then broke out of the reception line and fled. That was 25 or 26 years ago. I've seen her once since then."

He could barely finish the rest of the story.

"I'd taken a train to the wedding, a hundred miles, a hundred miles and I remember walking by the tracks from the church to the station so I could catch the rail home. And all the while I'm thinking: No, I can't do that. I can't do that. No, I can't do that. I don't know why I can't do that, but I just can't do that. I can't do that. No, no, no. I just won't do that."

"I wasn't talking about kissing Leanne, Sherry," he finally said. "I was fighting to cross the Westfield Bridge. For what I wanted to do was to lay my head down upon the tracks, then wait for the train to whistle me home."

# Mid-July, 2003—Mid-Race Dreams

*July 17, 2003, in Sedona*

*Dear Jacky,*

I needed a break so I took a week off. Jim (my boss) doesn't need me at work right now, so I cancelled Sherry, kissed Anne good-bye and left. But this is my normal Sherry day, so naturally I started thinking things through.

I told Sherry a few months back that if my fellow Hosanna High alum Jeff lives in a meringue tower, then my own towers are iron and stone. On the one hand, this means that sometimes I shut everybody out. The flip side is that sometimes things are so confusing that I don't know how to let anybody in. Stone towers are what I do best in those cases because I can hear myself think and I need to recognize my own voice before I can listen to others.

It's quiet here in Sedona and the nice part of solitude is not that the quietness lets me hear myself, but that it lets me realize that I don't even need to try to listen. I can just sit here and enjoy the silence. I want to stare at my navel and be empty, I want to go home and clean the house, clean the garage, clean my room, clean my desk up. I want to clean and be cleaned. I want to clean me.

There is violence in me. I fantasized today about hitting Leanne, then I whipped Deirdre and twisted clamps onto her breasts. My fantasy put Deirdre's husband in a little girl's dress, and I trained him to curtsey then kiss my feet and beg for forgiveness. I climaxed when I lifted his skirt in front of Deirdre and Leanne, then I took his ass.

I almost never have gay fantasies. And I don't have to do what I imagine, but I have to admit that I want to do it. I want to hurt, hurt, and punish Deirdre and Lee and as long as I fantasize then the pain is still controlling me and I'm not controlling it. I don't want to admit that I want to torture, but doing so gives it perspective. My sins don't want to be in the light so all I can do is to drag them there and let them go.

That's where I am today. I don't want to be there tomorrow. How do I get there? I'm tired of being ill. How do I get well?

One thing for sure: telling Deirdre that I want to rape her and gay-torture her husband is probably not the best way to repair our relationship, even if Ratfink deserves it.

I'm tired and there are too many questions, too many voices. I'll be better tomorrow. If I can't forgive Deirdre and Leanne right now, maybe I can listen to the quiet and rest. If their voices show up again, maybe I'll lock them back up for awhile. I don't need to torture them every day, maybe not at all.

Maybe I can let them out of prison one day. But for now, I want to enjoy the quiet without their voices. I'll go to Jerome tomorrow or perhaps a national park and do some hiking.

I love you, Jacky. I apologize for being so angry and I'll try to do and be different.

*Love,*

*Douglas*

*July 18, 2003, Jerome, Arizona*

If you've ever been to Jerome you know it's one of the few towns that really is uphill in all directions. You're constantly teetering on the edge of a precipice, some 5,000 feet above sea level, fearing your next step may sweep you down over the edge.

The sensation feels like skydiving, the pure and steady exhilaration driving more confidence. But Douglas also tensed in the wariness of always watching your step. He wondered how resident artisans coped.

He could not exercise his creativity here himself, not with fingernails desperately scratching out a lost message on the cliff walls, serving as a chalkboard, in a downward screeching fall.

He slowly wandered through the shops. A few were kitsch Navaho rip-offs for the tourists, but most shops offered the relaxed and mellow crafts and arts of hard-working hippies. He enjoyed a few paintings and nearly bought one, as his mother's voice talked him through how the intricacies of each brush stroke blossomed into the flowing gestalt of artistic expression. Instead, he satisfied himself with a decent latte and a great view.

You had to drop down 100 feet in a single block to see it, but his favorite spot scanned the crumbled ruins of miners' bars, dating from Jerome's old boom-town mining days. From there, you can scan skid row edgewise, as each bar establishment runs away from your field of vision in side-by-side columns. Each business was long and narrow, with just enough room for the bartender, the bar itself, a row of stools, and a narrow passage for customers to squeeze by. The layout reminded him of a chessboard.

After lunch, he drove back through Tuzigoot, enjoying the heat and fresh air in his convertible. It was quiet. And there was just enough time in the day to splurge on a helicopter ride at sunset.

The chopper pilot was glad to see another fare this late in the day, as it was off-tourist season and it had been a quiet day for the pilot as well. They took off with an hour left in the day, golden drifts just lighting the mountain peaks. Douglas dug out his digital camera and started shooting right away, amazed at the number of abandoned cliff dwellings dotting the landscape. He got off a few good shots then the camera batteries promptly went dead.

He rooted around for more and discovered much to his dismay that he was out. He laughed and the pilot asked him, "What's so funny?"

"You could make a fortune selling spare camera batteries up here. Twenty bucks a shot. I'm all out."

The pilot laughed too, "Damn, that's a good idea! I wonder if it's legal?"

Without the batteries, Douglas could only wonder at the cliffs and light and trees and ruins. But the pictures in his mind were nearly as good as any his camera could take, maybe better. The chopper skittered between two mountains, a tattered cliff dwelling shinning in the east, an aching ball of fire fusing into the horizon in the west. Maybe I should give skydiving a try after all, he thought, although he was still a little scared of it.

Back at the resort, he played Ping-Pong after dinner with the concierge then drifted back to his room. He watched *Woodstock* that night, both glad and sad to have been too young and conservative to go.

It had been a very good day. He didn't entirely feel mentally clean, but he'd at least washed his face and hands.

# Real Life

*July 24, 2003, in session*

Sherry's response to his gay torture fantasy surprised him. She said, "Good."

"Say what?" Douglas felt quite startled.

"Two years ago you wanted to commit suicide," Sherry continued. "To hurt yourself. Now you want to hurt someone else. Sounds like you're making progress, you're turning the anger away from yourself."

Douglas was confused, "But I still wanted to hurt someone, didn't I? Isn't that a bad thing?"

"You aren't doing it, are you?" Sherry responded. "You admit your anger and let it out constructively."

Douglas felt a warm flux of confusion and delight. He was making progress! But the muddle of emotions made him realize he still had a long way to go, too.

"Talking about sex is hard for you, isn't it, Doug?" Sherry asked.

He nodded, "Yeah. It's really hard to talk about, even here just a little. It's almost as if I can't *talk* about sex without *doing* sex and I'm not Jim Morrison."

"Jim Morrison? I know who he was, but I don't see what he has to do with anything."

"Morrison tried to sing and make love to his girl at the same time," he explained.

"Ah. Do you always make a joke of your difficulties?" She had a point.

He sighed, "No. But making a joke makes it easier to cope."

"Why not just respect yourself?"

"That's very hard to do," Douglas admitted.

"OK. It's the end of the session, so let's give you some homework. Every time you feel the emotional pain, let yourself feel it, admit that you've been hurt, then respect yourself for making progress."

The end of the session? Douglas felt like he'd hardly gotten started. But when he looked at the clock, sure enough. He'd taken a long time telling the story of his short vacation. Time to go to work. Whoop-de-doo.

*July 31, 2003, in session*

Every time Douglas headed over the hill he was glad he lived near Santa Brisa. The view of the ocean calmed him, the cliffs and waves.

Douglas loved his city. He didn't always love himself.

""Let's get back to '*Un dieu dans le ciel et une déesse sur la terre,*'" he started. "A god in heaven and a goddess on the earth." Something about the French pronunciation struck him as interesting, but he laid that thought aside. "I want to talk about a place in my letters where the two concepts connect."

"Good idea," Sherry said patiently. She thought it was a good topic.

Doug had already turned to the right area in his letters. "Yadda yadda yadda," he read, "Mushy stuff, irrelevant, irrelevant, more mushy stuff. Ah. Here we are:"

> *That's the thing I like most about Leanne—her eyes. When I look at Leanne's eyes, I find something to ground on, that I like Leanne and she likes me.*
> *That's the important thing: to perceive, recognize and understand in all respects that which is and creates what I call reality.*

He stopped there for a moment.

"There's still plenty of mushy stuff," Sherry remarked, a slight grin playing on her lips. The fact she could display even that much teasing reflected a growing amount of trust between them.

"Yeah. Isn't there?" he agreed. "But the important thing is that I was studying I John at the time. Here's I John 5:20 in the Amplified Bible." Douglas didn't have the Amplified Bible memorized, but had brought along his own copy.

> *And we have seen and know positively that the Son of God has actually come to this world and has given us understanding and insight progressively to perceive, recognize and come to know better and more clearly Him Who is true.*

Douglas deliberately modified this from knowing "Him Who is true" to "knowing reality." The change described how he perceived things around him. His eyes literally saw an aura around trees, for example, especially at night. The mystic was real to him because he saw it.

The change also expanded the range from "perceiving Christ" to "perceiving reality." He probably meant the cosmos, which may not be theologically sound (for a fundamentalist) but that's how Douglas was thinking at the time.

But the focus of the letter was Lee, not God, so Douglas kept reading. Yeah, verily.

> *Sometimes I can do it, don't ask me how. It's a gift from God. What really is important can be perceived, and it can be seen why and how it is important.*
>
> *Leanne understands me. I especially need her to make me feel.*

Leanne got under his skin. Yeah, you can say that about any first young summer romance. "I never really felt alive until I met <insert name here>." True.

Also false.

The true part is easy enough to understand—Douglas never really felt alive until he met Leanne. Enough said about the true part.

Let's talk about the false part. Douglas didn't handle emotions well in high school. No kid ever does, but Douglas was nearly manic-depressive. He'd be fine for a while and then explode at something, just go off on a rampage. Talk about mood swings, extreme and fast.

Religion and repression were the first two coping mechanisms he tried. What's odd about this is that there's nothing inherent about Christianity that says you must repress emotions. His mom, for example, was one of the most intensely emotional people Douglas ever knew. She taught art, drawing, English and history at Hosanna Christian High, directed two drama classes, mentored ceramics after school, and then produced local community plays in her copious spare time.

She was good at it, too. She could and did upstage everyone when she gave herself a bit part.

Yet mom was also one of the most religious people Douglas knew. She believed that Christians needed to learn more about the arts, to liberalize them. That meant she took her entire teacher's salary and plowed it back into the school. She built the stage, bought the curtains, made the costumes, thousands of them, bought the clay and a kiln for the post-school ceramics class. And when one kiln wasn't enough, she bought another, every bit of it to serve God as she saw best.

Back when Douglas was a kid, his mom was so dedicated that he used to confuse her with the Virgin Mary.

But that's another story. The point: what worked for his mom wouldn't work for him. He liked art and drama quite a bit but Douglas wasn't his mother.

"There's too much of my dad in me," he explained to Sherry. "If mom was the artist, dad's the scientist. If mom experienced emotions, dad explores thoughts and I put them together to know the why. I'm not satisfied with simply creating art. I like creating art but I also want to know *why* I want to create art. I'm really a philosopher."

Art to science, sex to religion, mom to dad. So many things were going on in his head back in high school that he couldn't control his own powers. The combination may not have been solely responsible for his roller-coastering moods, but it certainly didn't help any. Douglas flashed from up-to-down and the mix was volatile. Still is, but now he's much better at working with the competing factors.

To Douglas, Gothard represented religion and repression as wholly inadequate coping mechanisms. Instead of helping, Gothard urged that one should simply intensify one's religiosity and ignore or suppress the pain.

Oddly, Gothard made sense to the rest of his conservative family and IBYC creates a religion within a religion, a not-so-secret cult of the truly elect. On top of that, Douglas constructed his own rules and regulations, among them the not-kissing rule.

"But Leanne got past those barriers," he told Sherry. "She accepted my emotions as they were and cared about me. She nourished my mind, my body, my beliefs and my emotions and tried to love all of me. Leanne wasn't just my first romance. She ignored all the nonsense and was able to reach into me and touch my heart.

"Unfortunately, I walked into that relationship with Gothard's outmoded and peculiar teachings about women."

*"I especially needed her to make me feel."*

Or perhaps he meant, "I never felt complete until I met Leanne." She soothed pains he'd shunted aside from childhood, not that he could remember what they were. But Christianity is about resurrection, not burial and Leanne pulled away the stone he used to block his passions.

"And my anger," Douglas finished. "And any gar-Bawge left over from childhood." He stuck his nose up and affected an air, then became more serious. "Whatever internal balance I'd manage to strike before Leanne was lost and the result was shattering—to me and to Leanne, to us."

# A Crack Appears

The door to Sherry's office closed but didn't lock. He could leave at any time and was grateful for that. Maybe he could avoid the nice young men in clean white coats.

"Hello," Sherry said. She gave him a smile.

"Hello. Nice to see you again."

"Where did we leave off last week?" Sherry opened. Douglas knew that she knew, after all, she had all the notes in front of her, but that didn't matter. It was a way to synch.

"Talking about Lee," he responded. "We've pretty much covered how our romance started, so we can move to the middle of it. That'd be about August of 1975 through . . . oh, I dunno, maybe October or November of the same year."

Sherry nodded, "What happened during that time frame?"

Douglas shuffled through his own letters from 1975 before responding, "Mostly the type of things high schoolers normally do during the summer. I've got the records here for the week of August 16, 1975.

> *"Leanne and I went to the beach on Monday, then spent that evening with the combined high school and college-age groups at the riding park. We were both at a pool party on Wednesday, then went back to the beach with the church group on Thursday. We had a more formal date at a symphony Friday night."*

His memory filled in blanks from his thin recitation. Eddies at the beach, volleyball games barefoot in the sand, the cool air and smell of the grass at Lantern Bay Park on their date before the music started.

He drove Leanne home on Monday and as was their usual wont, they chatted before leaving. Then Leanne's mom came out and (not seeing Douglas) told Leanne that it was time for bed. Douglas pulled his wallet out of his pocket, then threw it into the middle of the street. His keys followed soon after.

Douglas thought he had done something wrong, something to displease Leanne's mother.

He lost his keys again on Thursday, buried somewhere in the sand. He had wondered even then: What's going on here? Am I doing this deliberately or is it an accident? He was never quite sure.

"I lost control," he admitted. "Neither problem was really all that big, but in both cases I made a mountain out of a molehill. I overreacted. It didn't affect our relationship then, because eventually I realized they were molehills and I soothed it out with Lee.

"But I followed the same pattern when genuine problems occurred. Instead of handling them normally, I overreacted and turned a real problem into an A-Bomb. I lost control."

"You were 17," Sherry pointed out.

"In August. I was 18 when we broke up," he added. "I remember telling you earlier that I need to forgive myself for being 17, or 18, for that matter, but you know. Sometimes it's dang frustrating anyway."

"Everyone goes through their teens," Sherry noted. "If they're lucky, that is. It's often an embarrassing and awkward stage of life."

"Tell me about it," Douglas agreed. "'Youth is wasted on the young,' they say. The older I get the more I realize that that says less about wanting to live longer and more about maturity. That is, I'd be willing to be 17 again with my current maturity level even if I died 28 years sooner because now I understand how to use my youth. And I don't have it."

Douglas paused. He'd wandered and realized that he was avoiding the hard topics. Time to try to handle it.

"But the problem wasn't just my age. I remember anger flashing through me, hijacking my brain. It was like . . . a seizure or something. I'd be OK for a while then I'd gradually feel . . . feverish, I guess. It's hard to explain the sensation. Sometimes I could tell it was coming in advance but couldn't stop it. It was . . . madness."

The anger flash felt like sleepwalking, like someone else was moving his body and tongue. It was not a comfortable sensation.

Sherry looked up from her notes. "Have you ever hurt someone, or yourself, while in a state like that?"

He shook his head, "No. Yelled at them, yes. Physically hurt them, no. But I don't like being there."

"I can imagine," Sherry was sympathetic. "Can you tell me more about how you feel when you're in that state?"

He shrugged, "A little. There are different types of . . . manic attacks, for lack of a better word."

"True mania lasts for days or weeks. How long does yours last?"

"Only a few hours. Maybe half a day at the most."

"OK," Sherry continued. "Why do you say there are different types?"

"Sometimes I'm manic and just talk a lot. Other times, I'm angry and manic and yell. And still other times, I'm manic and just get . . . weird. Here's another letter I wrote Jacky back in August of 1975." He pulled out his copy, with 5-inch letters scrawled all over the page. The first few words were coherent then the next eight or nine pages sprinkled hieroglyphs in random locations.

"I secret-coded it," he explained. "Or more precisely, it's a cipher not a code. Anyway, my point is that I felt manic and happy while writing it, not angry, but I still lost control."

Sherry asked the obvious question. "What were you writing about?"

"Haven't the slightest," he responded. "I spent an hour or so deciphering a few paragraphs then gave up. It just wasn't worth the effort. The topic itself was indecipherable, even after I broke the code."

There were some kinds of "me" from 1975 that Douglas needed to leave alone. It's not that as an adult he didn't have the same context now that he was mature. It's that, given the context, Douglas didn't understand what he wrote in the first place, even when he could read it. There was insufficient generative syntax to govern the semantics.

Sherry agreed with him. "Moving on" is not only a political or business slogan. It's a psychological necessity. The fact that he had lost control in more than one way as a teenager did not require him to do the same as an adult. An adult need not stop maturing.

❧❧❧

But it was the symphony with Leanne as a teenager that was still burned into his mind. She was prettier than a jewel that night. Her metallic white dress was long and lacy, preternaturally annealing into diamonds in the cooling August night. They'd gotten an early start so they took a walk near Morro Bay before the symphony, Douglas thinking that he was already blessed to "see" so much beautiful music.

"Girls do like compliments, you know," Leanne commented. He almost laughed at her blunt admission. Every moment with her was a compliment. 'Well, to me,' he thought. Perhaps it was time to return the favor, but he was terrible at the normal romantic conventions.

He struck a faux theatrical pose, "Your neck reminds me of Ivory," he started. Leanne raised her eyebrows. "Soap," he ended.

Leanne gave him an interested look, "Go on."

"Your cheeks are as red . . . as a crab." Leanne giggled.

"Your eyes remind me of pools. Cess pools." Douglas figured that as long as he was in this far, he might as well go the whole kit and caboodle. Leanne laughed outright.

"You do know what cess pools are, don't you?" He wanted to be sure.

"Oh, yes. But it's quite funny."

"Good. You're so important to me." He was quiet for a second. Perhaps his earlier thought could be turned into a genuine compliment, "Your presence alone is a compliment every time you're with me. I only wish I could do the same for you. It's not just your beauty, but your vibrancy, your joie de vivre."

She was in his arm in a moment not kissing his lips. Her breasts were close and soft, pressing against him and he felt virile or animal, masculine. Forget the symphony. This was good enough to last a lifetime.

◦◦◦◦◦◦

"My letter to Jacky at the time," Doug said as he ended the story, "adds that I can see how easy it would be to sin and defile Leanne."

"Defile," Sherry commented.

"Yeah. Later on I say that God has given me those feelings, but that may have been pro forma. It never occurred to me to think that if God gave me a desire for Leanne, then it wasn't defiling."

He looked glum. Sherry took yet another note, "So the two most important themes that month are losing control and defilement," she said.

"Yup. And they're tied together. If I lost control, I'd defile Leanne. So I had to be perfect all the time—Mathew 5:48: *'Be ye perfect as God is perfect.'* I couldn't deviate from perfection by a waltzing iota."

"And something was driving you to lose control," Sherry finished. "Find that and we can find out more about why you once wanted to kill yourself."

It was just past the usual end of the session. Sherry had sensed his thought was nearly complete and let him finish it. That was nice of her and he didn't expect it to happen often, if at all.

Douglas was weary, with a long drive home. Just after sunset, the traffic drifted away as the once hidden stars climbed into the sky.

*August 9, 2003, at home*

*Dear Jacky,*

I do get tired of talking to Sherry about my problems. It always seems like one big thing after the next, too much overload. I need more breaks than I give myself, but that's not a reason not to take a break now.

Big things. Hmm. I wrote you once about small things awhile back, eating a sandwich while watching a fly, so let's talk about big things today, really big things.

The odds of living in a perfect world are infinitely tiny. But this universe is so God Almighty Huge that there's just about an infinite number of worlds in it aren't there? Big!

It's tempting to believe that there's a planet somewhere with my name on it. Douglas's planet, the perfect temperature, the perfect woman, the perfect combination of sea and forest and desert. And I could wander around it forever, exploring, laughing, jumping and playing with the water. My own planet, my own little world to smooth and tune, to blow on like a dandelion, breathing into it the breath of life. No wonder the Mormons really believe in this.

But the universe is so dang big that no matter how much I control, there will always be something that is *outside* of my control. Entire galaxies I can't and don't control and don't even want to control. It's something I remind myself of on my bad days. The universe is bigger than I am.

*Eppur si muove.* "The Earth still moves." Although Galileo beat me to saying this so many years before, it is one of my mantras. The Sun does not revolve around us, we revolve around it. I don't constrain the universe, the universe constrains me, and I refuse to be as the Most High God.

Trust me on this one. I have no interest in becoming God—it's difficult enough to just be me.

# ALAS

# ALAS—The Gestalt

*August 14, 2003, in session*

"I'm learning to respect my own emotions about Leanne," Douglas said to open the next session. "But I'm still confused about Deirdre. When I pause to look at it, I want to torture Deirdre because I'm mad at her. Then I want to comfort her because someone tortured her (me) and she's hurt. Then I want to punish myself for hurting someone I love, then I want to make love with Deirdre because she's just so dear to me."

"That actually makes sense to me. At least I've gotten that far, but after that it's more of a muddle."

"Can you express those behaviors as emotions instead of actions?" Sherry asked.

"Sure. I'm mad at Deirdre. I love Deirdre. I hate Deirdre. I want to hurt Deirdre. I want to make love to Deirdre."

"Good," said Sherry. As usual, that was Douglas's cue that he'd better listen closely. "You cited five emotions: anger, love, hate, abuse, and sexual desire.

"But the fact that you experience five emotions all at once," Sherry continued, "does not make them the *same* emotion. Anger is not love. Love is not abuse. Abuse is not sex. Sex is not hate."

Boom! Sherry had just earned her salary for the year as far as Douglas was concerned. He knew he needed to remember what Sherry had just said so he made up an acronym on the spot: A.L.A.S. Anger, Love, Abuse, Sex. He wasn't sure where hatred belonged in that set just yet so he left it out of the acronym. Besides, 'A LASH' didn't seem like a good idea. Hatred was easy enough to remember as is.

"Wow!" he exclaimed. "Let me let that sink in a bit."

He took a breath and closed his eyes for a moment. "ALAS," he muttered to himself just to whack it into his head, "ALAS."

"It's downright messy," he finally said out loud. "Loving and hating simultaneously, to say nothing of anger, abuse and sex, is just so maddening. I want to retaliate. Hurt someone else because they hurt me.

"The good news, such as it is, is that I'm not torturing anyone at all—Deirdre, me, or even Barbie dolls. But I am trying to face my emotions and that's hard enough because I want to hurt. I want to torture.

I want to punish Deirdre and then myself. There is darkness within me and I don't like looking at it."

"Wanting isn't doing," Sherry reminded. "I thought we covered that."

"Yeah," Douglas stayed silent another moment. "But how to handle it? Maybe I can leave virtual Deirdre in virtual jail then visit once in a while to torture her, a voodoo doll. I don't really know what to do."

Sherry shook her head no. "That might be the wrong direction," she said. "Let's back up to what I said earlier. There are at least five emotions in your head that you experience simultaneously: anger, love, hate, abuse, and sexual desire. And they're all tangled up together."

"Sure."

"You're still trying to deal with the gestalt, with all the emotions all at once. And, as you might say, you just don't have the bandwidth. But the tangle in your head can be approached one item at a time."

Boom! Another year's salary. This had turned into a key session.

Douglas often thought of therapy as being similar to the problem-solving at his job. The more difficult the topic, whether technical or psychological, the more scattered the original source material. His strategy was first to comb through facts to find the various pieces to begin to sort and assemble them. Once there were enough puzzle pieces to collate, he would simply spread the scraps out like any other jigsaw puzzle until his mind flashed on the pattern. The pieces then seemed to fly together by themselves.

<hr/>

Thinking of puzzles reminded him of the time he'd scared his boss with a big one. Doug had been at his current job only a month when he realized that another engineer's documentation he'd been stuck with rewriting was very, very wrong—technologically wrong, not just poorly written—the Friday before a big Monday deadline.

So he just dumped the pages on the floor and started staring at it, doing nothing for an hour or two before a deadline.

And his boss's jaw dropped. Talk about panic! He walked into Douglas's office, visibly holding his temper and asked: "What are you doing?!"

"Doc's wrong. I'm rewriting it," was the only absent-minded response he got. In the meantime, Doug just stood there.

Jim barely managed to keep his composure. "Just be sure you make the deadline."

"No problem," Doug said distantly. What's all the big fuss about? he thought, it isn't *that* hard.

Jim left, but didn't quite believe him and (Doug found out later) stomped off to see his own boss. How the $%!&, he screamed, would Douglas make the deadline if he wasn't doing anything?

Sharon, the department VP, just laughed. She'd known Douglas at a previous company and told Jim not to worry. Douglas, she said, was full of surprises.

Just 24 hours later, Doug had rewritten all 50 pages and added a memo outlining several bugs and telling that engineer how to do the next 5 docs. Then he took the next day off; job's done. 'Geez. Let me get back to debugging, will ya? What's all the panic about?'

And his boss's jaw dropped again. He later told Douglas that the document was by far the best he'd seen.

∽✦∾∽✦∾∽✦∾

The key to such problem-solving, thought Douglas, is the gestalt. What picture does the software paint? What is happening in the rest of the department or company? What is the whole?

Doug usually creates a gestalt bottom-up. That is, he finds small pieces and assembles them into an unexpected picture, larger and larger. By contrast, plot can be created top-down. A writer can create an ending in advance, which the reader won't know, of course, then builds a chain of cause-and-effect to create that ending.

For example, "The Queen died" is a character study. But "The Queen died. The King died of grief" is a plot. One event causes the next until the author's desired goal is reached.

Douglas approached both such workday issues and therapy as gestalt. He was interested in the technology (or himself) "as built," the whole item or person as it actually is — the gestalt. He was much less interested in the item "as planned by the engineer." The two are rarely the same, as NASA periodically rediscovers when it bounces satellite probes off Mars instead of landing them.

Sherry's comment gave therapy two new roles beyond gestalt. The first was obvious: therapy can be broken into smaller pieces. The second is that each thread, each emotion, can be addressed "as happened." It can be seen as part of a plot. Doug loved Deirdre, Deirdre betrayed him, he hated Deirdre. The one event impacts the next until the current (undesirable) emotion is reached.

Therapy weaves a tapestry; the client fabricates the pattern of his or her life by braiding the threads. But therapy doesn't just work with the gestalt of the pattern. It lets you look at things one strand at a time. The idea was revolutionary.

179

Douglas Baign

*Before enlightenment: chopping wood, carrying water.*
*After enlightenment: chopping wood, carrying water.*

As with most epiphanies, the sky was still blue, the trees were still green, and the task the same. Douglas still needed to do the work, but his mindset had changed.

# ALAS—Thoughts on Anger

*August 20 and 21, 2003, at work, then in session*

Douglas abruptly walked out of Mike's meeting (always an impolite thing to do) rather than screaming "You're a freaking idiot!" He knew he was losing his temper and decided it was better to look rude than to be a jerk and make enemies.

So Doug decided it was appropriate to talk about anger the next day when in session. Which, alas, didn't keep Mike from being a freaking idiot but . . . such is life.

"I'm going to shift gears slightly, Sherry," Doug paused as he opened the session. "'Slightly Sherry.' Sounds like a new light wine for tongue twisters. But never mind.

"Up to now I've been focusing on people and events—Leanne, Gothard, L'Abri, the Catacomb service and so on—and talking about how I feel about them. But what you said last week about ALAS—anger, love, abuse, sex—is so useful that I want to examine each of those emotions in light of those people or events. I'm just reversing the focus."

Sherry nodded. "Makes sense. Those emotions tangle at those locations."

"Exactly. But now I can talk about them one at a time."

Sherry was relieved that Doug seemed to be getting it. It had taken awhile. "Go ahead," she said.

"Anger, love, abuse, sex," he intoned. "The first is anger. Damn it all, I thought I was done with GoatHerd and IBYC, but I obviously still need to work it out."

Douglas stopped then added, "'We can, we can,' sang Saints John and Paul."

"We can what?" Sherry asked, confused.

"'We can work it out.'" He sang the lyrics. "Sorry, but my head really does go there."

Sherry just shook her head, "Do continue."

Doug was tempted to say, "Oh, Yoko, Oh no!" but did as she requested. "I really hate to do this, but let's go back to IBYC's original barf statement on the Web." He quoted it from memory.

> *The goal of this seminar is to explain God's way of life
> and provide further training and resources for those who are
> committed to God's best.*

"Gothard supplied a syllabus to everyone who attended as the 'resource'. He pondered a bit, "Or maybe it wasn't a resource. Depends on what you mean by that, I guess."

"What was in the syllabus?" Sherry asked patiently.

"I guess you could say Gutter Snipes—I mean, Gothard's—night lecture notes. It was a fire-engine red, three-ring binder divided into seven sections, one per each major topic. Each section outlined Gothard's positions on that topic, illustrated points with drawings and gave biblical citations. The syllabus was actually polished and well-organized, which doesn't mean that I agree with it, of course."

"The syllabus sounds like a good resource to me," Sherry remarked. "Why do you say it wasn't?"

Douglas just shook his head. "Gad. Where to start? Hmmm." He sat still a moment, organizing his thoughts. "I may be over-generalizing, but I got mad about the syllabus for two reasons: direct and indirect.

"The indirect reasons are gonna be a lot easier to talk about, so let's start there.

"The syllabus was far too rigid and just flat out didn't make any sense once you started looking at it closely.

"I threw mine out for some strange reason, but I surfed the IBYC website (such a pleasure, I assure you) so I could give you a sense of what's in it. Here's a quote from 'Communicating with God,' with that particular page titled 'Understanding Postures of Prayer,'" like when Moses fell on his face before God."

Douglas struck a pose then continued in a theatrical voice. "Let your posture express the attitudes of your heart."

> Communication with God does not require a certain physical position, but postures do give expression to the attitudes of our hearts. Here we will look at eight postures of prayer, discuss their symbolism, and see how they relate to the (8) beatitudes Jesus presented in the Sermon on the Mount:

"The Web page goes on to describe how being flat on our faces represents humility, kneeling represents repentance, and so on for all eight postures."

"I don't know enough theology to comment." Sherry said. "What's your point?"

"You have to read between the lines." Douglas stopped. "No, that's not right. His positions are obvious enough, it's just that you have to know the Bible to see them. And I do know enough about theology to comment."

"And?" It was a good thing that Sherry was very patient.

"You gotta read it this way. 'Communicating with God doesn't require a certain physical position . . . unless you're feeling one of these eight attitudes of the heart. See list below. In which case, you are required to have that posture, and if you don't have that posture then you obviously don't want God's best.'

"Never mind the fact that those postures developed at least 5,000 years ago. And never mind the fact that maybe you have attitude number nine, or posture number 10, or have two broken legs and can't kneel anyway. That's it. Here are these eight required postures and they're backed up biblically. Obey or face God's wrath."

Douglas's voice was getting progressively sarcastic during the rant. Sherry waited a brief moment.

"He locks you into certain behavior patterns," she commented.

Douglas took a breath. "Yea. Not only that, but he locks you into *obsolete* behavior patterns. It's like he takes his own outdated cultural bias and dresses it in scripture.

"And the syllabus is comprehensive. By the time you've finished the course you can't so much as sneeze without knowing when God wants you to reach for which color of a handkerchief and which fingers to use while blowing."

Sherry smiled. "How did this impact you?", she asked.

"Mostly it just annoyed me. I was already in that culture so I was doing much of that stuff anyway. It's just that I didn't see my own bias as ordained by God. I was interested in other people—our family toured Europe when I was 12—and how they did things, too. So I thought GurdHerd was boxing cultures out when he didn't need to and when it was counter-productive."

"So it was an indirect irritant."

"Yes."

"And what directly caused you anger?"

"That's harder to talk about." Douglas stopped at that point.

"And?"

Douglas sighed. "Gothard's section on anger made me angry and that colored my relationship with Lee at the time. Our first argument, other than a minor tiff or two, was in . . . October, I guess, over Gothard. Yuck. It went something like this."

"I want to attend the Gothard conference anyway," Leanne said. They'd been discussing it for several days off and on.

"And I still think it's a very bad idea. I don't think it would be good for you."

"Why not?" Lee asked. "You haven't yet given me a good reason not to attend."

Doug was darn positive that going would be damaging. But it was more of an intuition. He still didn't have the words for it, even after arguing with PD. He struggled to find an analogy.

"The Bible isn't a cookbook, Lee" he finally said.

"What do you mean?" Leanne was puzzled.

"It doesn't give 'recipes' on how to handle every situation. So why does Gothard try to turn everything into a behavior recipe?"

"I don't think he does," Leanne replied. "Besides, the rules IBYC suggests are based on biblical principles."

It always boiled down to the Bible. If you didn't believe Gothard, then you didn't believe in the Bible because Gothard used biblical principles.

But what if he wasn't? Did the Bible focus on 'principles to obey' or 'how to love?'

Douglas thought this through in his head, but also knew that he didn't dare suggest that. Questions like this were far too dangerous within a fundamentalist environment. Besides he felt tongue-tied when he tried, his old speech impediment inflaming his own frustration. What to say instead?

"Calvin thought he used biblical principles, too," Douglas tried. Both of them were familiar with Church history, when Calvin developed a theocratic dictatorship in Geneva during the Reformation.

Leanne cranked up her own agitation, "Oh, come on! Gothard is clearly not Calvin."

'He isn't?' Douglas thought, but didn't say anything out loud. He was losing the argument and didn't want to lose Leanne as well.

"Look," Leanne continued. "You're angry about it. That's one of Gothard's topics so maybe you could benefit by going with me."

⁊⁊⁊

"Damn. That pissed me off no end, Sherry. It's the same double bind again because it assumes anger is a sin. I thought about breaking up with Lee right then and there."

"Why didn't you?"

"Because any couple has to learn how to deal with serious disagreements. Dumping her felt like giving up too early, like escapism."

"So how did you resolve the argument?"

"We didn't. I attended one or two days just to be with Lee, then told her I needed to study. Which I did, but it was also a way to keep myself from flying off the handle. I was starting to lose it."

"Ah," Sherry remarked. "That makes sense. So how do you feel about Gothard and his principles?"

Douglas looked puzzled. The question seemed out of sequence, "What do you mean 'How do I feel?'"

"You've been telling me a lot about how you think about him," Sherry explained, "so tell me how you feel about him."

He turned it over in his head, "Definitely angry. Confused. Trapped. Abandoned. Manipulated and devalued."

"Good," Sherry encouraged. "That's a good summary so that's a good place to stop. We can explore those emotions next week."

Doug unkinked his legs and stood up. "Thank you. This has been a good session."

Sherry smiled. "You're welcome."

At least he wouldn't have to deal with Mike today and probably not for the rest of the week. 'I wonder how Mike would react,' Douglas thought, 'if he ended up stuck in a Gothard seminar? Hmm. I wonder which one I should send him to . . . '

He laughed. The vision of the expression on Mike's face kept him going throughout the day.

*August 28, 2003, in session*

Douglas's workweek went blessedly well for a change, and he entered the next session ready to go. Anger wasn't his favorite topic, but it was better than sex and he knew he wasn't done talking about Gothard.

"Gar," he murmured

Sherry opened the session, "Last week you said that you felt angry about Gothard." She read her notes. "'Confused. Trapped. Abandoned. Manipulated and devalued.' Can you tell me more?"

"Yeah," Douglas had anticipated the question. "I'm not positive," he continued, "but my primary emotion is anger and the others explain why I'm angry. That is, I feel angry because I feel confused and so on."

"OK. Let's talk about each of those in detail." She gave him a smile.

He understood exactly what she meant. Split the emotions and handle them separately. He just hoped he could.

"Well, I'll try. I felt confused because there seemed so much disconnect between what I'd been taught by my church as a young child (love, gentleness, acceptance, and so on) and what Gothard and my

185

Church taught me as a teenager (follow the rules, closed-mindedness and so on).

"Go Turd's lures — I mean, Gothard's rules — seemed contradictory, both to each other and to other so–called biblical principles and sometimes even to their own parent principle. They also contradicted what I knew of psychology, even when I was a kid. It's easier now for me to find the contradictions when I sort through the material, but it certainly wasn't back then.

"Lastly, I felt confused because all these emotions and ideas were running around inside me and I didn't know how to get them out."

"That's a good start," Sherry praised. "That was well-ordered. Let's talk about the next emotion. Why did you feel trapped?"

"I remember feeling trapped the first time I read Gothard's material on anger. As I said last week, I don't have their syllabus anymore, but here's a direct quote about anger from their website."

Doug read from his printout.

> *"Anger is a serious problem. What causes it? The root cause of a spirit of anger is tension from past hurts and guilt. This mixture of pain and guilt is cumulative and it erupts in anger when new offenses remind us of past experiences."*

Douglas continued. "Contrast that to what Wikipedia says about anger. As if I need to tell a therapist what anger is, but reading through the definition helps me think."

He pulled out the next printout.

> *"Anger can occur when a person feels their personal boundaries are being or going to be violated. Some have a learned tendency to react to anger through retaliation as a way of coping. Anger may be utilized effectively by setting boundaries or escaping from dangerous situations."*

"Go on," Sherry said.

"OK, let's list my areas of disagreement," Douglas lifted a finger for each point.

"First, in the Gothard version, anger is only bad. It's a problem. Wikipedia states that anger can be bad (you retaliate) or anger can be good (you use it as a warning system to set boundaries or escape). I'm not sure good-bad dualities apply in a scientific environment, but never mind.

"Second, Gothard moves from talking about anger in the singular to talking about 'a spirit of anger' as if they were the same thing. They aren't, because being angry once does not engender a 'spirit of anger.' By which he meant someone who was constantly angry, or filled with a demon of rage.

"Third, Gothard defines anger as a reaction to the tension caused by a *past* hurt and guilt. Plus there is no 'or.' Hurt *and* guilt. So guilty of what? Being hurt?

"By contrast, Wiki attributes anger to a reaction to a *present or future* violation of personal boundaries. That plus personal boundaries has nothing to do with it for Gothard.

"Gothard's position is inaccurate and his deception made me angry. Which meant PD, my church and even Lee told me to read the Gothard section on anger and I felt trapped."

"Gothard's view," Sherry commented, "of 'tension from past hurts and guilt' is more true of PTSD than anger."

"Come again?"

"Posttraumatic stress disorder. Like the disturbed dreams or shock that rape victims or soldiers can get. PTSD victims can also get angry when something triggers a memory of the past trauma, like a firecracker reminding an Iraq vet of gunfire. That much of what Gothard says may be true of PTSD, not anger."

Sherry contemplated whether or not this was a good time to tell Douglas that he probably had PTSD, too, but decided against it. He was still trying to process what PTSD was in the first place. One thing at a time.

"Very interesting," Doug paused for a moment to soak it in but didn't continue.

Sherry finally prompted him, "What does this have to do with feeling trapped?"

"It trapped me into a negative cycle. I thought the red syllabus was wrong and deceptive, so reading the section on anger made me angry. Which meant PD, my church and even Lee told me to read the section on anger.

"But I didn't think anger was a sin even in junior high, much less high school. Back then, and you gotta remember that my dad taught me biology and animal behavior. By the time I was 10, I thought anger was part of the human fight-or-flight response. Anger can help humans; anger can hurt humans. It's just there. But Gothard treats anger as a problem or sin from the get go."

"Did you tell people this when you were in junior high or high school?" Sherry asked.

"Yeah. But they weren't going to believe what science said about anger over what Gothard said about anger because Gothard used 'biblical principles', even though the Bible doesn't agree with Gothard to begin with."

Douglas stopped himself. "Now that's an interesting thought."

"What is?", Sherry asked."

"It's a quote by Will Durant, who wrote a history of the Reformation.

> Protestantism was the triumph of Paul over Peter.
> Fundamentalism is the triumph of Paul over Christ. [1]

"That is, Protestants trust Paul's letters more than the Pope, Peter's heir, while Fundamentalists trust Paul's letters more than what Jesus said in the Gospels.

"To which I would add that IBYC is the triumph of Gothard over the Bible. That is, what Gothard *says* the Bible says becomes more important than what the Bible actually says.

"My church couldn't distinguish between the red syllabus and the NT." He shrugged. "Though I was probably the only person in the Church who thought that."

"So you felt abandoned," Sherry inferred.

"I was abandoned. No, wait," Douglas halted himself, his thoughts clashing with each other. "Or continue, whatever. Dang, this confuses me."

"Take your time."

He stopped, took a deep breath, then continued.

"It's true that I was abandoned, or at least I think so. But saying, 'I was abandoned' doesn't really get at what I want to say, so I stopped myself. But I need to say more so I began to continue. . . . So I'm stopping and starting simultaneously and got tongue-tied. It's very confusing." He paused again.

"To say nothing of damn frustrating. It's been more than 30 years since I had speech therapy and sometimes I still can't get the damn words out."

Sherry raised her eyebrows. Two damns back-to-back. "Can you go on with describing how you felt abandoned?"

"I think so. Take for example the fact that I thought Gothard wasn't biblical. I didn't have the skills yet to identify exactly where, even though I knew he was wrong. But when I gave my suspicions to PD or my family, they just blew me off. No one paid any attention.

---

[1] Will Durant, *The Story of Civilization: Caesar and Christ:* NY: Simon and Shuster, 1944, p. 592.

"If I talked to my Dad or John about Gothard today, which is probably a bad idea, but never mind that, they'd probably agree that Gothard was seriously Bad News. Not that this would help me any. I'm still stuck with the fact that they didn't believe me *then*.

"I didn't feel like anyone listened. They didn't give me any credibility, even as I grew older. If nothing else, I thought that if the sessions damaged me, then I shouldn't be forced to attend. It wasn't like it was a required class or anything. But they insisted that I believe in correct dogma instead of being human me."

PD offended Douglas once (30 years later Doug couldn't remember exactly how) and PD asked for his forgiveness. But Douglas wasn't so sure he could give it, because he thought PD would probably do it again. Why should Douglas encourage him?

Douglas said as much and discovered that following the dogma inverted the roles. The offender was good because he asked for forgiveness. The victim was bad because he wasn't sure he could give it. The actual behavior of the offender, current or future, was irrelevant so long as the offender followed the form.

The converse was true of the victim. The offender had asked for forgiveness, so the victim's current and future behavior was relevant, no matter how much pain or humiliation the victim had suffered. If the victim was still upset or angry or admitted his or her pain, then the victim lacked faith and had an unforgiving spirit. The victim needed to repent.

It was another double bind. Once the offender asks for forgiveness, then he is guiltless. If he repeats the offense, then a simple promise not to do it again sufficed, regardless of the actual behavior. Any further trouble is therefore the victim's fault. Blame the victim and sweep the offending behavior under the rug.

If you follow the rules, then you abrogate self-responsibility because you followed the rules. And if you don't follow the rules, then you're responsible because you didn't follow the rules. 'Under this logic,' Douglas thought, 'the only way to gain responsibility for yourself is to break all the rules.'

"Damn, this pisses me off!" Douglas felt himself losing it. "Maybe we should talk about something else for a moment."

"You're doing well so far. Why not continue?"

"Maybe. But I gotta take a break for a second, at least."

One night, Douglas and his friends Tabitha and Andy took a walk on the beach. They hadn't checked the weather report and none of them expected the red tide. Soon, it became an unrehearsed night of magic and moonlight, the three of them playing fingers and feet through the water, watching it shimmer and turn. With every wave there came another spin and rush of diamonds.

It was easy to find a place to wash themselves off. There aren't that many people on the beach at midnight.

Remembering that moment gave Douglas pause, enough silence and stillness to settle him down. Enough magic to take a breath and be quiet.

He took another breath and continued, "I felt manipulated and devalued, alone. Confused and split against myself. I was manipulated into attending and devalued because I didn't fit the mold. It was confusing. Part of me screamed to get me out of the Gothard conferences, part of me wanted to please my church, my family, my girlfriend, so I attended."

He sobbed and reached for a tissue. Sherry let him cry a bit then reminded him, "It's time to close. We'll have to continue this next week."

*Epper si muove.* The earth still moves, never pausing for our tears. There would be no magic or red tide tonight.

*September 4, 2003, in session*

A typical fantasy story shows the characters in awe of the magician. As fire bursts from his hands, people gasp in fear or applaud in appreciation. The wizard changes shape or summons demons and the audience sits stunned by his power.

Doug wondered about that. If magic really did exist in the world, wouldn't we just get used to it? "Oh, you turned the rock into a sapphire. OK. What do you want me to do with that sapphire, boss?" In a magical world, magic is normal. There's nothing special about it at all.

If you flip that around, then maybe we really do live in a world of magic and color, but it's so ordinary that we fail to notice it. A fire warms our hands or hot chocolate warms our bellies. Maybe it's all magic. Maybe it's an incantation. And seeing the ordinary as magic makes it special.

Or . . . maybe not. He didn't really know. There were probably lots of ordinary things that he never saw as beautiful every day, simply because they were ordinary. And maybe his idea was completely bogus. Maybe there was no magic at all and never had been. Who knew?

But coming out of high school, Douglas was positive about one thing. His girlfriend Leanne was magic.

"I can't help but wonder," Douglas told Sherry, "if I could have explained my doubts about Gothard to Leanne better if I'd had a bit more philosophical vocabulary."

"Go on," Sherry thought he was on the right track.

"At the time, I was looking for at least two words: exegesis and reductionism.

Exegesis is theological interpretation of the Bible," Doug explained. "In theory, you're supposed to do it without being self-serving, but no one's that unbiased. On the other hand, you can safely leave out David Koresh raping 13-year-old girls in his own church, even though he was otherwise really, really good at exegesis. Or perhaps casuistry, but never mind."

"OK. What's reductionism?"

"'An approach to understanding the nature of complex things by reducing them to the interactions of their parts,' says Wikipedia. Descartes disagreed with Aristotle's position: 'The whole is greater than the sum of their parts.'

"The philosophical debate," he continued, "is whether or not humans are 'greater than the sum of their parts', like Aristotle says, or can be 'reduced' to a set of parts that interact to form an automaton, like Descartes says.

"Fascinating stuff. I've written a paper or two on the topic which, of course, has nothing to do with what I want to talk about, so let's keep going."

"Yes, let's," Sherry said gratefully. "What does this have to do with Gothard or Leanne?" Maybe he wasn't on the right track after all.

Douglas nodded, "I was trying to tell Lee that any exegesis like Gothard's that reduces biblical principles to rules is suspect because the Bible facilitates a gestalt, not automatons. Humans may or may not be reduced to a rule set in a computer, but the Bible doesn't paint people that way. The Bible holds with Aristotle.

"'The Sabbath was made for man,' said Jesus, 'and not man for the Sabbath.' We are saved and live by grace, not law."

On one level, Douglas thought that was all he needed to say. It was a good summary.

But therapy isn't engineering. You don't stop when the problem is summarized. You stop when you come to terms with your own behavior. Until then your mind cycles over the same stuff, which reminded Doug of the Israelites circling Jericho until the Jews screamed in frustration and the psychological walls fell down.

Onward.

"Gothard's problem has more to do with exegesis, so let's talk more about that for a second." Douglas said after a moment.

"Before you get there," Sherry interrupted, "why are you talking about this?"

The question startled him. Doug had come into this session well-prepared, thinking out his positions in advance. But why was he doing it? The topic was anger, not exegesis.

"I guess because it's hard for me to express emotions," he said slowly, "as you well know. Sometimes I can write about my emotions. I'll write poetry and that helps. But I can't do that all the time and I can't talk about my emotions easily so some of them just stay blocked.

"But when I intellectualize a topic then I can approach my emotions sideways or through the back door, like what I did when I talked about Gothard's section on anger. I dissected it until I could say, 'I feel angry about this and confused because of that.' Then I could expand on the emotion to get at it."

"OK. You're not always digressing because it's fun, but because it lets you approach painful topics," Sherry said.

"Yeah. Though sometimes I detour just for the heck of it. English is such a marvelous language for that."

"It is, isn't it," Sherry agreed. "Go on with what you were saying about exegesis."

Deciding when to do exegesis can be tricky. The Bible is usually so clear that you don't need exegesis anyway or it's so muddied that exegesis won't help you.

For example, what's exegesis supposed to add to John 11:35, "Jesus wept?" That tears consist of water, lipids, and glucose with trace amounts of sodium and potassium? Simple things are best kept simple.

On the other end of the spectrum, we have Genesis 6:2.

> That the sons of God saw the daughters of men that they
> were fair; and they took them wives of all which they chose.

Ah. Here Douglas had gone through life thinking that the sons of eggplants saw the daughters of orangutans that they were ugly and took them as wives from those they didn't choose. Silly Douglas; clearly he needs to develop spiritual maturity.

No, seriously. How does exegesis help here? What does the verse really mean? Who are the "sons of God?" After all, the Book of Job lists Satan as one of them.

By the time Douglas got to JECU, he'd read Genesis 6:2 multiple times, shrugged, and decided it was irrelevant. There was no way to know what the verse meant. Nonetheless, Dr. Mildew took 10 minutes of Old Testament 101 outlining four explanations. Then he concluded by saying that we had to make up our own minds. There was no way to know what this verse meant.

"Any questions?" Dr. Mildew asked. Doug waved his hand, "Yes, Douglas." In a class of 50, the professor already knew who he was by week #2.

"Yeah," he asked. "Why have you spent 10 minutes on the topic if there is no way to know what the verse means?"

The professor looked annoyed, but answered the question anyway, "So you're familiar with the possibilities when you try to make up your own mind. Any more questions?"

At first Doug was going to take that answer on face value, then he realized that the answer didn't make any sense. Didn't the other students notice that? He waved his hand again.

The professor was going to ignore him, but no one else raised their hand, so resigned himself to calling on Douglas again, "Yes, Douglas."

"Yeah. If there is no way to know what the verse means, then how can we make up our own minds?"

Douglas soon discovered that he was not necessarily Dr. Mildew's pet student (guess his motivation level). But the point's the same: if simple verses are best kept simple, any verse too complex is best left alone.

Bringing his attention back inside Sherry's office, Douglas wiped his brow and brushed back his hair while thinking through his emotions, "If there is no way to determine an answer, don't bother trying," he said. "Go elsewhere."

"What Dr. Mildew has in common with Goth Turd is neither one thinks things through. Instead of doing the obvious, they're both misusing the Bible as a cookbook. Just open it up and answers mysteriously appear.

"Gothard isn't searching for God because he feels he has already found Him. Make up your own rule set, just like Koresh. Mildew isn't searching for God because he picks apart an inexplicable recipe. It's gotta have a secret in it somewhere. Neither of them wants to worship God.

"The reason why many of these people have so much difficulty finding the true spiritual hidden meaning in these confusing parts of the Bible is because . . . there isn't one. The message in the Bible is the obvious.

"It reminds me of the Emperor's new clothes. All the professors or Gothard pompously pontificate about pointlessness until all the JECU junkies or Gothardites bob their heads up and down obediently then bounce into boring obscurity. Then everyone pats each other on the patootie for becoming patriarchs.

"What a crock!"

193

"I ran into an acquaintance from JECU a few years ago," Douglas continued, "and he wondered 'Why haven't Christians had any great theologians lately?' They were thinking of someone like C. S. Lewis."

"I made some polite noise, but inside I'm thinking, 'Because you don't want one.'"

Douglas wound down while Sherry looked at the clock, "Do you think you can wrap this up in five minutes?" she asked.

He thought for a second, "Yeah. I'm done with the first point and the next two will probably go quickly."

"OK. Go ahead."

"The next step," he reiterated, "is doing the exegesis. But think about it. Between simple tears and sleeping dogs, the Bible doesn't leave much room to interpret the text without personal bias.

"I mean, come on! We've been studying the same New Testament now for nearly 2,000 years, at least 500 years more than that for the Torah. David Koresh was so good at it that he could fluently justify adultery, underage sex and murdering ATF agents. Sounds like 'personal bias' to me.

"That's the Federal Bureau of Alcohol, Tobacco and Firearms.

"I followed," Sherry said.

"Yeah. So enough said. Step #3: Applying (good) exegesis to a day-to-day situation requires some care. Just because Saint Paul picked up poisonous snakes without being bitten doesn't mean that God requires this behavior right up there with baptism. Common sense applies and everyone has different gifts. For some reason, I'm pretty sure that I don't have the gift of handling poisonous snakes."

Sherry smiled. "Neither do I."

He thought for a second. "Yeah. Anyway. I think that's one reason I got mad at Leanne. Even if the Bible were a cookbook, that doesn't mean it contains the recipe I need. I felt like she was applying Gothard's exegesis carelessly and I thought better of her. Yeah, I know she was 17 and I know she was in a conservative environment. But Deirdre was younger than Lee, I knew her at the time, and she didn't do that."

"We'll have to finish this off next week," Sherry said.

Doug felt glum about this all and sat there a short moment. Then he got up and bid Sherry good-bye. It was sad to realize that Leanne was human, not magic.

Then he had another thought as he walked to his car: maybe she was both.

*September 11, 2003, at home*

*Dear Jacky,*

Crap. 9/11 again.

9/11 is absolutely vital to me only because I must ignore it. Everyone else says, "We'll never forget!" and I try to pretend it never happened.

There are (count 'em) six tall bridges on my way to work every day. So I ignore 9/11 lest I stop the car, say, on the 101 bridge over Santa Ynez Valley and, like the dead of 9/11, never once cross it. "The only way to get rid of temptation," said Oscar Wilde, "is to yield to it." I cannot tempt myself to jump.

OK. So maybe I'm not patriotic. So be it. Unpatriotic slime bag that I am, I need a better way to control my life than by committing suicide. I must get smart.

From chaos to control, control back to chaos. "The best art is a controlled fury," so said my friend Tabitha. Oscar Wilde is sometimes a cold wind a-blowing. Tabitha's ideas I keep thinking about, a tapestry hanging inside my walls. It warms me.

Sometimes it felt weird in college when I wrote my best poetry during philosophy class, then outlined my philosophy papers during poetry class. UNIX, poetry; poetry, UNIX. But so what? If one is chaos and the other is control, then my best writing is Tabitha's controlled fury.

Some of my 1975 letters show the chaos, Jacky, as you well know. I have much better control in 2003 (took me long enough), but I can still only release the fury in small doses. Ah well, one step at a time.

My controls in 1975 were the rules of religion and self-denial mixed with a young man's idealism. My fury was much greater than my control and so I lost Leanne. But if I can learn why I lost control then (and it's gotta have something to do with sex) then maybe I can learn why it's still hard for me to control my emotions now.

Which begs the obvious question: when and where did I lose control with Leanne? And why was there so much fury in 1975?

*With love,*

*Douglas*

195

# ALAS—Thoughts on Love

*September 18, 2003, in session*

"Anger, Love, Abuse, Sex," Douglas said to open the next session. "We've talked about anger so the next one is love."

"Are you sure you're done talking about anger?" Sherry verified.

He exhaled slowly, "I think so. I'm never sure that I'm entirely done, but it feels that way for now. And I can get back to it later, if need be."

"Of course," Sherry responded. "Let's talk about love."

"Big topic," he replied. "I love Sharon, I love Catherine, I love Anne, I love saying that I love people, I love me, I love lemonade.

"Love is such a stupid word sometimes. Maybe we need another 37 different words for 'love,' like the 37 Eskimo words for 'snow'. Of course, that's just an urban legend, but it gets the point across. There are too many types of love."

Sherry had a suggestion, "Why not subdivide along the lines of what you were using earlier, love of God, love for a woman?"

"I like it," Doug agreed, then he thought about it some. "Except both of those things confuse me and I don't always know how to handle them. I can only try to accept them, to accept and care about myself. I love me. Let's add one more category: Love of self."

"Good," Sherry said. "Where do you want to start?"

The music immediately popped into his head and the question felt whimsical. Let's start at the very beginning. A very good place to start, he sang to himself.

"With love of God," he managed to say out loud instead. Love for a woman felt like a larger scale, and he wanted to key in on something simpler, or at least on a more minor pain.

## Love of God

The Bible is not God. There were times when Douglas wasn't even sure that the Bible is the Logos, the Word of God. After all, Jesus took that claim for Himself. But let's avoid that theological tangent for now, for as interesting as it may be, and focus on his relevant beliefs. The Bible is about people, not rules.

Matt and Rachel, who plopped themselves over each other at the Hosanna High Disneyland post-graduation party, dated through the summer of 1975. But in August they broke up over theology. Matt is a charismatic who believes in 'sign' gifts like healing or prophecy, Rachel is a Fundamentalist who does not.

It all seemed pretty silly to Doug. Both parties were more willing to marry their beliefs than each other. On that point, clearly they made the right decision. But from his viewpoint, even though he kept his mouth very shut, they were both more interested in yelling about who had the best way to love and honor God than to actually, say . . . love and honor God; or each other.

How human! We've probably been doing that for the past 8,000 years, at least.

But Jesus, Doug thought, didn't call us to stay still, He called us to move. He called us to *follow* (Him), he called us to *go* (forth). Christianity is organically active, not doctrinally passive. Jesus called us to be better than ourselves, to keep searching, to keep growing. The fact that we've been idiots the past 8,000 years is no excuse to keep doing it for the next 8,000. Why not start trying to love each other now?

It might take us awhile.

"Loving God," Douglas added to Sherry, "implies two things: intimacy and power. Power because you're talking about God. Intimacy because you're making the claim, true or otherwise, that you're on good terms with that power. That you love God at least in the way that I love ice cream. I'm familiar with it and enjoy the stuff. Of course, I obviously enjoy it too much. It's good.

"That may have been what attracted me to Philippians 3:10 back when I was dating Leanne."

> *[I want] to know Him, and the power of His resurrection, and the fellowship of His sufferings, being conformed to His death, if any way I arrive at the resurrection from among [the] dead.*

"Here's how I paraphrased that in 1975," Douglas didn't have that one memorized and had to read his notes.

> *That's the important thing; to perceive, recognize, and understand that which is, and what creates, that which can be called reality, and experience how it cannot be destroyed.*

"The paraphrase loses the intimacy of St. Paul's original words," he commented, "but underlines the power to see the resurrection as indestructible reality. I tried re-paraphrasing this just recently and got:

> *[I want] to perceive, recognize, and fellowship with the Jesus who is, and who creates, even in His suffering and in His death. Because while I'm in Him, His resurrection from the dead shows that neither He nor I can ever be truly destroyed.*

"Which still doesn't get it all. There's perhaps too much emphasis on intimacy, not enough on power, but let's leave it for now. It took me 28 years to work that much out so maybe I'll have a better explanation in 28 more. Who knows?

"The point," Douglas did have one, "is that Paul talks about a relationship. To 'know *him*.' To love not the rules but the person through their suffering. Married folks know this well. If you love, you will suffer and share the suffering."

And that took him back to Matt and Rachel. I Corinthians 13:13:

> *But now abideth faith, hope, love, these three; and the greatest of these is love.*

In 1975, Doug thought that the Apostle Paul was on to something. If you truly love someone, then differences can be worked out and certainly some strong cross-religion marriages have worked like this.

Yes, there really is a time and place to die for your beliefs and millions of people have done so. But is the baptism of the Holy Spirit one of those beliefs? Or not enough to die for but enough to break off a romance? For Douglas it probably is not. For Matt, it certainly is. He did it, but why? John 14:6:

> *I am the way, the truth, the life. No man comes to the Father but through me.*

The truth is not an idea. It's a *person*. The Bible doesn't fall back onto beliefs, but onto *relationships*. "In the beginning was the Word and the Word was with God and the Word was God." Then the Gospel begins to speak of Jesus as the Word. Or to put it even more simply "Love the Lord with all your heart, with all your mind, with all your soul" and "Love one another." The one is power, the other intimacy.

"Maybe the way I read scripture makes me a heretic," Douglas finished. "After all, here I am saying that loving God is more important than doctrine and analyzing scripture for myself rather than just trusting my pastor, perish the thought. And I really don't care. If loving God makes me a heretic, then so be it.

"Likewise, it is not my responsibility to judge who has the right theology—Matt or Rachel, as if I had the ability to know. There's too many ways to logic-chop the Bible to be sure of anything but the basics.

"But it *is* my responsibility to love my neighbor. And as far as I'm concerned, that's where I draw my lines. That's the time and place for me to die for my beliefs. Not to worry about dogma or abortion or gay marriage or the Iraq War, or God knows what all. Just to love Him and to love each other—to bring the power of God to man through love."

"You're passionate about this," Sherry commented.

"Yeah," he nodded. "What's the point of living if you don't believe your life has value?

"And if I don't know why I once wanted to commit suicide, that at least provides a reason for me not to. I can continue to seek and experience the value and beauty of life created by the God I worship and to share that value with others whom I love."

## Love of Self

*September 25, 2003, in session*

"To thine own self be true," said the Bard. We're all different. Anne woke up at 6:00 a.m. to beat the morning traffic. As a night owl, Douglas preferred to work late rather than to arrive at work early.

But to what extent was he himself similar to others?

Consider Matt and Rachel. If Matt and Rachel could break up over the summer, then so could Leanne and Douglas. They didn't, but a fear crept into his belly and he began to mistrust Leanne for no reason. It was like a demon. Something beyond theology drove him to doubt and fear and he kept on trying to squash it.

"You can't box up your demons," he began. "That's a lesson I've learned from you, Sherry. I've got to let my demons out at least long enough to admit that they exist, no matter how ugly they are. 'To thine own self be true.'"

"It's frightening," he elaborated. "I told you once that I wanted to beat you up."

"Yes. I remember that."

"I told you once that I'm afraid you'll tie me up and beat me up instead."

"Yes."

"I cross-dressed in front of you so that I could screw up the courage to tell you how much I fear women."

"Yes."

"I told you that I hate Deirdre. I told you that I want to rape and torture Deirdre then use her husband as my little slave-girl catamite."

"Yes. But where are you going with this?" She remained unperturbed throughout Douglas's litany.

"Denial," he responded. "Healing for me began when I stopped denying that those were things I wanted to do. 'To thine own self be true' includes the rotten and the evil."

Sherry agreed, "Correct. And wanting isn't doing."

"Yeah. I didn't see that clearly back in the '70s and suffered the consequences. Not sure about it, but there seem to be two ways to deny: deny that I want something healthy and deny that I want something that isn't."

"What do you mean by 'healthy?'" Sherry queried.

"Uhh . . . normal human behavior. Like, I wanted to make love with Leanne. But when I dated her I felt that *wanting* sex required me to *do* sex. It's what my church taught me, accidentally or not, that the desire is as bad as the act. I tried to deny that I wanted sex and that just screwed me up worse."

"OK. Go on." Sherry was on the same page now.

"Deirdre is on the other side of the same coin," he continued. "After we broke up, I wanted to do something unhealthy—to hate Deirdre. But denying the hate just turned it into torture. Denying that I wanted to torture someone else just meant that I tortured myself."

"There's a subtle pattern here. 'To thine own self be true.' If you deny the desire to do something bad or to do something unhealthy, then the demons get worse. Better start accepting yourself now, warts and all."

By this point Doug had been in therapy two and a half years. Life is easier, to say nothing of therapy, if you admit your fears and desires right away. The problem is that when you start therapy you're so crazy that you don't know what they are. Therapy works partly because admitting the confusion is being true to yourself. You move from the realm of denial to the realm of the possible.

The breakup of Matt and Rachel affected Douglas not just because he began to fear losing Leanne, but because he began to fear Leanne. Maybe she had a crazy agenda like Rachel. And he couldn't admit it to himself because the fear was irrational. Likewise, he wanted to make love with Leanne and denied that, too.

In 1975, Doug needed to admit both his unhealthy fear and his healthy desire. And he didn't, or at least, not enough. The result was that the demons continued to grow.

"I've got 28 years of perspective on that summer, Sherry," Douglas concluded. "And parts of it are still confusing."

## Love for a Woman

*October 2, 2003, in session*

Douglas started the next session by reading a love letter to Lee, one he'd never sent.

> *Dear Leanne,*
>
> *Thank you so much for just being you, for loving, for wanting me to be happy, no matter what you want. Thank you for your smile and your joy. Thank you for caring. Thank you for every little detail that you are. Thank you for giving me the confidence in myself that I need. Thank you for caring and loving me.*
>
> *Leanne, I owe you so much, and all I can give back is myself. This music expresses only a little of that, but I give you the music, how I feel it, to realize the beauty. Rivers trickle over moss and willows dance in the breeze. Leanne, you give me peace, the peace of a mountain. Each one stands firm to command all about it. Peace, peace that brings forth joy, wonder, and care. Peace that, "knits up the raveled sleeve of care."*

He looked up from reading. "And blah, blah, yadda yadda yadda, mushy goo. Bleh! My margin notes say I was listening to Beethoven's 7th at the time, by the way. That probably influenced my mood."

"Your words are touching," Sherry responded. "And you were young. Why be so hard on yourself?"

Doug felt embarrassed. "I mean I wasn't that great of a romance writer, not that I didn't love her."

Sherry confirmed his statement, "You most definitely loved her. Tell me more about your love."

A hint of red crept into his face. But then, he'd already read Sherry a love letter so maybe it couldn't get any worse.

"Leanne is a fox," he started. "There's just no other good way to say it. Fox, fox, fox. And it wasn't just infatuation. We were friends with each other before we dated; we were friends with each other after we dated. If it wasn't love, I sure did a good imitation of it for a few years. I mean, here I am talking about Leanne 28 years later, ya know? One gathers that maybe there was something long-lasting to it."

❧❧❧

"What are you doing?" she asked. They were strolling near San Juan Creek that evening.

"Talking to the trees," Douglas responded. "Smelling their summer freshness. Sometimes I can see a light in the crown of the trees, pulling me in. Then I touch the bark, pretend to be the tree, and listen to the rustle of their leaves."

"What are they saying?" Leanne was curious.

"Very little. Mostly they're waiting for someone to look at them." He smiled. "We can be the first."

"The ordinary is magic," she said.

"Exactly."

When Leanne wasn't around, Douglas would tell the trees his troubles while they listened in silence, letting his voice grow and rumble. The trees had no agenda, no demanding tapes to play. They just listened. And he trusted them with both his hands.

He remembered talking to Leanne back then, smelling her springtime perfume. He'd see the light from the crown of her hair, pulling him in. He'd touch her face with both his hands and wonder:

Can I trust Leanne the same as the trees? Do I really like her? Does she really like me? What is her real motive for liking me? What is she hiding?

The shift was jolting. For a moment, he'd been walking near the creek amid the sunset, his nostrils full of oak and chaparral and listening to the trees. Now he was sitting back in Sherry's office, his nostrils full of office bland and listening to the hum of the air conditioner.

"Ja," Doug used the German word. "There I was with a beautiful, young, woman in my arms, yet I worry about justifying our relationship. I kept trying to intellectualize it while at the same time denying the passion. But there she was, gently folded inside my embrace.

"Remember. I was a strait-laced choirboy in the Independent Baptist 1970s. Our hugs were not exactly 'hands up the dress.' Besides, she was wearing a pretty white, full-length skirt that night. I'm talking about a normal hug, arms around the waist face-to-face, cheek-to-cheek, no kissing."

He paused before continuing, "I loved a woman and I felt just horrible about it."

He paused again, sitting there. He stared up at the white ceiling tiles for a minute.

"Go on," Sherry prompted.

"I don't know how," Douglas answered. "Anger, Love, Abuse, Sex. When I pick up the snarl and look closely, the threads seem so impossibly tangled."

"So you're getting stuck on 'love for a woman,'" Sherry commented.

"Yeah. Exactly."

"OK. What can you tell me about the snarl?"

He thought about it. "My emotions slide freely from one to another at this point," he finally voiced. "It's one thing to admit that my anger became abuse, as I said about the fight when we broke up, because anger strikes me as close to abuse anyway. But it's another to admit that my love crossed into abuse."

He shook his head, ashamed.

"But it did. I never hit Leanne but I abused her nonetheless. I yelled at Leanne. I screamed at Leanne. Then I screamed at me and yelled some more. I cut myself down in front of her. And I did it again, and again, and again. Emotional abuse is worse than physical."

"Oh God, this hurts to talk about," Doug's pain showed clearly on his face. "Then I get stuck when I try to talk about it. I'm sorry I can't be clearer about it. But I can't."

"I understand," Sherry flipped through her notes while he composed himself. "Back in May," Sherry said after a moment of searching, "you commented you were terrified of touching Leanne and of her touching you. Even panicky."

"Yes."

Sherry continued, "So of Anger, Love, Abuse, and Sex, you get stuck on loving women and sex. As different topics, I mean."

"That's about the size of it," Douglas agreed.

"Then why don't we move back to discussing sex?" Sherry suggested. "We were going to anyway."

"Because I'll just get stuck again?" Doug queried rather than stated.

Sherry was more optimistic, "Perhaps not. That was four months ago, you've made good progress since then, and you can talk about sex within the context of your relationship with Leanne."

"We didn't have sex."

"But you were sexual. You held hands, embraced, stroked her hair and so on."

"True enough."

"Then let's just leave 'love for a woman' alone for now and discuss sex. We can get back to love later."

It made sense, Doug realized, but he still felt petrified. On the other hand, Leanne was still magic. Maybe some of that magic could still rub off on him.

"All right," he said, looking at the clock. "Though I suppose it'll have to wait till next week."

Sherry glanced in that direction, "Yes. But this has been a good session."

The praise warmed him. By no means did Doug have all his behavior under control. He still felt forced to play with Barbie dolls, for instance, minus the hitting. But he felt much better and let's not argue with success, he thought. Committing suicide would put a sudden halt to my efforts to learn to like myself.

# ALAS—From Love to Sex

*October 9, 2003, in session*

Douglas was grateful to CalTrans every Thursday morning on the way to Sherry's office. To Douglas's native eyes, the brown hills with rock and green bits of shrubbery near the highway looked lovely.

"OK," he started, "here's a letter I wrote Jacky in 1976 that talks about my sexual relationship, such as it was, with Leanne in 1975. I was still dating her at the time."

> *Dear Jacky,*
>
> *How does touching Leanne feel? I'm not sure. I've tried to explain only I can't get any words out. Holding Leanne makes me complete. It helps me to realize that Leanne Loves me. Leanne's body just seems to melt into mine. Together, we're melded into completeness.*
>
> *What is it like? It's like rain, so still and quiet and peaceful. It's like the wind, driving through my hair. It's like watching the sunset. It's like all those things put together and then multiplied by the beauty of running.*
>
> *When we lay close to each other on the small football field yesterday, I put my hands under her coat and over her blouse then placed my hands on her hip. And Leanne was just snow in my arms. I could feel her breasts close, soft, and pressing against me, almost inside me.*
>
> *Leanne flowed. She just fit into me so well. We matched in an unbelievable way. She was just molded into me. It was better than anything else I've known.*
>
> *I don't know how to say it all.*
>
> *Love,*
> *Douglas*

"Nice letter," Sherry commented.

"Thanks, though I never did send that to Leanne, just Jacky. At any rate, that letter reflects one mood of how I saw sex. Here's the other. Blah, blah . . ."

*Dear Jacky,*

*I feel guilty about it, but can't dwell on if embracing her was wrong. That's a fantastic way to ruin myself. But maybe I should change my behavior. Maybe I need to fight against putting my arm around her or to fight against touching Leanne at all. I need to think of what's good for her.*

*Touching Leanne tempts me to want physical marriage. Sex. I can see how easy it is to sin and defile Leanne and I need to keep her pure. Thus, I must block those feelings and I'll need God's help to do that. I'll have to keep my mind on Christ first then let him do what He wants to do.*

*Frustration is imminent. Good! A little frustration is good for the soul.*

*Love,*

*Douglas*

Doug's reaction was succinct, "Bleh."

Sherry's reaction was more long-winded. "Your romance is colliding with your religion over sex," she said, taking a more active role than normal.

"Right. *Un dieu dans le ciel et une déesse sur la terre.* And my religion set man as 'head of the woman.' Which in turn meant I was responsible for keeping my wife (or girlfriend) 'pure'—whatever that means.

"Religion, sex, and purity. Aargh! I'd whinge about how long it takes to talk about each topic, but then I'd have to whine about how long it takes to whinge. Best that we just continue."

"You're learning," Sherry encouraged.

"Yeah. Well, maybe. At any rate, I was in the process of separating God from the Church, which in the long run was definitely a good thing over that summer, but I hadn't gotten very far.

"I knew what God, or at least the Bible, says about sex. Hebrews 13:4: 'Marriage is honorable in all, and the bed undefiled.'" Doug quoted from memory again. "One of those places where you don't have to do exegesis. The meaning is clear.

"So why do I try to prevent myself from wanting something God thinks is honorable? God must turn you down cold when you pray for strength to deny the reality He creates.

"I was trying to keep myself from wanting to make love with Leanne—not a good idea."

"But wanting isn't doing," Sherry reiterated.

"Exactly," though he was still chewing it over. "That's one therapeutic truth that I'll have to keep repeating to myself until I get it right. There's only one good way to make an erection go away and breaking it in half isn't it.

"But what the Church showed me by example was that sex is bad and actions speak louder than words. There were lots of spoken or unspoken gender rules in the Church, to say nothing of the school. I knew that the Church wasn't working for me, but I didn't know how to make structure for myself.

"I relied on law because that's what I knew, and the rules I made as a substitute for my Church's rules were inflexible. Fine. Don't make love with her. But why not a kiss or better yet let myself make mistakes? Why was I so harsh on myself?"

Sherry agreed. "That's a good question. Why were you?"

He exhaled noisily, "I don't know. I don't understand my behavior in 1975, even accounting for the fact that I was 17 or 18 years old. Just *listing* my behavior is about all I can tolerate right now. Maybe it's time to move to purity."

"And we'll have to explore that in more detail next week."

"You say that every week," Doug grinned sardonically.

Sherry smiled back. "And you keep coming back. You should feel good about your progress."

Douglas wasn't sure whether or not to believe her. He felt empty, not proud of his progress. But on the way out to his car, he decided to take the long way to work. It was an extra five minutes, but taking the rest of Route 33 west to Interstate 70 touched against a creek and a long notch full of trees.

*October 16, 2003, in session*

"Hello, Sherry!"

Sometimes Douglas wondered what it would be like to have Sherry as a friend, not as a therapist. Not that he expected such a thing, but he liked her. Ah, well. He'd take what he could get.

"Hello!" Sherry retorted with a friendly smile. Douglas enjoyed listening to her voice—salesman smooth with nothing to sell. "How are you today?"

"Oh, not too bad. Work's a pain, but that's pretty normal."

"Ready to get started?"

"Right." Actually, Doug was more than ready. He could have just hopped right into the session, but following the social protocols was important. "We're talking about purity."

"Go on."

"The topic got me thinking about the pilgrims," he started, "who believed Puritans weren't 'pure' enough so they moved west across the

207

Atlantic. If you examine colonial history, the pattern repeats. Every once in a while, there's a religious revival, folks decide that their current society isn't 'pure' enough, and they move west to create their own religious paradise, multiple times across the frontier.

"If we keep on going west," he concluded, "then the purest American Christian possible is an Independent Baptist missionary surfing the west coast of Guam—surfing China would be un-American."

The analogy startled Sherry unexpectedly and she laughed.

Douglas grinned back. "I'd hate to point this out to those same Independent Baptists," he continued, "but if you go west far enough then you'll discover that the world is in fact . . . round. A constant search for purity will only take you 'East of Eden.'"

Sherry laughed again then calmed herself. "That's all very interesting . . ." she commented.

Doug interrupted her, "'But how does it apply to me.' Yeah."

"Exactly," Sherry did not seem perturbed by his interruption.

He shifted positions while sitting on the sofa. "History suggests that there's not really any such thing as purity. It's simply a concept that people manipulate this way or that for their own purposes."

Sherry didn't see where he was going with this, but at least he was becoming more specific. "Go on."

"OK. Consider our ancient Roman non-ancestors. One vestal virgin angered the emperor somehow. But before she was executed, she made the mistake of pointing out that it was illegal to kill a vestal virgin; they were too pure.

"'No problem,' said the emperor, who promptly raped her publicly then had her executed. After all, he had to make sure the public understood she was no longer pure."

"Ouch," Sherry commented.

"Yeah. Not that really being a virgin helps any. Agamemnon sacrificed his pure virgin daughter Iphigenia on his way to 'rescue' Helen of Troy, who was decidedly impure. There's something Freudian in there somewhere, but the Greeks already knew this. Just read Sophocles."

"I've never read him," put in Sherry.

"Interesting guy, but back to virgins. Even before Helen and Iphigenia, the Hebrew Judge Jephthah promised that if God gave him a victory he'd sacrifice the first thing he saw in his village when he got back home, which was his virgin daughter. Oops.

"If you're a virgin you're sacrificed for purity and if you're not a virgin you're murdered as impure. Damned if you do, damned if you don't. And maybe you'll be sacrificed by a simple mistake. Oh, well.

"I'd suggest that we just sacrifice the virgin Eve and go back to meiosis and mitosis but somehow, life doesn't work that way. Either God created sex to be pure or God created humans with the evolutionary imperative to be impure." He paused. "Pardon my roundabout approach, but I can't seem to get at this directly. But I think I've finally figured out my point."

"Which is . . ." Sherry prompted.

"If women are pure and sex makes them impure, then what am I? Guilty just for wanting sex? In this case, I mean just 'wanting,' not 'doing.' And if I'm impure because I want to 'degrade' women, then how am I supposed to protect the purity of my wife in the first place? She becomes impure just by marrying me because I'm already impure. The whole game at Lands Baptist seemed back-asswards."

Sherry agreed. "It does sound distorted. How did this impact your relationship with Leanne?"

Douglas's response returned to indirect: "How did she see the situation? Did she think sex was impure?"

Back when Doug was a young kid, churchwomen would all gather around the latest baby and, at least from the point of view of a six-year-old kid, coo themselves silly. By the time he was 11, the church leaders taught Doug to "guard his thoughts." Men could think "bad things" about women and if he wasn't careful then he'd think about "denigrating girls."

Douglas's assumption, of course, was that girls don't want to be denigrated. Not that he knew what sex was at the time, but whatever 'it' was 'it' was bad. And 'it' happened in marriage. Why did women get married if 'it' was so degrading? Did they want to be degraded? Or did girls simply put up with sex in order to have children? Could any woman really love a man? Just to love him?

If 'it' was so denigrating but women did 'it' anyway, then women had to be getting something out of it.

Babies. The women weren't cooing themselves silly over their husbands, now were they? All their attention was on babies. Making babies involved men in a way Douglas didn't quite understand but that didn't matter. Marriage was a trade-off: sex + denigration = baby + revenge. Simple.

"Damn!" Douglas exclaimed, "I was ten or 11 years old at the time. And it just hit me while talking about it now. I was 10 years old. And it wasn't just religion, I dreaded sex *before* I dated Leanne. Sex with women, or even wanting to have sex with women, made me impure.

"But it was more than dread, Sherry; it was horror. That's sex with anyone, not just Leanne. I know it isn't rational and I can't tell you why I felt like this. But I can tell you what I was feeling—terrified and confused. On the one hand, my hormones were panting:

> *Leanne is a fox. There's just no other good way to say it. Fox, fox, fox.*

"While my heart was singing the harmony.

> *Our fellowship is an unconquerable power, final resistance, and ultimate authority.*

"So far, so good. But my amygdala was screaming at me.

'RUN! She's going to get you! She'll fuck you over then beat you with a whip! Then she'll trample you and laugh at you just for fun!'"

"Most adolescent boys in a sexual situation are afraid of being laughed at."

"No, no, no, no, no. That's not what I mean. I wasn't afraid of making a mistake in a sexual situation. I was afraid of being *in* a sexual situation to begin with. Mistakes were OK. Girls were terrifying. No. Past terrifying. Horrifying. No, that's not right either because it's not horror. Absolutely overwhelming panic and dread."

Sherry nodded. "Go on."

He took a deep breath. "It felt like the act of making love with a girl was evil in and of itself. I earlier said that I felt like sex *defiled* a girl, that I committed a sin by Doing It, even with someone I deeply love.

"I can't explain this, or at least, not yet. It simply doesn't make sense. All I know is that my heart and gonads went one way, my limbic system another. I was head over heels in love with Leanne and wanted to make love with her. And I was horrified that she might return my love and want to make love with me: screaming, pounding terror. It split me inside.

"Anger, love, abuse, sex. There's a connection between love and abuse and another between abuse and sex."

Sherry did not seem surprised. Of course, she didn't express emotion frequently anyway, but Doug noted that she seemed more controlled than normal.

"And we'll have to explore that in more detail next week," was all Sherry said.

"I've heard that before somewhere," he responded.

Sherry smiled, but there was nothing to do about it today. The session was over.

# Recognition

# ALAS—From Love to Sex to Anger

*October 23, 2003, in session revisiting 1975*

The next event that summer in 1975 was a planned week off from Leanne. Leanne had paid for Teen Tour before they even started dating and PD asked Douglas to be a junior high camp counselor on the same week.

The break gave Doug time to think and realize something crucial. He loved Leanne enough to marry her. Their youth didn't bother him. His mom (19) and dad (18) married young, too, and that was a fast romance. His brother and sister both had slightly longer romances, then married at age 20.

Douglas had precedents. Wait a year or two, find a job, marry Leanne, or go to college as a married couple. Nor was he worried about the marriage lasting. His parents clearly were still madly in love after more than 20 years and his siblings both had strong marriages.

"But I panicked at the idea of making love with Leanne," he told Sherry. "Not 'religiously upset,' though that was a factor—terror. Sex was evil. Sex was hatred. Sex was how women attacked men.

"I called Leanne as soon as I could after camp and started to pull her closer to me in love while simultaneously pushing her away in fear. That's the only way to make sense of my behavior from junior high camp until we broke up four months later—the Tacoma Narrows Bridge. Push and pull then rip apart."

"This is painful to discuss—very, very painful.

"I wrote Leanne and asked her how she felt towards me sexually. I don't have a copy of my letter. But I wanted her to reassure me that she was honestly attracted to me physically and didn't want to manipulate me. Did she want to make love with me because she . . . loved me? Or was I simply a necessary evil, a chess piece that she pushed around, to get something else that she wanted? Like babies?

"My letter to Lee didn't explain any of this and it probably should've. I just asked her how she felt towards me sexually. On the other hand, I'm not sure I could have explained myself. I was that terrified.

"I do have Leanne's response letter."

*Douglas,*

*Boy is this going to be hard. Two answers—the easy one first. "You've come a long way, Baby!*

*The next isn't so easy—choice E. I'm not sure exactly what you want so I'll just tell you what I want—specifically early Sat. afternoon. I wanted desperately for you to kiss me. I had my head on your shoulder, looking up into your eyes and my stomach did a flip-flop. I think you felt the same way by the way you reacted. You looked frustrated, maybe that you couldn't kiss me.*

*I enjoy being close to you and want to get closer. You're so strong! So masculine! All I want is to be Loved by you. I'm find[ing] it hard to come right out and say it, but I want to tell you. I'm going to write it as though it is to myself. I can't come right out and say it so look for the implications.*

*At certain times of the month I can be walking along and into my mind pops this thought, "If Douglas were to make love to me now, I could have his baby." It's a neat thought.*

*(No implications, I don't think.)*

*There have been certain times when I felt so protected in your arms, so small and Loved, cared for and held close to you, that if I had not been brought up in a Christian home, was not a Christian, and if you didn't have any principles, things could happen very easily that both of us would be sorry for later.*

*Don't think bad things about me, please. You asked and I told you about my "sexual desires." They're slight temptations but I can easily overcome them.*

*Douglas, I Love you more than any other person! No one else has made me—physically, emotionally—and spiritually—the way you do.*

*With all my Love,*
*Leanne*

Doug read the letter to Sherry slowly, thinking it out, "I misinterpreted her letter. This was a rotten thing to do, but I did it. It sounded like Lee wanted exactly what I feared. Sex for babies was great! But sex because she *loved* me was something both of us would regret.

"What were men—chopped liver?

"Why did Leanne think wanting to make love with someone she loved (namely me) was tempting? Why wasn't it a joy? If Leanne was *tempted* to make love with me - and temptation only applied to something sinful—then was *actual* sex with me a sin? After marriage as well as before? Did she think that sex was really that dirty?"

"You thought Leanne fit your stereotype of women," Sherry suggested.

"Right. Maybe she just wanted a baby and revenge for being denigrated. Maybe she didn't love me. Maybe she just wanted power. Maybe she wanted to abuse me for making her do something dirty."

"Anger, Love, Abuse, Sex. If it's still difficult for me to separate between sex and abuse now, I couldn't do it at all when I was 17. Sex was abuse. Abuse was sex. There wasn't any difference and it felt like Leanne reinforced the link, however unintentionally, when I needed her to break it."

"Let's explore how that impacted your relationship next session," Sherry said.

Doug was hardly surprised, but for once he was glad the session was over. He had handled the situation with Leanne badly and wasn't proud of his behavior.

*November 6, 2003, in session*

"Shall we get started?" Sherry didn't seem to be in any rush, but time was passing.

"Certainly."

"Good. Last week we were talking about your reaction to Leanne's letter about sex."

Douglas was usually the one who picked the opening topic, but it looked like Sherry had an agenda. The topic was close enough to what Doug thought he needed to talk about anyway, so he decided to just go with it.

"Right," he fell silent for a short moment then added a caveat. "I can talk about my reactions, but you have to understand that it's a very painful topic and my reactions weren't rational."

"I understand," Sherry's body language showed that her comprehension ran more than skin deep.

Douglas's eyes thanked her even as he continued, "I decided that Leanne was just like any other woman. Or at least my misimpression of what women were like. She said sex was something we would both regret. That suggested that she didn't really love me. She must only be manipulating me to have a baby and to retaliate for making her do something dirty."

"Not that that makes any sense."

"Go on," Sherry was listening more intently than usual.

"I wrote Jacky about it later that night," he rooted around until he found the copy.

215

*Dear Jacky,*

*I feel like Leanne isn't dependent on me. It's like she read a book about how to get a boy to really like you, and she's followed those rules with me. But she just wanted the prize, not me. Maybe she didn't accept me because she wanted to, but because that was the best way to jeer.*

*I know that Leanne loves me, but (a bad word) will she submit herself to me? Or perhaps Leanne submits outwardly, but does she submit because she wants to or because she has to in order to keep me as her toy?*

*Obviously, there's a good way to find out, and I think I'll try it. I'll turn myself into as much of a jerk as I can (in a loving manner, of course. I must forgive her first and feel the pain). I'll ask Leanne to submit to the dumbest things I can think of, and react as stupidly as possible. I want to break Leanne down and to make her cry. But I have to do it in the right way and that'll be very tough to do.*

He broke off reading and groaned, "God, this is just awful!"

"My reasoning was that if Leanne still loves me when I'm a complete asshole, then maybe she's serious about me. And if Leanne wasn't serious, then I could punish her for manipulating me into the relationship.

"This was a mean and rotten thing to plan. I sinned. But why the hell was I thinking like this way in the first place? Why is there such a cross-circuit? 'I love Leanne so the best thing I can do is to make her cry so I can build her back up again.'

"Leanne had done absolutely nothing and there I am planning revenge. For what? Looking beautiful? Serious crime, that—what's going on here?"

Douglas was distraught.

Sherry thought she knew the answer, but she wasn't sure about it. How to verify her idea and how to tell Doug what it was?

She waited a bit through his tears. "How would you summarize that letter?" she asked finally.

Doug was honest about it, "I wanted to hurt someone I loved. The idea felt good. And I didn't like myself for wanting to hurt someone I loved. The idea felt bad.

"That felt ridiculous in 1975, even when I was writing it. What surprised me was that I was in fact writing it. It felt like another person pushing the pen, because I usually didn't act that way."

"All right," Sherry prompted. "Can you tell me anything about why you wanted to hurt Leanne?"

He thought about it. "Yeah, I think so," he responded, "at least a little."

"Go on."

He gulped, but managed to continue. "I was scared shitless of getting close to Leanne because I was sure that the closer she got to me, the more she would want to make love with me."

"And making love is . . . what? Sinful?" Sherry tried to step Doug through his own conclusions slowly.

"That's part of it. But the bigger part is that I was afraid Leanne would use making love to me as a way to manipulate and hate me. To strike at me."

He stopped himself, puzzled, "I'm just repeating myself. So let's go on. Thinking that she wanted to strike at me doesn't make sense because I could tell her feelings towards me were genuine. Why would she suddenly turn around then use making love as a weapon?"

"I don't know," Sherry mirrored. "Why would she?"

Doug chewed his fingernails while he thought about it.

"She wouldn't," he said slowly. "I knew Leanne that well, anyway. So why did I *think* that she would?"

It was a vital rhetorical question. Sherry let him stew for while then was about to prompt him when he continued on his own.

"I know I'm just repeating myself here," he added "Again. But let me go over the same thoughts from a different viewpoint."

Sherry smiled, "Good idea."

"OK. Push and pull. I loved Leanne and wanted to pull her closer to me. That's easy to understand. The push side, not so much. As near as I can figure it, I eventually realized that Leanne was innocent, so there was no reason to hurt her. But if I hurt *myself*, then I could still push her away. She wouldn't want to be around someone who was self-destructive and that would let me avoid hurting her. And I loved her."

"Why did you want to push her away in the first place?" Sherry decided that if Douglas could repeat his answers in a different way, then she could repeat her questions in a different way.

He brooded while looking out the window.

"Because I saw myself as dirty," he finally said. "Leanne was pure or at least innocent and I was dirty. Being close to her would make her dirty, too, and I loved her and didn't want to hurt her, so I pushed her away."

"And that still doesn't make any sense," he stopped again, feeling baffled. "Why would I be dirty? Because I'm male?"

Sherry's eyes reflected the question back to him but stayed quiet. Douglas was closing in on something.

He didn't directly answer. "If I'm really honest about it," he said instead, "watching women coo over babies isn't enough to make me think like this. To see women as manipulative or men as dirty. Other boys I knew at church didn't have the same issue and they went through the same thing. Something else must be going on? But what was it?"

"You don't have any ideas?" asked Sherry.

"No. The answer escapes me right now, and I don't see any stone tablets dropping down from heaven. Besides, with my luck, the answers would be in Arabic anyway."

Sherry smiled briefly. "If you don't know why you felt dirty, can you describe more of what being dirty feels like?"

"Oh hurrah," he responded. "My favorite topic."

Sherry was supportive but insistent, "Just give it a try. Start with 'I feel dirty.'"

He paused for a moment to gather strength, "'I feel dirty,'" he started, stopped, then started again. "I feel so guilty and dirty inside. I deserve to be punished. I want to be punished."

"Go on."

Douglas felt red creeping into his face, but continued, "I dressed like a little girl the other day and crawled into my closet. I closed the door and knelt down to worship one of mom's costumes. Then I asked mom to please beat me, to hit me. I want to hurt myself. I wanted mommy to punish me. And I begged her to love me, please love me.

"But I can never, ever please her. It's not just that mom died 16 years ago. It feels like I couldn't please her even if she were still here. I feel like shit. I'm just her worthless, broken toy. I feel so awful inside. I feel so sad, so confused, so angry, so lonely, so hurt and ugly and all the things one is never supposed to be inside. I want to die because sometimes it hurts so much."

The confession was grueling and painful.

"Good work," Sherry praised. "Those symptoms are consistent with abuse. Abused children often want to abuse themselves."

"That doesn't make any sense," Doug replied. "Mom didn't abuse me and dad wasn't around much."

"Maybe someone else, then," Sherry persisted. "But we're running out of time for today."

Doug exhaled. "That was tough. And I have no idea who could have abused me."

"Think about it," was all Sherry said. "Anything else you want to add for now?"

He sat there briefly, "I'm not sure what happened," he added. "But this much I can say. What I cherish with my heart and understand with my head are two different things and the object of therapy is synthesis.

It might take me longer to get mentally healthy than most people. But I won't stop trying."

Doug finished the thought, "The worst part of insanity, having been there, is knowing that you're insane while not knowing how to get out of it. I just want this over with. I want to live again and be clean."

*November 7, 2003, at home*

*Dear Jacky,*

I just came back from the beach with lots of sand on my feet. Funny how the beach does that to you. Walked into the house with it, too. Oops.

But I needed the break. I don't have to solve the mysteries of the universe when I'm at the beach. I don't have to understand the light, see beyond the great illusions, grok the inner oneness. Hey, it's enough trouble for me to remember to wash off my feet.

The universe doesn't revolve around me, but there is also a picoscopic corner of the universe that is mine. All I have to do is let myself wade into the waves. I can feel the hard, crumbly sand beneath my toes and let the water shock my feet. I have 15 minutes on the beach where I can understand the lights, feel the small illusions, and grok the outer twoness. Water, sand—sand, water. I like it when it's simple.

The waves are cold at night. But if I want to wade in, I wade in, clothes and all. Yeah, it's cold enough to hurt, but I need the smell and sound and feel and touch and taste with salt around me—shivering.

At the beach, I can start now. I can touch now. I can see now. I can let the waves touch me. Now. It's mine and I love it. I can stop thinking of the stupid things I've done, the times I've missed, the games I've played. I can just be me there for that itty-bitty stretch of time. Water, sand—sand, water.

I decided that I could forgive myself some. Maybe I can forgive myself a little more tomorrow or the next day. I don't have to do it all at once. I can just stand on the beach, the tug of waves pulling at my knees.

And I can let myself weep, Jacky, if only just a little. I can let myself weep.

*Love,*

*Douglas Baign*

# ALAS—From Love to Sex to Abuse

*November 13, 2003, in session*

People die one by one, though the Nazis certainly devised destructive ways to hurry along the process. But it was a depressing thought. All individuals die, a mystery only known to themselves.

Douglas's Grandma Schneider had died over the weekend. They weren't that close and he wasn't grieving. After Momma May (Grandma Schneider never let him call her 'Grandma') rammed her fingers into his stomach and asked him why he wasn't a multimillionaire like his cousin, he didn't even like her very much.

Actually, he hadn't liked her before that loving event. May put him down every chance she got. Douglas never owned 15 percent of a startup bought by Apple.

"Are you doing all right?" Sherry asked him. "You've had a death in the family."

"I'm OK," he assured her. "Not great, but I'll be fine soon. Grandma May—I'll call her what I want, now that she's dead, was a serious pain in the gluteus maximus. She kept comparing me to my cousin, among other wonderful, loving things and I'm neither famous nor rich. I'm just me.

"And I think I'll stay that way," Doug added. "Neener, neener, neener."

"Well, I'm certainly glad to hear that you're you," Sherry commented.

"Yeah. Reminds me of one of my favorite jokes." Douglas pitched his voice down to a bass. "I'm schizophrenic."

He spoke again in his normal voice, "No, you're not."

Pitched up into a falsetto: "Shut up and let him talk!"

Sherry laughed. "Actually, that'd be dissociative identity disorder. But that's still a good joke."

"Yeah. Thanks."

"But do you really want to pay me to listen to your jokes?" Sherry wanted to get him back on track.

"Might be worth it," Doug retorted. "Might be the only way I can get folks to listen to them."

Sherry laughed again.

"But you're right," he continued. "Let's get on with it. My only caveat is that I'm clearly not in the mood for anything deep and meaningful, so I'd rather focus on happy memories."

"Sounds reasonable. Did you have one in mind?"

"Yes," Doug did actually use the normal affirmative on occasion. "My 18th Birthday; Leanne gave me her gifts a few days in advance."

*Happy Birthday, my Dearest Douglas.*
*Your gift has three parts,*
*The first, you've been wanting,*
*It isn't really a present*
*Just a reminder of me.*
*Yes, Douglas, today I got my senior pictures*
*And I'd like to give you one.*
*Whenever you're blue or lonely*
*Pull it out and look at my smile.*
*That smile is for you*
*And shows you all of my Love.*

Doug looked up from his notes. "I tossed that pic, more's the pity. There's a picture of Lee in Anne's Senior JECU Annual, for as strange as that may be. At least I've got one. But to continue . . ."

*Think back now, almost three months*
*to a wedding and the waterfront*
*And posters hanging on a wall.*
*Yes, Douglas, I picked one,*
*One which says what I want to say.*
*Take its meaning fully*
*And share your life with me.*
*Share all the small little things*
*And listen to me share.*
*Be my friend and also my helper,*
*My protector and my teacher*

Douglas stopped again. "I think this gift was a journal to write in, though I'm not positive. In any case, Leanne was one of the first people to encourage me to go into writing."

*This third little thing*
*Comes from the heart*
*Not from the hand.*
*You have said before*
*That I have free reign.*
*Do I still have that?*
*Answer me yes so I can go on.*

"By now I had an idea of what she wanted to do," Doug commented, "but I try not to go back on my word. So . . . I said yes."

*I want you to know*
*Just how I feel*
*And I can say it, true.*
*Or I can show you now.*
*Yes, Douglas, I love you.*
*But actions speak lower than words.*
*So here is my gift, third, but not least*
*I give it from the bottom of my soul*
*Take it Douglas with the same sincerity.*

"Then she kissed me," Douglas reached for a Kleenex. 'This is getting to be a habit,' he grumbled to himself. But he wasn't serious. It was time to respect himself.

"That was more than 28 years ago, Sherry, and it's such an important moment in my life. It wasn't just a first kiss. It was more than a beautiful girl loving me. It was *that* a beautiful girl could love me and that I could be loved.

"I'd made mistakes with her, I'd mistreated her once or twice and there she was kissing me. After all of my idiocy, after all of my anger, with all of my flaws and awfulness. Leanne kissed me.

"A goddess kissed me. A beautiful woman cared enough to give me her body. I meant something to her. I was attractive to someone, not because of what I was but because of who I was.

"My heart pounded, softened, folded her into my soul where she has never left and can never, ever leave. I took her in my arms; she gently laid her arms around my neck, pressed me close, and softly kissed me on my cheek; and heart. And mind, leaving herself behind and in me forever and ever. I cannot leave that moment nor do I ever wish to. She was there for me that once and I will not let that go."

"You were valuable to her," Sherry stated.

He gave her a quizzical look, but "Well, yeah," was all he said.

Sherry restated her point, "Think about what that means for a moment. You were valuable to Leanne. Doesn't that mean you're valuable? Not just to her but to yourself. You're valuable."

Doug looked startled. "I never thought of it that way."

"You should," Sherry continued. "You called Leanne a goddess. Would a goddess love just anyone? If she's a goddess, you're a god. If she is innocent and pure, so are you. If she's valuable to you, you're valuable to her. You are her equal and you're valuable."

He sat there for a moment, "That's a hard one to swallow," he finally said. "I'm used to thinking of myself as dirty." He had a feeling about what Sherry would say next and he was getting edgy about it.

"You aren't dirty," Sherry stated emphatically. "You aren't now, you weren't then. So why did you think of yourself as dirty?"

Doug exploded at her. "I don't know and I've told you that before, damn it!"

Flash anger. It faded as fast as it came. "I'm sorry," he apologized. "You didn't deserve that."

The anger just slid by Sherry. She didn't react to it at all. "And you didn't deserve whatever happened to you," she explained.

Douglas couldn't quite meet her eyes, "I don't feel that way." His voice trembled.

"I know you don't. But you're not dirty. You're not sinful for wanting to make love with someone you love, you're human. Or if you don't trust my judgment, trust Leanne's. Leanne would never have kissed someone she thought was dirty. You're not dirty."

Doug flushed but said nothing, lost in his own uncertainty. Sherry let him stay still for a moment, then brought him back into the room.

"Several months ago, you said the idea of touching Leanne was terrifying. I want you to do an assignment this week. I want you to think about why. I know you have a block there, but just run it through your head and see what happens."

He looked even more doubtful, "Are you sure that's a good idea?"

"You're making progress," Sherry answered, "so yes, I think you can do it. Promise yourself that you'll just think about it. Ask yourself this: why were you terrified of touching Leanne? Was she that holy?"

"OK," Doug said. "I promise." He wasn't sure he could keep the promise but again, he realized he needed to try.

"Good. You're making good progress, Douglas. Keep at it."

The praise pleased him.

*November 15, 2003, at home*

*Dear Jacky,*

I can't sleep now. Every time I nearly fall asleep I hear you saying, "You promised that you would talk to me about it." OK, I can't sleep anyway, so I'll bite. Let's talk. What are we supposed to talk about?

Sex. Why were you terrified of touching Leanne? Was she that holy? Why did you feel dirty?

Oh. This again.

Yes, this again.

I don't want to talk about it.

You promised.

Come on, Jacky. It's 1:15 in the morning! Can't we do this later?

You promised. Besides I know you. If you put it off you probably won't do it.

Do I have to?

You promised.

It's embarrassing!

You promised!

Now?

Now!

Sigh. I can't talk about this without doing this, so give me a minute here while I get out some stuff . . .

I'm dressing like a girl now, feeling silk and taffeta around me. I like to curtsey and smile and flutter my eyelashes. I want to primp and mince my steps a little, looking in a mirror. I like wearing lipstick and rouge and feeling an earring and wearing a bracelet on my wrist. I especially like the shoes and the straps around my ankles. I want to wear this all day then go to sleep in this, feeling soft and feminine and loved.

I feel safe this way and very delightful. I like being feminine, and I wish Anne would let me kiss her feet or cower in front of her. I want to feel vulnerable and humiliated. I want to be punished. I want Anne to force me to kiss panties for hours, feeling my long skirt flowing down my legs, touching each wrinkle and bow and lash and bracelet. I want to be a little girl.

I want to be male and force a woman, feeling her trembling body ache to my touch as I undress then fuck her. I want a slave beneath me, spreading her legs, begging me for forgiveness, for wickedness, as I lash her to a bedpost.

This is all so confusing. It feels like a different person, someone else who wants to cross-dress then be hurt, someone else who wants to fuck and torture. But I am the one who was hurt and wounded. I am the one who feels like I must either cower or rape. And I am the one who wants neither this nor that, but only to be healed and on the road to feeling clean.

I am a little child. Why are you doing this to me? I don't feel loved and yet you say you love me. I feel so dirty inside. Don't do this to me. Don't do this to me. Stop. Please stop. I am naked and afraid. Take me away from here. Don't do this to me anymore. I need to go away forever. Take me away.

I am limber. I am strong. I want to protect myself and be a boy. I am no longer one and yet I am one here and now. I'm feeling so lost and confused. Help me find myself. Help me love myself.

I am not a girl. I am not a rapist. I am a little boy and I am a middle-aged man. Let me be me, let me be both of me. Let me practice being me, piano and math and chess. Let me write poetry. Let me weep about this. Let me be scared. Let me fear so that the fear never more will drive me. But that I am in control of it. Let me be who I am.

Sometimes I feel the most me when I am sexless. But I also remember Leanne, when I was male and she was female. I liked being close to her. I want to be male and loving and yet experience a powerful, powerful femininity soft and tender and loving beneath me, not in anger, but just inside her, pulsing.

I still feel confused by this letter, Jacky, but I told myself that I would do whatever it takes to write— dressed like a girl or not. I started it one way; I'm ending it the other. I remember something Pierre or The Marker once said. The emotions are just there to experience. Maybe, maybe not.

I feel like I need to keep writing, but 2:00 a.m. isn't the time for it. Still, I've done what you asked of me and now I can sleep. Thank you for helping me to keep my promises. And thank you for listening when I am confused and afraid.

I'm all yours, my dearest Jacky. I'm all yours.

*Love,*

*Douglas Baign*

*November 20, 2003, in session*

"You have two polar views of love and sex:" Sherry said to start the next session, "dominant and submissive. But a man and a woman often make love with each other because they do love each other."

That hurt. Douglas had a hard time preventing himself from crawling back behind the sofa, dressing like a little girl again, playing with his Barbie dolls and sucking his thumb. He felt guilty and dirty for thinking such things, for not seeing the obvious. He was ugly, naughty, filthy. It was his fault

Another part of himself wanted to attack and deny. He wasn't that way. He was a good boy.

He took a deep breath instead of doing either thing. He felt his face flushing, embarrassed. Then Doug took another breath and tried to keep his voice steady while asking.

"Why am I so stupid? What can I do about it?"

Sherry shook her head. "It's not your fault," she said. "You're not stupid. You're wounded. Someone hurt you very deeply and very badly, probably before you even learned how to talk."

"Can you explain that further?" Doug managed to ask. He reached for a tissue and wondered if Sherry reused the empty boxes as piggy banks. The tears ran down his face, despite his unspoken attempt at humor.

Sherry nodded, Douglas was ready to let her explain. "Think about your symptoms: disturbing thoughts and feelings, distorted dreams, a risk of suicide."

He smiled behind his tears. "Sounds like me, all right."

"True," Sherry continued. "And those are the symptoms of PTSD. It's not your fault," she repeated. "Something happened to you that caused you trauma. You're not stupid. You're wounded."

Sherry had hinted at this before, but this time he found himself listening. Then he realized that he could take that in more ways than one. Douglas hadn't just found himself listening.

Douglas had found himself. And he was a wounded and shattered child.

"I don't completely understand," he said. "Only partly. Why do I sometimes want to cross-dress and smash dolls? What does that have to do with PTSD?"

"Traumatized children," Sherry responded, "don't always show the distress, but their play sometimes reflects their memories. I think part of you remembers, but you can't talk about it because at least some trauma occurred before you could talk. So you smash dolls instead. It's iconoclastic. You're breaking the idols that have ruled you."

It made sense. But it was a lot to adjust to. Douglas kept wanting to blame himself or to hurt and punish himself. But it wasn't his fault.

He repeated the thought, "It's not my fault."

"Right," Sherry confirmed. "Asking 'Why am I so stupid' is the wrong question, because it's not your fault. Think about what you said while describing that experience of cross-dressing."

Sherry consulted her notes, then quoted Douglas's own words back to him.

*"I am a little child. Why are you doing this to me? I don't feel loved and yet you say you love me. I feel so dirty inside. Don't do this to me. Don't do this to me. Stop. Please stop."*

Sherry continued, "You didn't do it. Something was done *to* you. As you might say, reverse the direction of the pointers.

"The question to ask is what was it and who did it? You've said that your mother never molested you, but the signs point to you being molested by a woman. If your mom didn't abuse you, then who did? What about the rest of your family?"

Douglas understood what Sherry was saying, but felt battered by too many revelations, "Gimme a second, will you? This feels abrupt. There's too many things hitting me at once and I'm feeling pummeled."

"Certainly," Sherry let him sit for a moment.

It was unusual for Sherry to say this much in a session, much less to be this blunt. It was also unusual for Douglas to stay this in control of his emotions—such as it was. He still felt the urge to cross-dress and hide behind the sofa. Perhaps the two and a half years of therapy were beginning to yield results.

"I don't know," he said finally.

"You don't remember anything at all." It was more of a query than a statement.

Doug thought through his relationship with his mother. It'd been a roller coaster, tumultuous at times, blissful at others. There'd been a rift between them after L'Abri, one that they both worked on to repair while she was dying. But she had died before their relationship was more fully healed. He missed her.

Of course, there was that one time when . . .

No. He didn't want to talk about that yet.

Doug didn't say anything at first, just staring out the window. Then he repeated her question, musing. "'If my mom didn't abuse me, then who did?' I keep on wanting to ask what's wrong with me even though I know that's the wrong question," he finally said.

Sherry smiled, "It's progress to understand even that much. And asking who abused you *is* the right question."

He still felt moody about it, "Not that that helps me any when I can't remember anything. Why can't I just lead a normal life? Why me, God?" He threw up his hands theatrically in mock despair, but truth be told, he hurt.

"You'll never guess how I'll respond to that," Sherry returned.

"'We'll have to talk about that next week?'"

"Yes. Have a good week."

*November 22, 2003, at home*

*Dear Jacky,*

It's a mess this is. But the emotions are too distant right now for me to answer. Maybe it's because I debugged a Perl script at work today and that can be draining. Or maybe it's because it's 1:00 a.m. and I'm rushing to get to bed. Or maybe I'm just out of the courage it takes to face my behavior.

It doesn't matter. No matter what the cause, I don't have the energy to study the chess pieces of my problem.

When I get this tired and can't move to a solution, then the best thing to do is to admire the problem and let it move me. Sometimes therapy can be like engineering. You just sit there and ask yourself recursive questions. "What question should I ask? Here's the problem in the mirror—what am I looking at?"

If my mom didn't abuse me, who did? I was a boy. Was I just an object to be manipulated and tossed away? What happened to me before I met Leanne? What happened to me before I was 10?

And I dunno. I can't remember. But maybe someone else in my family can. It's time to ask them.

"Love your neighbor as you love yourself." The crazy thing about being crazy is that you can only learn to care about others by learning to care for yourself. I need to learn selfishness. And damn it, Jacky, you're right. I don't have to be a jerk now and that fact alone gives me another chance.

Let us hope, let us hope. Thanks for listening, Jacky. And please help me to write yet again.

*Love,*

*Douglas Baign*

*November 26, 2003, at home*

*Dear Jacky,*

Jesus fucking God.

Forgive me, Jacky, but that's the only profanity that even comes close to my feelings. Jesus fucking God.

Go back to Sherry's question. 'If your Mom didn't abuse you, then who did?'

I asked dad. Of course, you can never ask dad a direct question. He doesn't answer them. But Grandma May Schneider isn't around anymore and she was a full-time hassle. The roundabout approach with dad was to ask why Grandma May was such a pain before she died. Why was she such a b . . . witch?

Dad just glanced at me and said, "You remember her boyfriend-of-the-week club, don't you?"

228

Then it hit me. I've never told you about my early childhood, Jacky, and dad's words triggered a key memory. My grandmother slept with a new boy toy every week, usually on Friday night. She was insatiable.

And she was our landlady. May lived in what was literally the grandmother cottage behind our house for nine years, and she owned both houses.

Yeah. Leanne was right to say I had problems with my mom. And I was right to tell Sherry that I don't remember my mom molesting me because my mom never molested me.

The problem is that I was raised by both mom and by Momma May until I was nine. My birth mom was my mom. And my grandmother May was my guardian, my other momma. And when May ran out of men she could access a child.

Me. For nine years—any day of the week.
*With love,*
*Douglas Baign*

# Entr'acte

# Reboot

*November 27, 2003, Thanksgiving, at home*

*Dear Jacky,*

No Sherry this week for obvious reasons, damn it. Just when I need to talk to her.

If my mind is like a boardroom with different folks in my head trying to negotiate with each other, then remembering abuse is like having a dirty and very badly bruised kid escorted into the boardroom by security. Tricky because that kid holds 51 percent of the stock.

There is simply no way to let him vote; the vote won't make any sense. But you also can't prevent the little fella from voting.

My mind keeps circling. What to do, what to say? How to handle it? Can I just give myself a bath and let him go? There's something cruel about that, something cruel in even thinking that way. But everything else has ground to a halt. I can't think, I can't function, I can't do my job. I find it difficult to write in here. I'm not very good with children, much less abused children, and here I discover that I am one.

Aargh.

Don't touch me. Leave me alone. Don't touch me.

OK. That seems clear. The problem is that I'm stinking up the boardroom and leaving dirt along my path as I pass by others sitting at the table. Hmm. How to handle this? Maybe I can give myself something to eat and drink plus a few napkins. Like . . . a few hundred? Would you like a glass of water?

Cheese. Water is OK, I guess.

I get the impression that I prefer milk. Tell you what, here's some water and cheese and I'm going to go look for some milk. In the meantime, I'm going to leave you some nice thick executive towels. I'll put them over here on the sofa then walk away so you can feel safer. There's a bathroom just off the boardroom if you want to wash up a bit.

OK.

OK. We're good for now and from the way he's devouring the cheese, we may become friends here. Something we have in common. Still, I need to move cautiously and I'm really just not very good at this. How to handle it? Got any suggestions?

Douglas Baign

*With Love,*
*Douglas Baign (and Douglas Baign)*

*December 2, 2003, at home*

*Dear Douglas,*

First, let it be said that your words are touching. Your sense of wonder, your breaths as you touch Leanne, the tender threads of your life's tapestry running through your hands are precious. Sherry is right. You're valuable.

You ask for my advice and I will give it. Consider L'Abri. You were torn apart when you walked back down the mountain that day, fixing your eyes on the snow crests over Lake Genève. But if you made any mistake, it was to stitch various parts of yourself back together while your wounds were still open, exposed and dirty. They only festered.

Now, here you stand, facing the deep, snowy slope, ready to clean and bind old wounds. One gets very few chances in life to do that. Approach the task with caution.

"Whatever you bind on earth shall be bound in heaven," said Jesus. To bind is to grant power. Even with wounds, the way you bind can make a difference.

Sauron, of course, is the opposite. "One ring to rule them all," he said, "one ring to find them, one ring to bring them all, and in the darkness bind them." With the predictable results and that takes me to my second suggestion. When you find wounds that deep, then bind them in the light.

Take your time and do it right. Take time to grieve.

Listen to yourself. Help yourself mature. A child can get so used to abuse that he becomes angry when it is taken away. Children are too easily confused by love mixed with abuse.

There's a lot there, but there's no reason to do it all at once. If you can't take a big step by talking about May, then take one small step by talking about Leanne—Neil Armstrong was right. You'll still get to the same destination, though presumably you're not interested in being either loony or a Moonie . . .

*With love,*
*Jacky*

# Denial and Control

*December 4, 2003, in session*

Douglas opened the next session with what seemed to Sherry like a non sequitur.

"Momma May," was all he said. It wasn't a non sequitur to him. To Doug it was the answer to a question and the obfuscation let him approach the topic obliquely.

"Momma May?" Sherry asked.

"Yeah," he responded. "Momma May. Remember how I use to attack three Barbie dolls and I named two of them Leanne and Deirdre? The third one is named Momma May."

"Who's Momma May?" It was the obvious question.

"My maternal grandmother. I mentioned her once or twice before. She's the one who made me the stuffed Dalmatian. But I talked about that more than a year ago. I was molested by Momma May."

"Ah. How close was the relationship?"

"Extremely," Doug was emotionally blank for the moment. "She was more responsible for raising me than my mother until I was nine. My grandmother was, to all intents and purposes, my sur-mother up to that point."

"Wow. That would explain a lot. The abuse was severe enough that you couldn't even think about it until your grandmother died."

"Yeah."

"Do you want to talk about it now?"

"No," Doug was still closed. "There are too many topics to discuss. Leanne, my grandmother, control, grief, sex, love, abuse, Gothard. I know that Momma May is key to a lot of them, even most of them. But it took a lot out of me just to recognize that fact. I don't know that I have enough yet to discuss her."

"One issue at a time," Sherry rephrased.

"Yeah. And the issues with my ever-loving grandmother are still too fresh for me to deal with right now."

"All right. What do you want to talk about?" Sherry wasn't happy about it, but understood his reticence.

"Grief. Does that make sense?" Douglas asked.

235

"It doesn't have to make sense to me; it has to make sense to you," Sherry responded.

He thought about it, "I'm not entirely sure why, but yes, it does make sense to me."

To grieve. We often say "Good grief!" as if there were something good about it. But grief can contain so much anger, so much hatred. When his mother died, Doug wanted to curse. Curse God, curse the universe. Anger can be part of grief.

Denial, anger, bargaining, depression, acceptance —in that order, if you use the Kübler-Ross model of grief. Doug went through most of those stages when his mom died, but not in the order of steps Kübler-Ross described. It was more of a round robin or spiral pattern: denial, depression, anger, acceptance, anger, depression, denial, anger, acceptance. In as much as anyone gets to acceptance; that is, you don't stop missing someone you love.

"I never really did the bargaining bit," he added to Sherry. "I mean, I just don't see God as the negotiating type. How would you bargain with God? 'Hey God! I'll give you two galaxies and a super-massive black hole for three extra years of life and a paid medical bill. Come on, God! It's a bargain!'

"Yeah, right. When it comes to God, we ain't got no chips. The black holes are God's to begin with." He paused for a moment. "Though I can't figure out why He wants them in the first place," he added.

Sherry allowed herself a smile. "You don't bargain. But what stages of grief are you good at, Doug?"

"Denial. The key is to focus on something realistic, something possible. For example, I didn't pretend that mom would get better. I knew damn well that she wouldn't. I simply denied she was sick to begin with. She was alive, vibrant, and I couldn't reach her because she was probably sorting costumes with the troupe. Denial focuses on what is possible, not on what you know is not."

And the pretense let him get through another day, another day without going mad. Denial is a gift when the world moves too fast for you to be angry or to cry. The trick is to keep moving because the Earth certainly isn't going to stop while your mother dies. Or to quote Stephen Crane:

> A man said to the universe:
>   "Sir, I exist!"
> "However," replied the universe,
> "The fact has not created in me
> A sense of obligation."

*Epper si muove.* The Earth does not stand still for your pain. What kind of universe would it be if it did? Is a death more meaningful if the universe stops for that person or more meaningful because it doesn't?

"Where are you, Douglas?" Sherry asked. Her voice was more gentle than normal.

He looked out the window again, almost in shock, wondering if he could still hear the trees. Would the trees still bother to talk to him if he stopped by to listen?

"Remember that I'm good at denial," he said finally. "And sometimes I have to deny I was molested just to get through the day. My mother abused me, or grandmother, whatever. I get them confused.

"But the pain from my grandmother stays with me."

Sherry picked up on his thoughts, "And the fact that the universe has no sense of obligation doesn't prevent the pain."

"Yeah."

"What mechanisms do you use now to deny the abuse?" she asked.

"Mostly I play games. Civilization is very interesting, challenging and fun."

Games get Douglas into what psychology calls "flow," where you're really good at something but it still remains a challenge. In sports, it's sometimes called "the zone."

As a good immersive game player, Doug could master closed, rule-based strategies then sink into the trance to brilliantly bluff and hide his pain.

"Sadness and pain are better than denial," he summarized. "And that's such a depressing thought."

"Good."

"Huh?" he was quite confused. "Why is depression good?"

Sherry explained herself. "You've broken the cycle of denial just by recognizing it. You've moved. And now you're progressing to the next stage of grief, from denial to depression. And, as you pointed out, the universe isn't going to wait for you to catch up."

Good enough.

*December 11, 2003, in session*

"I hate Christmas," Douglas told Sherry after the preliminaries. "I'm always afraid I won't get the right gift for Anne. Terrified is more like it, or say the right things to be merry enough.

"Besides, it can sometimes get gloomy in Santa Brisa this time of year, and if it's gloomy outside, it's gloomy inside. It's so easy to get depressed. Rush, rush, rush. Traffic, traffic and trying to look Christmas cheery. God save me from Christmas."

"Did you want to talk about Christmas?"

Sometimes Sherry's reflective questions drove Doug mad. Of course, he figured he was already mad to begin with. How much worse could it get?

Actually, he didn't want to answer that. He already knew.

OTOH, Doug understood Sherry's goal— to keep him on track. Talking to her cost about $2.50 a minute, less whatever insurance covered, which wasn't much. Was his phobia of Christmas the first priority?

He tapped his teeth while thinking about it, "Not really. But my despair at Christmas is worth mentioning. Maybe I'll bring it up again later."

"All right," Sherry pushed. "Last week you talked about grief. Do you want to talk about that?"

Douglas shook his head no. "Only indirectly; I want to talk about control. We often grieve over things we can't control, like my mother dying. I want to reverse that and talk about things I can control, like my own life. How do I gain more control? Do I talk more about Leanne or my grandmother?"

"You're far enough along now," Sherry remarked, "to know that's a good question to ask."

"Yeah. But I don't know the answer. I need your help for that, and getting help means I've lost control, and control is what I'm trying to gain in the first place."

"Ah, and what do you propose to do about it?" Sherry asked.

It was another reflective question. On the other hand, if Sherry simply handed him an answer, he wouldn't be developing control, now would he? Time to come up with a strategy.

Control, he thought, came in three stages: (1) admitting your feelings right now, (2) deciding what you don't want to be, and (3) finding a role model of what you do want to be.

Of course, he knew there was no guarantee that this was actually the right way to go, but it gave him a place to start. He felt confused, despite having temporarily chosen a direction. There were still days he felt suicidal, despite the meds, yet he'd joke about it in session. The line between pain and humor is thin. Was he a victim or a comedian? Both?

"You're a hurt human being," Sherry suggested.

"Yeah." he responded, "No matter how many times I try to write it out, talk it out, act it out, or just plain barf it out, there's still so much pain inside. I still cross-dress, I still hurt myself, I still play games to hide the pain.

"But knowing what happened—my grandmother molested me— doesn't remove the pain. I hurt. I hurt. I hurt. As if saying it 500 times makes it go away or convinces you I hurt. But what type of response do

I really want from you? What comfort can I give myself? How do I gain the control I really need?"

He was afraid—afraid that he'd never know how to deal with this. Afraid of telling Anne how desperately he wanted to be a little girl in front of her. But if he acted out, would he be more of himself or less? Would he be gaining or losing control?

"I am my grandmother's slave catamite," Doug exclaimed. "I am my grandmother's little Barbie doll and she dressed me as one once. I am May's little sex slave, her sex toy, her little plaything. I am hurting because of this!

"But how do I stop being my grandmother's sex slave? How do I learn to live for myself, not her?"

"Stop there for a moment, please." Sherry was still writing notes.

"OK. What did you have in mind?"

"If you want to stop being your grandmother's sex slave," Sherry responded, "then tell me: how did you feel when she dressed you as her Barbie doll?"

Douglas was puzzled. "What does the one have to do with the other?"

"It's a variation on control. Do you express your feelings or do your feelings express you? One way to control your feelings is to express them. So how did you feel when your grandmother dressed you as her Barbie doll?"

Douglas felt the red creeping into his cheeks.

It started when his grandmother decided to make a dress for his sister Rose. Douglas watched her work on her rebuilt sewing machine ("I'll have to tell you that story later," Douglas added.) and after awhile Momma May wanted to size the dress.

"Hmm," his grandmother pondered. "You're about the same size as Rose so I'll just size the dress on you."

The thought was horrifying. Plus Rose wasn't that far away either, so was that what Momma May really wanted to do? But there was nothing Douglas could do about it and a few minutes later he found himself wearing a dress.

He remembered the fabric slipping over his head, the embarrassment and the pleasure. The dress went down to his knees and the softness made him feel guilty and special. He tried not to move in it, but the hem still slowly rubbed against him.

"He-he-he." She cackled. "My instincts are still there. You're the same size. I wonder what else I can do?"

Sizing the dress on Douglas hadn't been enough for her. Soon enough, his grandmother found some lipstick nearby and carefully

---

dapped his lips. "That's better." She commented. Then she found some clip-on earrings, added them to Douglas's ensemble and had him turn and pose.

"How old were you," Sherry asked.

Douglas was glad for the interruption. "About 7 or 8," he said. "I feel guilty about it."

"There's no reason to feel guilty. There was nothing you could do to change the situation."

She'd said that before, but it just seemed so hard to do. He wanted to go back and make different decisions, but it hadn't been his decision to begin with.

"I am Douglas Baign," he summarized. "There will always be something I can't control, but I vow to love myself nonetheless. I just gotta keep telling myself that even if I don't feel it a bit. I love myself, I love myself, I love myself, I love myself.

"All right, so I don't know how to solve all those problems. Maybe I don't need to. What I have to do is love myself today, resolve to love myself tomorrow—love myself, love myself, love myself. Maybe someday I'll get it straight."

Sunrise, sunset—days may begin in gloom, but can end in glory.

*December 13, 2003, remembering February 17, 1976*

I sat down that day on a patio bench at UCSB, the spring of my freshman year. The leaves fell from nearby poplar trees and scattered around my feet, brown and red and golden. They reminded me of bloody hands reaching for me, and I nervously fumbled through the paler leaves of my binder to write.

> *Dear Jacky,*
> *Leanne said she was uncertain how she felt towards me, mixed up by flirting with Michael. I've been on both ends of the flirting business. Good! This is challenging me.*

The patio sits below a beautiful walkway connecting floors between two science buildings, with arches like a Roman aqueduct. I like it there, but the bloody leaves unnerve. I was worried. Could I connect this idea to that as prettily as the walkway? I felt both pressured to perform and relaxed by the quietness.

The pronouns shift from meaning Jacky to meaning Leeanne.

*I know what to do and how to do it, yet it's hard, humiliating, and very frustrating. So I won't be able to go with you Saturday night. OK. A lot of good things come about from it. For one thing, I save $9.50, but somehow, that doesn't really bother me. I never cared about saving money or spending it. I only use it to trade in for something I cannot have otherwise—you.*

I put my pen down, knowing it was a form of denial. A lot of good things did not come about from it. Instead, everything around me whirled about. Starting as a college frosh was bad enough, but I felt like I had no home. Mom and dad weren't around. My Church keeps repeating the same message. I had just yelled at my first girlfriend, whom I deeply, deeply love. What is going on with me?

*Anyway, what have I been doing wrong? I have to swallow all my pride and let all my principles go to pot to become humble. I have to admit I must be doing something to displease your parents. I haven't shown any improvement over the past three weeks. OK. I'll ask God to squelch my pride. I'll ask why—why haven't I improved? What can I do to show a change of attitude?*

There's a lot of culture shock at UCSB, but I had already anticipated that. But I still feel torn apart and I don't know why. I ache. I need help and there didn't seem to be anyone to turn to. I'm sad, angry, helpless, and confused. The roles and beliefs of my Church aren't working and no one offers a good replacement.

I turn back to writing Jacky as if she were Leanne.

*I know that you're watching all this breathlessly. You want me to accept your parents' moratoriums with a smile, or at least without complaining. Well, I'll try. I'm severely disappointed, but I'll try some more anyway. Brace up! Hey, don't you know that Leanne loves you? I have to convince myself of that without asking you to help me anymore than you have. OK. I'll try Leanne, but I may not succeed. Please, Leanne, try to accept my efforts. Try to accept me.*
Love,
Douglas

❦❦❦

Worst of all, I couldn't admit the problems to myself. Maybe I would later perhaps, but not then.

Douglas Baign

Instead, I decided to rebuild my brain's computer, calculating to use it to dam up my feelings so that everything would be OK. Instead, my emotions breached the dam and the torrent hurled me downstream.

*Believes, beliefs.*
*Be leaves to hold*
*and crumble in my hand.*
*I saw a leaf once*
*and touched it.*
*That is enough of a miracle*
*for me*

# Role Models and Victimhood

*December 15, 2003, at home*

*Dear Jacky,*

Ha! I ran into Leanne's parents yesterday at a church Anne and I visited. Coincidences do happen. At any rate, they didn't recognize me nor did I bother to tell them who I was. Why would I?

I never did find out what bothered them about my relationship with Leanne— possibly that I wasn't a stable, conservative beau. Well, duh, I was 18. I suppose Dear Abby could say that it all worked out for the best—at least for Lee, but I'm not so sure about that myself. Protecting your daughter is too narrow a viewpoint. Or perhaps not informing the beau of expected behavior is too broad a notion. I was a boyfriend. Not a mindreader.

But I digress; on with the show. Let's go back to something I said in a previous letter and move it in a different direction.

> *Leanne said she was uncertain of her feelings toward me, mixed up by flirting with Michael. Good! This is challenging me. Ah, so! It's opportunity time!*

That's a PD catchphrase. The trials and travails of life are always spiritual opportunities to grow in praise!

You know? Even at the age of 46 sometimes I still hate PD, no questions asked. Which, I suppose, just goes to show that I'm an immature, spiteful SOB. But hey, you gotta start somewhere. OK. So I'm an immature, spiteful SOB. So be it. It's good to know who you are.

"Rejoice with those who do rejoice. And weep with those who weep." There is a time to dance and a time to mourn. I was hurt when my on-again-off-again girlfriend starting to flirt with other guys. Sometimes fortune favors you and sometimes fortune favors Michael because "The Great Mandala" will "Turn! Turn! Turn!"

But you gotta admit the pain.

Again, Dear Abby would argue that it's her choice. It's good to find out sooner rather than later, and if she's not dating me that seriously, then I have no right to be jealous. Yadda yadda yadda.

All of which is no doubt true, but that doesn't change what you feel. I needed to admit Lee's actions hurt then to weep about it. Instead, there I was trying to be the happy little rejoicing Christian. Sometimes you must cry for yourself before you can rejoice for someone else, and I wasn't mature enough to cry.

*"Rejoice with those who do rejoice and weep with those who weep."*

IMHO, PD only preached the first half of the verse, at least while he was my youth pastor. Rejoice with those who do rejoice! If something went well, he "Praised the Lord!" so consistently that I often wondered if he really knew what he meant. And if something went badly, he rejoiced because he was challenged! Praise the Lord! It's opportunity time! Rejoice in the Lord always and again I say rejoice!

But what about the weeping? What about my tears? Life with PD was thorns and never roses for me.

PD was not only the youth pastor, he was the main bus driver at Lands Baptist. Between the Bible memorization, youth mentoring, bus driving, and constant rejoicing, he pushed himself too hard one day a few years after I graduated then fell asleep at the wheel of a bus full of kids. Fortunately, only one person was hurt.

That was the day Pastor Dan accidentally killed his own daughter.

*"Rejoice with those who do rejoice and weep with those who weep."*

He truly wept that day. Not that it helped me any. By the time PD killed his own daughter, I'd already been damaged by his behavior, and he never wept for me. Why should I care? What's one daughter more or less? He had four.

Yeah. I'm angry. PD just pisses me off. And yeah. Maybe I'm so callous that I don't weep for him when I should. Yeah. Maybe I'm so royally jerked at that slime-pit monster that I didn't really give a crap.

Maybe so. After all, PD was my Christian role model, and he never wept for any of my pain, did he? So why should I weep for him? Let us rejoice instead!

So yeah, PD! I'm glad your daughter died! It's challenging you! It's opportunity time! Fuck you, PD!

*"Rejoice with those who do rejoice, and weep with those who weep."*

The words don't go away, you know, and they still tell us to weep. Do I have to forgive PD in order to mourn for myself? At the very least, if I'm going to ask someone to weep for me, then I need to be willing to weep for them. Even PD.

And if I don't have it in my heart to forgive PD, then maybe I can mourn the girl who died. Janis was a friend of mine, not just PD's daughter. Did she deserve to die? I lost a friend.

Sometimes the best and only way to praise God is to weep, PD. I'm sorry your daughter died. I'm sorry Janis died.
*Love,*
*Douglas*


*December 18, 2003, in session*

"That's one major issue in a nutshell," Doug said to start the next session. "The daughter of the pastor who wounded me was my friend. The grandmother who played and laughed with me is the grandmother who abused me. The folks who hurt me, at church or elsewhere, are the same ones who nourished me. Does following their example lead me to heaven or to hell? Is Momma May my role model or not?"

"Last week," Sherry chimed in, "you said you were going to talk about both role models and victims. Are you starting with role models, then?"

"I can talk about both role models and victims at the same time," he responded. "But let's start with role models."

The ultimate role model for a Fundamentalist Christian is Jesus. In the 1970s, "following Jesus" meant that Douglas would read the Bible, pray, go to Church, and try to ace all his classes at Hosanna High. What it means now for him at age 46 is to follow his conscience and let his conscience be influenced by his beliefs, which include Christianity.

Christianity is not defined by what you do, at least in the sense that "doing" church or Bible study doesn't make you a Christian. When the Apostle James says, "Faith without works is dead," Doug takes that to mean that an individual's outward actions need to line up with their interior belief system. James says to work in-to-out. The role model on the inside manifests itself on the outside. Faith without works is dead.

Of course, psychologists say that acting as if something is true on the outside can make it true on the inside. Out-to-in—any politician or scam artist knows this one.

"Not that there's any difference between the two," he snarked to Sherry. "But never mind." Keep repeating your lies long enough and the population will believe you.

Sherry's position (out-to-in) is that Doug must learn to pick the systems and role models that work best for him (in-to-out). He tried "acting" like a Christian, by 1970s standards, for a long time and only part of it sunk in. He tried acting like everything was OK for even longer, and the only thing he got out of it was looking down from a bridge and calculating how long it would take to go splat.

Nope. That didn't work either; time to try something else.

Funny thing, what. You think differently about yourself after you attempt suicide. In Douglas's case, trying to get his external actions to generate an internal belief system didn't work out. He started to get better when he admitted that he hurt. He had a problem. Then he got even better when he admitted that he couldn't control the problem; it was controlling him.

"Alcoholics Anonymous would no doubt call this step #1 of their 12-step program," he decided.

"To admit the problem was controlling me. But I don't believe in them either. My mess was not of my own doing. I wasn't downing Bacardi 151, I was a victim when my grandmother molested me when I was five; different story, that."

"And that takes me to the topic of victims," he paused.

"Go on," Sherry encouraged.

If Christians make the mistake of trivializing victims (Doug so often heard, "Just read the Bible, pray and things will be fine."), non-Christians can do the opposite by adoring the victim. There's such a worship of vic-dumb-ology these days that pain begins to lose its meaning.

For example, Mister Bill sent Kim Jong Il a nuclear power plant just because he figured that Kim was having a bad hair day. Pooooor starving North Koreans. "I'm sure this will make them feeeeeeel better." Right and the Great Leader might feel even better after he removes Los Angeles from the map, too. Here's hoping he has a good hairdresser.

On second thought, if he really nukes L.A., who will miss it?

Back to roles and role models.

If your role is to be seduced, says Gothard, then there's no such thing as abuse in the first place. Everyone has sinned, so there is no "victim." God allows, or perhaps even encourages, the childhood abuse to occur to teach the so-called victims, who really aren't ones, to cry out to God and confess their sins.

"You're kidding," said Sherry.

"Unfortunately, no," he replied. "Gothard printed a worksheet in about 1995 titled "Why Did God Let My Son Be Molested?" The worksheet is phrased to advertise the advantages of being molested."

"Oh, my God."

"I looked it up before coming. For example, reason #4 about why God 'let' your son be molested is (and I quote)":

246

> *4. To transform aroused desires to spiritual power.*
> *When molestation takes place, sexual desires are often awakened. Sexual energy, however, can be transformed into spiritual power as we yield up the members of our body to the Lord on a daily basis and hide God's Word in our heart.*

Sherry put her head in her hands and took several deep breaths. "Give me a moment, please," she asked.

Actually, Doug felt the same way. Some childhood experiences seemed . . . warped. But Gothard's positions weren't just abstract nonsense. He'd lived it. For example, when he was six or seven Doug thought that his God-given role in life was to be an abused kid. God had created him to be abused and he certainly believed in God.

Doug also believed in his grandmother. She was his mother. It was very confusing then and it's still a bit confusing to him now: Mom and Momma.

It's back to ALAS: anger, love, abuse, sex. Love is not abuse, but when you're the abused kid you can't tell the difference. Douglas believed that he was loved, because the abuse was love. Momma May loved him, Momma May abused him. What's the difference?

As an adult, he understands something of the difference. As a five-year-old, he did not.

"But this much I do know," he declared. "Victims do not want justice for their abusers, or at least, *I* don't. I don't want revenge. I want power: power for myself, the power to lead my own life. I didn't jump off the Westfield Bridge in part because it meant abrogating control. Jumping meant gravity governed my destiny, not me."

Where Doug found himself sadly agreeing with victimology is that you *feel* powerless, swept along by the banzai race of your emotions. It's easy to do bad stuff to yourself—he enjoyed cutting himself for a while. It's also easy to do bad stuff to others—Doug never raped, but he understood the impulse. Raping gives the rapist the illusion of control, but they're not yet mature enough to realize that true power comes from controlling yourself, not others. The ultimate role model is you.

Where Doug disagreed with victimology is that you know something is wrong, even if you don't know what it is. Self-cutting is not something humans normally do as part of their daily hygiene. "I can just see the Clinique marketing campaign now," he commented to Sherry. "'Buy Eau de Sang Contaminé now! Only $50 for 2 ounces!'

"One reason why it's so hard for us crazies to become sane," he continued, "is that things are just so damn confusing. I've been there, OK? 'Ah ha! Cutting myself isn't working out so well. Maybe I should kill myself instead. That will solve the problem permanently!' Yeah, you really do start thinking like that."

"Oh, I believe you," Sherry agreed.

This all reminds Doug of what Anne calls "the first rule of holes." When you find yourself in a hole, stop digging. His only disagreement is that, pardon the expression, you must start with whole numbers. The zeroth rule of holes is that you must recognize that you're in a hole to begin with.

The internal conversation goes something like this:

> *Gosh, I'm cutting myself. I wonder why I'm doing this.*
>
> *Maybe I'm in a hole. Do you suppose jumping off a bridge will improve the situation?*
>
> *What the heck am I saying? I'm still digging and I can't seem to stop myself. Whoa! This is definitely not normal. Jesus, God Almighty, I'm in this way over my head! Help! Help! Help!*

Sometimes ya just gotta hit the panic button. It's there for a reason, you know.

But it was really, really hard for Doug to admit that he needed help. It's back to control again. Douglas wanted to control his life so badly that it was hard for him to grab the rope when someone tossed it down, because *they're* pulling you up. Not you. It hurts while you're being pulled up, too.

"God, it hurts," he exclaimed. "Dear God, it hurts. Please God, I'm not blaspheming. Dear God, dear God, it hurts."

But he grabbed that rope when it came down, tied it around his waist, and yelled at Sherry to start yanking. He didn't have to know why he was in the hole or what made the hole. Just grab the rope.

And Doug did it for the best of all possible reasons: self-preservation is the ultimate act of empowerment. If you're going to follow God, then you have to be alive to follow Him.

Of course, getting out of the hole is only the first step. You need to mark where the hole is so that you don't fall back in, then repair as much damage as possible.

One step at a time; the hole may be bigger than you realize until you start getting out of it. Ya just gotta keep climbing. Even the Grand Canyon has a rim.

*December 20, 2003, at home*

*Dear Jacky,*

Can I still trust my dad? Do I still trust my father? I had to ask myself that when dad asked me the other day if I remembered having a tumor when I was seven.

God damn it!
*Douglas*

# Three Years Later

# Dad

*Dear Jacky,*

Three years: I stopped writing anything personal for three years, including to you, Jacky. I simply didn't know what to say. That I didn't trust my own father? I'd already said it.

Three years - and things in my life are much the same as they were three years ago. Same job, same lack of progress on my job, same frustrations, same problems, same spouse, same house, same louse of a boss, and no doubt the same mouse gnawing on my cheese. And now it's time to stop grousing.

If I can't trust my dad, can I trust any of the other ways out of the loop?

> Endless loop: *see* loop, endless.
> Loop, endless: *see* endless loop.

Dad has always been a constant. When I wasn't getting along with mom, when I was heartbroken, when I was homeless, my dad was always there for me. Mom, May, dad, the Church, Leanne, Deirdre, L'Abri: of all the major components in my story, I always trusted dad.

Now I can't trust him. The taste is gone when there is no one left to trust. I started thinking about that bridge again and it wouldn't even take that long. *Un, deux, trois.*

I haven't jumped. So let's pick up with where I left off. Let's see here. The last thing I said – three years ago - was . . .

> "Can I still trust my dad? Do I still trust my father? I had to ask myself that when dad asked me the other day if I remembered having a tumor when I was seven."

Yup, I sure do. It was a big hard ball glued to the base of my spine. I'd been aware of it a day or two, but it didn't really bother me until I sat down and my back just didn't feel right. Mom noticed me sitting oddly at dinner one night and you can take it from there. I ended up at Dr. T's office pretty fast with a long needle in my spine. That was the level of 1964 tech, I'm afraid. The doc tried to freeze the tumor off.

253

Maybe I should have told Dr. T not to bother, because I could feel that tumor's cold, hard grip on me. That tumor just did not want to let me go. Dr. T froze my back for nothing and we moved to surgery.

The surgery itself is mixed up with other hospital visits as a kid (I'll have to tell you later about nearly going blind), but I remember waking up and the doc telling me that the tumor was "encapsulated." That was a big word for a seven-year-old, so dad translated it as "benign" and told me I was OK; no problem.

My back felt empty for a while. I kinda missed the lump. Then it felt OK and I stopped thinking about it. I've been filling out the med forms for 25 years on my own now and I just rattle off my surgeries: broken arm (twice), eye surgery, kidney stones, benign tumor.

Except it wasn't benign! It was cancer, glioblastoma multiforme, and that has a 90 percent death rate. Yes, 90 percent! Fucking cancer, the same shit that killed mom! A tumor wrapped around my cancer and contained that nasty, nasty sucker from getting into my backbone. The cancer was "encapsulated" and I got lucky.

What it was doing at the base of my spine, I don't know (the doctor was surprised about it, too) but I don't care. I'm still here and that's what counts.

But damn it! I got mad at my dad. I wanted to grab my father and shake him. Just take him by the throat and squeeze. Don't you understand! You're withholding something that I need! Don't try to protect me anymore! I'm an adult, dad. I don't need protection!

I'm not mad that dad didn't tell me when I was eight. I'm mad because he didn't tell me about it when I was 18. It's not the med forms. It's my heart, my emotions, my conscience. I can't trust my own father. He withheld information from me when he didn't have to, when I needed it as an adult.

It's easy to just blow it off. Dad was 43 when I was 18 (I was 46 when he told me, 49 now) so he was probably going through the same "busy, busy, busy" shit that I've got. But he had a son; I don't. He was responsible for me and he failed that responsibility.

*Pause.*

How do I feel about it? What does it mean to me? Does it really change the medical forms that much?

But it's different somehow. Part of me is missing. Not just the tumor, but the cancer of trust and misgivings. It's my grandmother. What does my dad really remember? Can I trust anything he says?

Dad claimed the other day that we moved away from Grandma May so all us kids could go to school in the same district. (John was in a magnet school.) Yeah, right. So why does Rose remember mom begging dad to get us away from May? Dad lied. I need your damn memory, dad! I need your information!

Dad's avoided too many questions, then says things I know are lies. I had a tumor and it wasn't benign. I'm a cancer survivor. It's surprising how such a little thing made such a big difference for the three years I didn't write.

I love you, Jacky. I'm sorry, I'm sorry it takes me so long to write.
*Douglas*

*November 9, 2006, in session*

Sherry's office had moved closer to Doug's commute route, but held much the same configuration: next to a garden, with the same photos and plants inside. The layout provided some much-needed stability.

"You're writing avocationally again," Sherry started. "That's important to you."

"Yes, both nonfiction and music. Some photography. It feels good, though the writing still doesn't cover the anger and disappointment about my dad."

"Was there anything you could have done differently?"

He shrugged, "Maybe. Maybe I could have written more while I was still angry. The writing now feels like undigested pulp. No grit, no fire. But on the other hand, maybe I was too angry to write."

"What brought you back into it?" It was the obvious question.

"Two things," he responded. "First, I talked to Uncle Tony and Aunt Cheryl. They both had lots of stories about my grandmother."

Uncle Tony remembered recommending to Doug's dad that the family leave their housing situation ASAP because Momma May was damaging the kids. Uncle Tony wasn't sure about the details, but his memories were important. Douglas wasn't crazy. Someone else (an adult when Doug was a child) remembered the truth and knew his dad was withholding information.

Doug commented on that. "My guess is Dad will take whatever he knows with him when he dies, but pushing him won't help and would damage our relationship. There is a time to just leave things alone."

"Secondly, I talked with my VP Sharon and Anne. They both said something similar—don't trust everyone with everything. You can be selective. For example, Anne said I can always trust her to support me, but not to put her shoes away when she comes home. She's more likely to toss them into the middle of the living room floor, where I can trip over them.

"Maybe I can trust dad to still give sound, practical advice, but not to tell me anything about Momma May. I'm not satisfied with that solution, but it's the best I can get right now. If nothing else, I'm not suicidal and I'm back to making progress here. The deadlock is broken."

Sherry smiled. "So what do you want to talk about next?"

"I'm not ready to talk about Momma May just yet and she has to do with ALAS. The obvious hole is JECU."

# From UCSB to JECU

*December 12, 2006, remembering June 6, 1976, at home and on campus*

### June 6, 1976, at home
*Dear Jacky,*

*Restless is the way I feel now, restless. UCSB classes are over. I have one final on Tuesday then I've finished my fight. I've completed the course. Not as well as I'm mentally able, but as emotionally well as I could. Now I'm through here and with my past and with Leanne. It's time to go somewhere else, to something different, to someone new. I had yesterday, now I have tomorrow. "Second star to the right, and straight on till morning."*

He took a walk in the rain that day at UCSB, smelling the leaves and wet pavement. It was quiet and the rain was comforting, dashing here and there like laughter. Naturally, Doug was thinking about his future at JECU, as well as Leanne and Deirdre, trying to understand his broken emotions.

*I want to fight for something, something I believe in. I have never really fought for much yet. Well, running, but now I can't run so I can't depend on that. That's God's point, I'm sure, only to rely on Him. But fight for God? I want to fight for something easier to grasp, easier to understand.*

*Maybe I can fight to be me. You think that's hard? YES! For me it is! But it's important to me to be me and not lie to myself. It's important for me to express my ideal, to think for myself, to stick my neck out.*

And the rain came down to soothe him, gently washing Doug to make him clean. It was better than taking a bath because the rain followed him everywhere and he desperately needed its coolness.

*I'll have to go one step more. I must also accept Leanne for what she is and refocus on how I can help her out. Moving my focus away from attention on myself will probably be good medicine. I'll need God's help, which is exactly what God intends, I'm sure. I'll need God's love, but that's what God wants.*

The words felt uneven—up, down, back, forth, swaying. The writing is good only in the sense that the words matched his emotions. The writing lacked confidence because he lacked confidence. The letters were stilted because he felt stilted.

*One last thing and I'll quit. God keeps putting it in my mind to train as a minister. I haven't accepted it yet and I'm not willing. Would that I were and the sooner the better! Who knows?*

But Doug knew that he couldn't mention his doubts to anyone because his church would say he was unspiritual and lacked faith. Instead, his letters still jangle through Bible verses and internal thought experiments on why he should be a pastor, or what Deirdre was teaching him, or what God wanted him to learn.

*Verses God showed me:*

*Forgiveness and prayer for help. Psalms 25*
*Forgiveness of sins. Psalms 51*
*Claim for God's protection. Psalms 26*

*Enough rhetoric, but that's the way I feel. What more can I ask for? Perfection? No longer. I'm learning how to live with myself, and one way is to admit when you're not perfect and to simply accept it.*

A small corner of truth. It wasn't to last.
*Yours,*
*Douglas Baign*

*December 14, 2006, in session*

"I'm not sure I can express the frustration," it was his next session with Sherry.

There were other things he did in life, like develop information systems, play games, write music, take photos or paint, but the sessions consumed him in the effort to understand and accept himself.

"I want to be in contact with the 18-year-old me," Doug continued, "and my letters from that time frame are my best investment. Yet they leave me feeling cold. Does any of the emptiness come through to you?"

Sherry smiled. "I'm not a literary critic. The question is: do you see any of the emptiness and if so, what are you going to do about it?"

"Yeah. One would think I would know that by now," but he didn't seem to be repentant. "How do I talk to me then? I was so different, yet that young man is still inside me and he is still hurt. What can I do to tell him that I care? That I am here for him? What can I do to tell him that I love him?"

Sherry was just as adamant that he answer that for himself. "You tell me."

He looked out the window while he thought about it. Different office, different garden, but the green still calmed him.

He thought about it some more.

"What do I need to remember about my second and third quarters at UCSB and what don't I?" he finally asked. "Not that I expect you to answer that. I'm asking myself because I'm trying to transition in my head from UCSB to JECU. What do I need to address and what don't I?"

Sherry was patient with him. "And what conclusions have you reached?"

"I'm not positive," he responded, "but I probably only need to remember two things. They're both in the first paragraph of that letter."

"'I have one final Tuesday, then I've finished my fight,'" Doug quoted himself. "'I've completed the course—not as well as I'm mentally able, but as well emotionally as I could do.'

"Rotten year, what, I only had a 3.65 GPA—just awful.

"And that's the first thing to remember. There's less and less correlation between my emotional stability and my mental performance. I felt more isolated and depressed. The clouds moved into me faster and faster and faster. But during the same time frame, my study habits improved and my grades went up."

"I should have stayed there at UCSB," he continued, "at least in terms of developing relationships and emotional stability, plus getting a B.A. But that's not what I was looking for. I wanted to find God. I wanted to know God. Maybe God was there at UCSB anyway, but I certainly couldn't see Him there.

"And that takes me to the second thing to remember." He didn't look happy about it. "'Completing the course' is a PD thing stolen from Saint Paul in II Timothy." As usual, he quoted from memory.

*"4:7 I have fought a good fight, I have finished my course, I have kept the faith."*

"I wrote that a year after arguing with PD and there I am still swayed by him," he explained. "Aargh.

"But it was hard to get away from PD anyway because the high school and college groups had joint activities. Maybe I needed to go to JECU simply to break the patterns I knew in Santa Brisa."

It was a depressing thought, given how many friends he had in Santa Brisa, and how much he liked it there. Starting over wasn't his forte. That was another reason he probably should have just stayed at UCSB, lived on campus, and developed relationships there. It didn't happen.

"Of course," Douglas continued, "I'm not in the photo prominently displayed on the 'Friends of PD' Facebook page either. Thank heavens." He paused.

Sherry let him sit for a moment then prompted him. "What's the significance of the photo, Doug?"

He had a peculiar look on his face. "Of all the photos taken during 40+ years of two or three high school trips a year, the one pasted front-and-center on the PD fan page shows the youth leaders of the Arizona bicycle trip in 1975.

"That's the trip I skipped to run a race for my track coach. If I hadn't decided that I was my own muse, not PD, and run the track race instead, then I would have been in that photo.

"I left PD's personality cult to search for Jesus. Terrible man that I am. Not being in the photo counts for something."

The truth was that he still hadn't dealt with all the garbage left over from PD or from his grandmother. And if you don't deal with the root causes of the garbage, the damage will continue.

"I love me, I love me, I love me. I love me, I love me, I love me," Douglas repeated to Sherry. "I can't change what happened between UCSB and JECU. I can only love myself now. I love playing the piano, I love writing. I love bright colors and pretty sounds. I love the deep bass of music rocking my bones. I love me, I love me, I love me.

"When I doubt, when I'm confused, which, I confess, is still most of the time, I keep trying to repeat my mantra: I love me, I love me, I love me. I don't have to understand everything about me. I just have to try to love myself. The understanding can come later.

"I don't understand myself. But that is one reason I continue to come here."

"And that's all the time we have to talk today," Sherry said.

Doug just whacked his head. "Time flies like an arrow" he said while getting up.

"Doesn't it?" Sherry responded. Doug stood up to leave, "and fruit flies like a banana," he thought.

*February 1, 2007, in session*

"Mom would have been 77 this week," Douglas started. "I still think about her so often."

Her death still shook him, then Doug gathered himself and told Sherry more about that summer of 1976.

Douglas's mom and dad went on a short-term mission trip in Europe after UCSB, leaving Matt and him to house-sit and tend the garden. The two BFFs planned to paint the town blue (not red, they were both quite conservative), date a different girl every week, play lots of beach volleyball, and take walks.

Instead, Matt fell in love with Theresa and Doug hardly ever saw the guy. He understood that part, being in love was something he wanted to do himself. But guess what, Doug was alone again.

He indulged himself by editing the book of I John—editing, not paraphrasing. Doug liked the book, wanted to get a better grip on it, and the four Bible translations he had weren't cutting it. His original edit was bad ("I kept a copy," he admitted), but even *doing* an edit was another step away from the Church. A Fundamentalist does not edit the Bible for fear of changing the meaning.

Revelations 22:19 automatically flipped into Douglas's head:

*And if any man shall take away from the words of the book of this prophecy, God shall take away his part out of the book of life, and out of the holy city, and from the things which are written in this book.*

Lands Baptist used that to avoid changing *anything* in the Bible. Douglas thought it only applied to the book of Revelations but did find it amusing that the verse didn't appear in the *Reader's Digest Condensed Bible.*

Editing the Bible in the '70s was simply a part of moving away from the Church. The drift made him feel yet more isolated. He talked to Sherry about it.

"When I get that lonely," Doug said, "sometimes it helps to look up at the stars. Who or what made the universe? If no one made the universe, then the universe made itself, either by existing forever or because the Big decided to Bang. Human wonder is a good antidote to human loneliness."

The stars may not care anymore than the universe of Stephen Crane. But for Doug the stars were personal, close, magical points of light amid his blackness. He stayed quiet a moment, gasping in wonder at the nebulas in his memory.

"It was a Dark Age," he finally told Sherry.

"What was?"

"The time frame between UCSB and JECU. For that matter, JECU certainly wasn't the Renaissance, so maybe that was a Dark Age, too."

Sherry nodded. "What happened during your Dark Ages?"

"Another bridge to cross to get to here and now," he responded. "Let's see here. It's a bit of a muddle, but some key events come to mind so let's start there."

1. "Lee and I finally break up for good in February of 1976 because I'm hurting myself because I was afraid of hurting Leanne by being close to her. Because I was afraid of Leanne herself. Because my grandmother molested me. In the end, I lose my girl, but still have good study habits.
2. "I dated Deirdre off and on between March and June before she and her missionary parents went back to Venezuela.
3. "Matt and I spend that summer at dad's house—just talked about that.
4. "I transferred to JECU in September 1976 to continue my search for God. This was a mistake and the transfer process worked very poorly—long story. In the meantime, I lose good college study habits but still have good Bible study habits.
5. "I drift though college for a year, losing more study habits along the way. Got pretty good at Ping-Pong, but my pool playing was so-so. My grades went in only one direction: down.
6. "I worked between June of 1977 and January 1978 as a janitor to earn money for L'Abri. I don't want to talk about this time frame much because . . . not much happened.
7. "L'Abri treats me like $%! in February of 1978. I've told this story. I lose good Bible study habits. God apparently thinks I'm not worth His time.
8. "Last, but certainly not least, either I convince myself that Deirdre cheated on me, she really did, or Leanne lied when she said Deirdre did. It doesn't matter. In any of those cases, I lose everything.

"I've already talked about #3, 6, 7, and 8, so let's take the others one at a time, front-to-back."

He paused, "Hmm. That's such a hack phrase. I wonder what would happen if people addressed problems back-to-front or two at a time?" he mused. "But I ain't gonna do it that way. Besides, even Homer knows it still starts with 'Doh' even if you sing the song backwards."

He moved to #1 and #2 on the list.

One difference between Lee and Deirdre is that Leanne tried to get past Douglas's walls to heal. And the reason she failed is that he was too scared of women. Doug believed that Leanne was there to rape and hurt, just like Momma May. That was, after all, what women wanted to do, wasn't it?

On the other hand, Deirdre assumed folks outside Douglas's walls could help him, especially authority figures. What Deirdre didn't understand was that the authority figures were indeed the problem in the first place.

"My mother raped me," he summarized. Doug meant his grandmother but was still getting his mother and grandmother confused. "You think I'm going to trust women or authority figures? Besides, the rape made me feel dirty. And that meant I had to keep my yuck and sin away from those I loved. Which in turn meant that I had to drive them away before they got too close to me, lest they become yucky too."

"Feel dirty," Sherry commented. "Not be dirty." It was an important distinction.

"Yeah," he responded. "Feel dirty." He paused a moment, thinking it through. He couldn't help but wish he'd made that distinction when he was 17. It's a sorrow still with him, pain, a lump in his throat.

"But I wounded Leanne," Doug said, "someone I loved, and that hurts. There is so little that I can do about it now except live with it. It's just that living with pain is better than not living.

"I wish I knew how to ask for Leanne's forgiveness. What I'm afraid of is that my very asking would wound her further, and I care too much for her to do that."

Sherry looked at him carefully, "You can't do anything about her, at least not right now. But there is something you can do."

"Go on," he said. "What is it?"

"Forgive yourself. If you can't do it all at once, then forgive yourself a little at a time."

It was time to end the session and he was glad of it. There'd been too much pain. But Doug remembered Sherry's words: to learn to forgive himself, if only but a little.

*February 8, 2007, in session*

It was cloudy and there'd been a trace of rain today. Douglas felt gloom in the gloom, despite the meds, despite precautions. February through April, when his mother lay dying, was the worst part of his year.

He managed to swing into Sherry's parking lot without killing himself, another small victory.

Doug was still thinking about Leanne as he started the session, "Protecting Lee by hurting her first, before I could hurt her even more with the baggage from my grandmother," he said, "reminds me of

Vanauken's book called *A Severe Mercy*. Vanauken's logic, after his wife died young, is that God is merciful when He hurts folks a little now instead of a lot later."

Doug didn't buy into that partly because he saw it as deceptive. Vanauken portrays something bad (pain) as something good (mercy) and Doug didn't see God saying, "Oh, wow! I've created deception and cheating! And lo! It is very good!"

"It's not *A Severe Mercy*." Douglas continued. "It's pain. Besides, if you follow Vanauken's logic reductio ad absurdum, then God should just kill everyone now to save us the pain we'll accumulate before we die of old age. Wouldn't that be just terrific? No one's in pain—and no one would even be sinning—because everyone would be dead.

"Whoopi! Now I'm in Heaven! The ultimate gold burg!" His frequent bouts of sarcasm beat his infrequent panic attacks any day, he decided.

If God wanted bad shit, Douglas thought, He probably would have put it there from the get go. Vanauken, with a bit of help from C. S. Lewis, is an idiot. God uses bad shit because *Homo sapiens—not-so-sapiens*—put it there and that's what we gave God to work with. The Earth is our domain.

"God isn't in control here," Douglas told Sherry. "We are. If my wife or Vanauken's, or C. S. Lewiseses dies early, it's still a tragedy, not a mercy. Been there, mom died young.

"Vanauken is just the PD thing, 'Rejoice evermore!' but never, never 'Weep with those who weep.' Even if your wife dies, even if your daughter dies. The first real mercy is to admit the pain."

Sherry generally agreed with him, but thought he was intellectualizing, holding his own pain at bay. "All right," she said, "But what does this have to do with you?"

"I hurt Leanne," he responded. "I don't want to be like PD or Vanauken. I caused pain to myself, to Leanne. What I did hurt people, her and me, and I have to own up to it."

"Go on," Sherry supported him.

"Vanauken's book came out the summer right before I transferred to JECU, and my friends or authorities recommended that I read it to help make sense of my struggles. I thought it was sappy nonsense, just some arrogant holier-than-thou bragging about how cool he was because he turned pain into mercy."

He thought about it, "I still feel that way, pretty much. Except I committed some of Vanauken's mistakes, to see hurting Leanne as a way to help her. But by the time I'd read the book I saw things differently.

"Damn," Doug was having a hard time of it. "There was so much going on and I just didn't have anyone to talk to. I felt so isolated that I actually looked forward to starting JECU so that I'd see some friends there. Several of my Hosanna classmates were attending.

"Leanne said I was attending JECU simply because she was, but my letters to Jacky during that time frame don't back that up. By then I was looking to date someone else. That's what Matt and I planned that summer, drat the guy. So I thought going to JECU would be a clean start, let me focus on something new.

"Little did I know it was another big mistake."

"And we'll have to talk about that next session." Sherry said.

"Yup." Doug didn't want to go to work that day. He had some vacation saved up and wondered if he should just go to the beach instead. But working through a Perl script would probably get his mind off things. There was something valuable about the shift.

*February 22, 2007, in session*

Douglas skipped a week before seeing Sherry again for the simple reason that seeing a therapist once a week for 10 years is expensive. Money was tight and he wondered how often he'd have to skip.

The topic was transferring to JECU but the results were beyond disappointing. His 48 UCSB quarter units transferred as 24 elective semester units and eight units towards a BS in math. That is, if he wanted one.

JECU completely ignored the following UC requirements: foreign language proficiency, one to three writing classes until you passed proficiency, two more literature courses, economics, art or drama and advanced physics.

"Physics, or any other science class, is an elective?" he bitched to Sherry. "At the college level? What did this tell me about how seriously JECU treated education? The good news, from JECU's viewpoint, must have been that their students didn't have the communication skills to engage in debate or to write a good protest."

Doug of course did, having already passed the required UC exam. Not that JECU actually had an appeals process—nothing. Students, not even ones who spent three or more years at a Christian school, couldn't even appeal the requirement to take 30 units of Bible classes—no exceptions.

The required Bible courses included Theology 101, which literally stated that God created the Earth in seven days and Jesus was born of a virgin.

Really? He had heard that before from somewhere. So what's next on the road toward Christ?

Doug tried a verbal appeal. But the happy little JECU administrator told him to relax. It was a bummer that they'd ignored 24 units, but hey, look on the bright side. His next math class would be easy, right?

"As if I wanted to take it," he continued. "Besides, what were their math classes going to teach me, addition? No, wait. I got it, economics! If you charge your clientele twice for general education, then it's easier to stay in business because it takes longer for you to get out of there."

By contrast, when Doug finally got his B.A. 10 years later, California State University expected him to take three years to complete the degree. He had acquired a huge mélange of college-level units by then so he said no way and successfully used the school appeals process seven times to halve that time frame.

JECU had nothing, *nada*, the big zippo-rama.

"Fucking bastards," Douglas swore. "I was angry and that's when I first started playing games. Sigh! My excessive gaming isn't just a sign of depression, though that can be part of it. It's a sign that I'm angry—at Anne, at my job, and at events or people in my past. Or maybe just that I'm playing the game poorly."

The only thing that might have made JECU worthwhile to Doug is if he had learned more about his relationship with God. But he had been there less than a month when he realized JECU didn't help him to know God, it helped me to know *about* God. He learned theology, not Godness. It was like trying to learn cooking by only reading the recipes. At JECU he never chopped the vegetables or even turned the stove on.

"Who am I and why am I here?" Admiral Stockdale (Ross Perot's VP candidate) joked during their presidential campaign, but it's a crucial question when you're 19. The idea of a good college is (in part) to help students build their own identity and self-confidence either by teaching them subjects one thinks they need to know or by helping them to specialize in what they want to know.

JECU failed to do that; it offered indoctrination, pure and simple.

He continued, "I could rant about JECU miserably for the next half-hour or so, but ya know? Ranting wouldn't help any." Doug was on a rampage again, despite himself.

"All I can say is JECU failed me. I'm still unhappy about it. Yeah, sure, that was 35 years ago and I'm supposed to just let it go. Obviously, I haven't. It doesn't matter. I hate JECU. And despise it. And I won't ever make that mistake again.

"Annnd," he stretched out the conjunction, "if I crucify myself for not forgiving JECU earlier, then I'm just digging myself in deeper. So let's move on to the next topic."

Sherry smiled at him, "Good. But take a deep breath and let's think about this a moment before we move on." She waited while Doug tried to calm down.

"JECU screwed up," Sherry continued. "That's a given. Their behavior should make you angry. They did the wrong thing. But you gain some control over your anger by admitting that the other party is wrong. You didn't make the mistake, did you? JECU screwed it up. But if JECU made the mistake, not you, then you can say, 'I'm OK.' And if I'm OK then why get angry?"

"'They're not OK, but I'm still OK,'" he paraphrased. "I can continue going in my own direction."

Sherry gave him one of her prettier smiles. "Exactly," she said. "Turn that around. What happens if you don't admit that that other party is wrong?"

He thought about it. "I'm not sure about other folks," he decided, "but I feel dirty."

"Right. You know that something is wrong and you think the other party is OK, so you feel dirty."

"Aargh," He was upset about it. "That's where I'm at now. I feel dirty. If you feel dirty, then either you have to retaliate or you have to hide the dirt, which is usually what I try to do."

"Right." Sherry was on one of her rare rolls. "Retaliation might temporarily make you feel better, but it won't take away the dirt and so you have to retaliate again and then again and again and again."

"Ugh," he exclaimed again. "I know where that's at. I've verbally retaliated against people who've made me angry. I know what goes on inside of a murderer's head, not that I am one. But I've retaliated and I still feel dirty afterward, even dirtier if I've hurt someone I love.

"Then you want to punish yourself for hurting people, and I guess that's one reason why some serial murderers get caught. Part of them wants to stop their own behavior. They can punish themselves permanently by being caught and executed."

If you hide, then the only person you hurt is yourself. But if you continue down that path, you can suddenly find yourself standing on a bridge, gazing down at the crevasse, quietly counting the number of seconds before you 'make an impact' with your life. A sure death offers one way of hiding but also of fully revealing self to self.

Doug had done a little bit of each. He tried to hide and hide and hide some more, while part of him kept leaking out to retaliate. Maybe his root anger started at JECU, or more probably at his grandmother, or maybe it was something else, whatever. The point is that Doug was OK when the anger first occurred because he was actually innocent and his anger was legit.

"But then I started to retaliate and hide," he admitted. "Deliberately. I hurt Leanne. I hurt Anne. I've hurt myself. I've made poor choices. I've wasted large parts of my life, gotten drunk, screamed at my mom, laughed in anger. I've hit, struck, burned, and cut myself—literally for the fun of it.

"Along the way, I've not been OK. Other than trying to make restitution to the ones I've hurt, the only thing that I can do is show my sins in the light, change my behavior and learn to forgive myself. And that is terribly, terribly hard to do. It's easier for me to forgive JECU for hurting me than it is to forgive myself for hurting Anne or Lee."

It was the end of yet another session. But there was one more thing on his mind that he managed to get it out before Sherry dismissed him.

"The human mind is not as logical as it may seem," he wondered. "How do you make restitution to yourself?"

*February 22, 2007, at home*
*Dear Jacky,*
I ended the session today by telling Sherry:

*"The human mind is not as logical as it may seem."*

. . . Nor should it be. Ignoring the amygdala is as dangerous as ignoring the frontal lobe. I'm not saying that the amygdala creates poetry. I'm saying that the limbic system is there for a reason. Instincts are part of who we are as humans. I don't need to ignore my lower brain functions in favor of logic—I'm not a Vulcan. I need to cooperate and appreciate both: poetry, philosophy, writing Perl, writing here.

It gets back to what I tell my boss, Sharon. I can only play the cards I've been dealt, even when my hand contains a Tarot, Mahjong, poker, an MTG card and a blank round chunk of cardboard. And people wonder why it's sometimes so difficult for me to focus on any one topic.

My friend Daniel said something interesting about this once. He commented that I'm a wanderer, a little of this, a little of that. Maybe becoming a painter would be a good idea.

So maybe the direction of my writing or my life doesn't deeply matter. If I'm going to wander, then I can just pick a direction and begin to wander.
Love you!
*Douglas*

# JECU

*March 8, 2007, in session, remembering October 1976*

Douglas started the session by reading a note he'd written in 1976.

> *October 18, 1976, at JECU*
> *Dear Jacky,*
>
> *I'm writing to see if I can alliviate that funny feeling in the pit of my stomach. I can't focus my mind on anything. I feel disconnected. I can't study well, even the Bible is difficult. I can write poetry, but I can't concentrate enough to write essays. I couldn't even study for my math test Thursday. Instead, I'm restless; walking aimless; playin' Ping-Pong or just standing there.*

Doug's high school essays rarely made the same spelling mistakes. But two years later at JECU, his writing and thought process deteriorate possibly because of depression. He just didn't care anymore. What difference did it make?

> *Why? Something's bugging me, but it's hard to put a finger on it. Well, why not try to analysis the situation.*
> *JECU boxes me into places where I just don't fit. I have to take this Bible class, I have to be prayerful tomorrow, I have to worship God at 11:30 in the morning. Blah, blah, blah. By the time I finish listing the "have to's" and "can'ts" I end up saying that I can't be myself. If I'm going to worship God, I'll worship Him when I can, not when someone tells me to.*

JECU required students to attend chapel at 11:30 a.m. unless they had a class immediately before or after. The result was that full-time students were punished (time was taken away from them by required chapel) while lazy students got lazier (because they could avoid attending chapel in the first place). It was just another example to Douglas about how JECU failed to take education seriously.

> *They're trying to tell me what to think, feel, do, or be, and what they tell me to be is not who I am. Why can't I just be myself? My roommate says that I put myself where I don't belong. Well, where do I belong?*

Again, there was a sense of cookie-cutter indoctrination, without thinking through the consequences of administrative decisions. It wasn't just chapel or the lack of an appeals process. Doug got the impression that the school was simply moving him from point A to point B without thinking of him as a person.

Doug had been treated with more care and love at UCSB than at JECU. For example, UCSB broke large classes into small study groups while JECU did not. His fundamental mistake in attending a Christian college, he admitted to himself, was the assumption that it was in fact Christian.

> *I want to be master of my own destiny. But shouldn't God really be my master? Who am I to tell God what to do? "In everything give thanks." So, God, I give thanks for all the crummy situations I'm in. Help me to have a positive attitude.*

The question wasn't just how JECU acted but how he was supposed to act, regardless of what JECU did or didn't do. It was back to L'Abri founder Francis Schaeffer question: "How should he then live?"

*October 20, 1976, at JECU*

> *Today stands out in my mind because God taught me how to cope with depression. My depression stems from my overactive imagination yet "courage," says Gothard, "is the capacity to face what is imagined." But iff I have an overactive imagination, then I'm imagining things that can't happen, use up too much courage, and become depressed.*

> *But if I trust God then he will give me the ability to cope with the imagination and fear. "Perfect love casts out all fear." Maybe I can learn more of this at JECU to be a better Christian.*

Doug kept blaming himself for the depression. The problem wasn't a lack of serotonin, it was a lack of faith, or a lack of prayer, or a lack of reading the Bible. Even before L'Abri, even before Deirdre, he kept saying that he had finally learned what he was doing wrong and was now going to fix it. Then he'd quote some meme or biblical verse to back it up.

But the next day he would be depressed all over again. His best writing from 1976 describes what was happening and admits his depression.

*October 22, 1976, at JECU*
*You know, I'm just really learning how little I know about anything. I thought I knew about Christianity but I guess it's so hard to actually apply it to one's life.*

The paragraph was true, but unintentionally. The black-and-white attitude in the fundamentalist community back then was that if you weren't going forward with God (constantly 'learning' more about God) then you were going backwards. You were either for Christ or against Christ. Thus, you had to show continual growth, continual 'learning.' So Doug wrote that he was *learning* to try to convince himself that he was *growing* at JECU 'spiritually.'

Of course, given that he eventually dumped the place on the road to sanity, one could say that he was in fact learning. But it certainly didn't have anything to do with the idea that JECU was helping him to be a better Christian. Rather, it was the growing realization that JECU was *preventing* him from being a better Christian, which is why he went to L'Abri.

*What a lousy attitude I've had! I've been assuming that I didn't have anything to learn and therefore I would get mad and frustrated, working myself into a depression.*

Douglas had "a lousy attitude." Douglas 'worked himself into a depression. Serotonin had nothing to do with it and the authorities, of course, were blameless leaders handing him God's will on a silver platter. He was unspiritual if he didn't take it.

Once you play theological Jenga then many of your assumptions flip on their head. The people you thought were deceiving you are telling the truth. The people you thought were great are deceptive. Most of all, they aren't the leaders, *you* are the leader because you take responsibility for yourself.

"I needed to admit to myself that I wasn't doing anything wrong at all," Doug told Sherry. "Or rather, anything that I was doing wrong, any bad attitude I had, wasn't really the problem. The problem was what was done *to* me, not what I had or hadn't done. The problems I had at JECU. The problems I had with women—Momma May, my mom, maybe Leanne a little bit.

"A woman betrayed me long before I decided Deirdre did. My mother raped me. That's how it feels inside. I had two mothers, May and mom. May raped me. My grandmother mother raped me. God, that's confusing. I am hurt by that. I am wounded. It is not what I have done, but what was done to me."

He stopped a moment. "I'll probably repeat that to you 50 times, Sherry, until it sinks into my head. My apologies in advance."

"It comes with the job description. Go ahead."

"*'Un dieu dans le ciel et une déesse sur la terre.'* I started talking about JECU and here I am talking about my two mothers. The problems I had with God are crisscrossing with the problems I had with women. And *that's* confusing, too."

"One at a time."

"Yea. But let me describe the crisscross before we get there."

"OK."

He took a deep breath. "We've talked about these three or four things before; it's just that we've never connected them. The first thing is the impression I got from my dear old Grandma May—that women just want power or booze or whatever."

"The first schema."

"The what?" he asked.

"The first schema. A schema," Sherry explained, "is a belief about oneself or another person that influences how you act and what choices you make. For example, the schema 'I am a good person' will give you confidence when you make choices now."

"Gosh, that's a useful concept."

"Quite. But I interrupted. You said the first relevant schema that comes to mind is that it's all about a woman's agenda: power, booze, babies, orgasms —whatever she wants. The woman is in control. What's the second?"

"A man's role is to make women happy. To *give* her what she wants. Grandma May was the landlord—I mean, the landlady—so even Dad did what she wanted, providing raw manpower or skilled labor. Dad's an amazing mechanic and handyman."

"All right. Those are schemas you learned from your grandmother. Where's the crossover to schemas you learned from the church?"

He nodded. "That's the third thing. The church started telling me in junior high that 'Men think dirty thoughts about women.' Women apparently didn't and that's where the short-circuit occurred.

"The church *reinforced what I learned from my grandmother.*" Douglas's face went red, so he took a breath, then continued. "It's not just all about a woman's agenda, like my grandmother said. It's about a woman's agenda *because* she's pure and the man isn't, like the church said. Two more nasty schemas for the price of one."

Doug kept getting progressively upset, but managed to keep talking.

"Many other schemas evolve directly from that combination. For example, when I was 12 or 13 the church was teaching girls to be demure and submissive. But I was already convinced that women were in control, so obviously the girls were being taught to be demure both as a way to camouflage their power and as a way of training them how to use that power. Being demure just let girls pursue their own agenda without getting emotionally involved with men.

"If I was attracted to a demure girl (nearly all of them) then I was just walking into an ambush. In addition, God programmed me to like women, but sex was dirty so God had obviously programmed me to *want* to walk into an ambush and be used then abused.

"The schemas interlock.

"It was all very unhealthy. By the time I was 17, I'd grown a bit and wasn't so sure of this. OTOH, why did women make love if it wasn't for their own selfish agenda?

"But no one reached out to help. It's not just what the church or the women in my life *did* do, it's what they *didn't* do. There was no career guidance when I left Hosanna. My mother (I mean mom, not Grandma May) ignored me. For that matter, so did Grandma May, assuming she had any parenting responsibility. Dad was too busy. The Church just shrugged. Wasn't I just supposed to join the mission field?"

"I fell through the cracks and into the cesspools of despair. It felt like no one cared at all except to say that I should be rejoicing in the Lord.

"At what? At the fact that my heart and writing grew bitter? At being laughed at? At being molested and raped? Rejoicing with those others who do rejoice begins when someone is there weeping when you do weep."

And indeed, he was weeping. Sherry just sat there without saying anything and let him cry. At first Doug wondered why that felt better than being comforted by the fundamentalists he knew. Then he realized Sherry was letting him weep without exhorting him to rejoice.

*March 22, 2007, in session*

Douglas wasn't sure how well seeing Sherry every other week was working. It certainly made it more affordable, but it also made it harder to stay on track. Well, who knew? It was too soon to tell.

He started the session.

"Remember my story about being promoted from the Bluebirds into the Yellowbirds in Mrs. Looney's 4th-grade math competition?" he said. "I liked math, so I finally decided to make math my major at JECU. But my heart wasn't in it, nor in JECU. I was quite depressed. I couldn't study so I did very poorly on my first test—38 out of 80.

"I knew I hadn't done well, but was pretty sure it wasn't that badly so I went back over my answers. Several seemed OK to me, so time to talk to the prof."

"Makes sense," Sherry commented.

"Right. But back in the Bluebird story, I also said that my 'Dad believes that it's results that count, not the way you get there.' Not that JECU shared the same approach, of course.

"Professor Thorebotum didn't like the way I proved the theorems on the test, not that the test required you to prove them in any particular way, mind you. I finally walked the good professor through every step of my proofs. Why he couldn't follow them in the first place, I don't know; after all the guy has a PhD. But never mind. Thorebotum finally agreed to raise my score 18 points to 56/80. A C+."

"That's quite the improvement."

"Yeah. Well, one would think so. Except for the tiny detail that Thorebotum marked one proof as zero points even though he agreed that I had in fact correctly proved the problem—the rat."

Sherry was puzzled. "Why did he do that?"

"I asked him the same thing, and he said and I quote: 'It's bad mathematics.'

"Really? Your test required 'good mathematics'? It certainly wasn't there in the instructions. I had read the instructions very, very carefully. Nope. No 'Good mathematics is required.' Nor was there any injunction to use a certain means of proof. What's 'bad mathematics'?"

Doug was puzzled by that phrase. Either you prove something or you don't. If a computer program gives you the correct results, do you argue that it's a "bad computer program"? Bad computer, bad computer, bad, bad, bad.

Remember that at JECU "bad" had the connotation of "evil." So while there's lots of ways of making efficient, well-designed or fast computer programs—or math proofs, but ("as I told you before, Sherry") Dr. Thorebotum didn't ask for any of that before the test. Why was the proof "bad"?

The same situation never occurs in the UC system. Instead, if you prove something by some bizarre method the professor will look at the test to see if the problem required a certain approach. If it didn't and you still had the right answer anyway, end of story. You got the points (and the professor might change the next test).

But at JECU, Dr. Thorebottom deducted 10 points simply because he didn't like Douglas's answer. The rule or ritual served no purpose, religious or otherwise.

Doug felt discriminated against.

Doug stopped taking JECU seriously. The problem wasn't just that he felt they were trying to control his religious behavior, but that they were trying to regulate his *non*-religious beliefs, too, when there was no reason for it.

Or to put it into a nutshell, if UCSB denied the spirit but accepted the mind, then JECU denied both. JECU buttonholed everything into a box, just like Gothard, without seeing the complexity and beauty of life.

"JECU clearly wasn't there to educate," he concluded, "but to indoctrinate. Even in math. Why one must indoctrinate students in 'good' Christian mathematics is still a mystery to me but never mind. The classes didn't make sense. So I stopped studying, with the expected results in my grades. Surprise!"

The semester after the math debacle, he read all of Schaeffer's existing material carefully, while going through the motions of attending class. Schaeffer made sense to him and answered some of his questions. Perhaps if he went to L'Abri on his own, then more of his questions would be answered.

Doug dropped out of school after two semesters to earn money for L'Abri. Deirdre returned that summer from Venezuela and they started dating immediately. He kept the job during the fall while Deirdre attended JECU. They kept dating consistently while he lived with his mom and dad and visited JECU on the weekends. By January 1978, he was about ready to go but decided to visit Deirdre another time or two.

"That brings us back around to L'Abri story, Sherry." It'd been a very long trip.

*April 5, 2007, in session*

"I love Deirdre. Deirdre betrayed me. I hate Deirdre. There you have it," he concluded. "A plot. The difference between love and hatred is betrayal.

"Deirdre betrayed me, or at least, I think she did. It doesn't matter. It is up to me not to betray her or myself and through that to learn to love myself."

It felt like the end of the story, not the beginning. But in releasing his feelings about life at JECU and his trip to L'Abri, he was left struggling with the aftermath.

"But this is a psych session, not a novel," he thought. "What's important is not what happened, but how I cope with my feelings about what I *think* happened."

"How do you propose to do that?" Sherry asked.

In response, Douglas's mind was awash within an ocean, calming in its ebb and flow, glittering in the sun. But his words were unreliable and confused. Somehow his thoughts just didn't connect with the working of his tongue, like tangles of rambling seaweed on the ocean floor, they seemed chaotic amid the reassuring waves that arrived and retreated, rhythmically uncovering sand and hidden creatures, only to obscure them again.

"Pardon me if I wander around some before answering that question," he said. "I don't know how to get at my thoughts directly, so I just have to let myself wander while I figure out where I'm going."

"All right," Sherry responded. It wasn't the first time he had taken this approach.

"Events with Deirdre still hurt, whatever happened," Doug loped off on his usual tangent, "I don't know how to deal with it, though torturing people does come to mind. I don't know how to cope. I don't know how to lessen the pain. I don't know how to get rid of it. I don't know how to be different.

"It's all I can do right now to just *admit* the pain. One of the hardest, hardest things to do is to admit that my pain exists, because saying, 'I hurt' is somehow supposed to make pain go away. Well, it doesn't."

He paused, filtering his words for clues to where he was going. Nothing there, so he kept going.

"There's such an expectation for cuckolds to forgive their ex-spouses with open arms, so to speak. Well, we didn't do anything wrong, so why are we supposed to forgive our betrayers? Shouldn't they be doing something about it? Society treats forgiveness these days as something to reward the betrayer, not the person who was betrayed."

"I know what you mean," Sherry empathized.

"Then there's the 'Dear Abby' approach," Doug added. "Reward neither. Forgive them if only so you can get on with your life. My boss Jim even said something like this at work. It didn't matter how we had gotten into such-and-such a stupid situation. You put it behind you then manage it. You think about now.

"But I am not there either. If we don't remember how we got into this mess, I told Jim, then we're likely to repeat the errors that got us there in the first place. That may make it difficult for us to solve the problem now. Learning how you got in, can tell you how to get out. Forgiveness is not forgetting."

Douglas snapped his fingers. "That's what I'm talking about."

"What?" Sherry was naturally curious.

"Forgiveness. What is the nature of forgiveness? Deirdre's actions were wrong. I certainly won't justify her actions by forgiving them, nor create a situation where she can betray me yet again. But how do you forgive someone without denying the validity of your own wounds? What do you forgive and what do you forget? If I honor my pain, will it then control me? And if I don't, then how do I control it?"

Sherry laughed, "That's too many questions. Where do you start?"

He thought it over, "Well, you don't start by forgiving or forgetting your betrayer. You start by admitting that you hurt and don't want to forgive them—or yourself, for that matter. You start by remembering the pain. Forgiveness, perhaps, has three stages: (1) admit something happened, (2) admit it hurts and it hurts you . . ."

He stopped there. Sherry waited for him to continue with step #3 but Doug didn't say anything, so she prompted him.

"Do you want to know the third step?" she asked gently. She was pretty sure she knew.

He shook his head. "No. Not yet." He was still processing the pain.

Forgiveness has no moral force until the victim realizes that he or she was damaged by the act. If you ask a victim to give forgiveness while they're still in shock, then the words have no meaning. It's that simple. Forgiveness can exist only when the victim recognizes that something is wrong.

The problem with some Christian Church and anger management classes is that they want you to forgive without the moral force of admitting the pain. Something bad happened; you don't want it to happen again—ever.

"My first mother — Grandma May — raped me. My second mother— mom—failed to stop it" Douglas told Sherry. "I am not at the point of forgiveness. I am at the point where I realize that it hurts and that I can let myself cry."

*April 19, 2007, in session*

The session started as Douglas wiped his brow. "I've covered most of the territory I need to, except my childhood before that Bluebird math contest." he told Sherry, "But my childhood stories are chaotic and distressing. I need to tell them, but don't always know how to tell them accurately."

"They don't need to be perfect," Sherry responded. "Just tell me what you remember. I won't prompt you or make suggestions. Besides, the schemas you develop during childhood may be more important than the actual incidents that caused them."

"*Ja.*" Doug used the German Momma May sometimes used. "I can see that. But let me talk about something else, *por favor.*"

"Go ahead."

"I was in the bathroom yesterday," he continued, "when a typhoon of emotions slammed into my head—like a headache or an urge to commit suicide. Or maybe like a simple panic attack, the kind that my meds are supposed to prevent—waves of pain, anxiety, hatred, sex just storming through me."

Sherry was concerned. "Did you take your meds properly?"

"That's the first thing I checked. Yeah. I took my meds. I'll probably talk to Dr. H about the incident, but I don't know what to make of it."

Dr. H is Doug's prescription MD.

"Do talk to him. Is there anything else you know about that incident?"

"Not really. The typhoon came, the typhoon went. I had to put up with a half-hour attack of the . . . weirds. That doesn't happen very often at all, but it does happen. I'd hate to be an epileptic or someone else who gets real seizures on a routine basis. Once in a blue moon is bad enough.

"Not sure it was a seizure, though," he added. "I was conscious the whole time."

"Not all seizures are epileptic nor must you lose consciousness while having one," Sherry replied. "You may have had a focal seizure. One that's localized."

"Thrills. You're just full of good news, Sherry." He paused. "I apologize. It's just upsetting, that's all."

"I understand. Do you have any idea what may have caused this?"

"Not really. I usually have a hard time of it this time of year because mom died this month, so many moons ago. I could probably talk to her about these issues. She could help me to remember stuff and dad won't talk. Besides, mom was such a tremendously beautiful woman in so many different ways."

"You love her deeply."

"Yeah. But we really do need a better word than love. Something combining love—*hiraeth* and *toska*."

Sherry shook her head. "I've not heard of those words before."

"I found them on a website of untranslatable foreign terms. Useful bugger. *Hiraeth* roughly means homesickness for something that no longer exists. *Toska* is 'a painful sensation of great spiritual anguish, often without any specific cause,' to quote that website: 'a longing with nothing to long for.'

"I *hiraeth*/love my Mom and missing her is close to *toska*."

"Yes, useful words indeed." Sherry saw the value in it.

"But if I'm going to talk about my mom, I'll need to separate her from Momma May, assuming I can do it," he added, "And that's a long story. Up to now, I've told you about my family by going through the main entrance, so to speak. If I'm going to tell about my life before the age of nine, I'll have to enter through the side door."

# Mom and Momma

# Infancy

"I was born just after midnight in the hospital waiting room, and the physician came straight from his own birthday party, festooned with ribbons as it were, to attend. I don't remember any of that, of course. But I do remember my parents later saying they didn't want to check in before midnight because they would be charged for an extra day in the hospital. So maybe I was born on the cheap."

Douglas paused his narrative. "I've been in therapy six years plus and I've finally been born. Yeah me!"

Sherry smiled. "That's a long gestation period."

"Yeah. Only happens to monsters."

"That's another schema," Sherry responded. "You're not a monster. But you've developed an internal belief that you are and it influences your actions now. Not all schemas are negative though," she added.

That made sense to him. "How do I get rid of the ones I don't want?"

"Identifying that you have it is the first step. When the thought crops up again, you're more likely to notice it then you can consciously contradict that schema. Beyond that, just keep coming here and we'll work on it."

"I can do that," he responded. "Besides, it's not clear to me that I'll have this job forever and that will leave me with free time anyway."

"Which will make it easier for you to come here."

"Exactly."

"Yes. Well, did you want to continue your story? We've got time left."

"Sure."

∽✌∾∽✌∾∽✌∾

Douglas's birth mother won an all-expenses-paid trip to Paris for a month. Baby Douglas was only three months old, but she didn't want to give up the chance, so she left her infant son with her mother, Doug's grandmother, Grandma May, and departed.

It seemed all right at the time. The Baign family had just moved into a small house, doubling the space for a growing family, and after all, Grandma May lived in a cottage on the same large lot. She was the family's landlady and it was easy enough to move from one house to the other. Just walk out the side door of the front house, cross the patio and take the cobble stones. The rent was low.

But his mother's decision was just the beginning of a habit of convenience. She left her youngest child with Momma May while she first finished her college education, completed her teaching credentials, and accepted a job as an inspiring and dedicated teacher. She became to all eyes a pillar of the church.

One of Douglas's earliest memories is being in Momma May's arms, not his mother's. Douglas was reared by two women, mom and Momma, for the next nine years, starting from when he was barely three months old.

In fact, Momma May was more of a mother to Douglas than his mom. This was not the best of situations, to say the least.

❧❧❧

Douglas rubbed his eyes, "I feel like I haven't covered very much ground, but that was tiring," he said. "I'll be getting into my early memories, such as they are, at the next session, so I need a break. Can we schedule our next appointment four weeks out?"

"Certainly."

*June 27, 2007, Zion*

*Dear Jacky,*

Miracles happen one-by-one: a rock, a leaf there lie quietly against the cold. The wind blowing the trees suckles them into the night.

My miracles are rarely so grand. They grow on me slowly as I hike through red walls and canyons to find a place to lie down. I find it, river water splashing on my face, the drowsy grass accepting me.

Should I laugh at the climbers on those walls? They're crazy! Or maybe it's just that their miracles are greater than mine.

I came here as a child, skipping stones across the water with Rose, climbing trails, throwing Frisbees with John and dad, drinking phosphates with mom, clinking the chains on the trail to Angels Landing.

So much has changed here. "More people, more scars upon the land," but truly the land is not so scarred. Zion has not changed so much as the people have changed. At one time, there was clean loneliness. Now the bustling, tearing mob jostles onto the waiting buses.

But the rocks are still here in my land, my Landing, the trees still speak to me, the river still flows into me and I am rich to see this. I am richer yet to see miracles happen once again, just the still pebbles, or the groan of cliffs dripping the rain of a thousand years ago.

What is here is mine. Yes, mine, my miracles, my journey. My soul lives here, so I can laugh with and smile once again.

I am myself here, coming back into myself once more.

I love you, Jacky. What's more, perhaps I'm learning to love myself.
*Love,*
*Douglas*

# Early Memories

*July 12, 2007, in session*

Douglas's earliest memory is sitting on a wooden floor, listening to Bach and Beethoven on his Dad's old Philco. He was fascinated by the cascade of musical notes rising, falling, repeating. Doug soon learned the patterns and began to predict notes in advance, his first steps into the dazzling world of math and art.

He remembered his mom talking about Buddy Holly, but isn't sure if that was before or after Buddy died, while his mom reminisced.

But he remembered the surprise of seeing a TV for the first time. His family tuned in to see Eisenhower's farewell speech, a face inside a TV, just like a face in his jack-in-the-box!

"It's difficult to pick out which early memories are important, Sherry," Doug was uncertain how to proceed. "For instance, I can remember playing with Tabitha, our lovely cat, on the porch or the delicious smell of our wonderful hope chest, full of hidden nooks and crannies, knickknacks and doodads. But are the stories relevant or not?"

"I can't answer that for you," Sherry responded. "But what's your goal? What are you trying to accomplish?"

He thought about that a bit. "I'm not trying to detail my childhood, not yet anyway. I'm trying to deal with being abused as a child. It feels so heartless toward my inner child, limiting my wanderings, but what do you talk about and what don't you?"

"You tell me." Sherry's answer didn't surprise him, but he still couldn't help wishing she had a magic wand. He shrugged.

"Dunno. Or rather, I'm not positive. The hope chest was marvelous, but it doesn't feel relevant somehow. Maybe I'll get back to it. Tabitha, on the other hand . . ."

One day Tabitha jumped out of Doug's arms to chase something across the street, only to be run over by a car. Their precious Tabitha turned limp and lifeless. Rose and Doug buried her in the side garden, near a rose bush. Doug wondered where she was a few days later, so Rose took him over to the rose bush and they exhumed poor Tabitha's body, just to make sure she was dead. She was.

The memory made him feel sad and ill. "I remember thinking," he continued, 'this is how dirt is made.' Tabitha's body turns to dirt. It was my first experience with death.

"Some of my early memories are precious roses, Sherry. Others are stiff, rotting corpses, turning into dirt. The problem is that those memories lie next to each other and I don't always know how to separate the two. I constantly ask myself: is this memory a rose or simply poor Tabitha?"

"Why not just try to describe what happened during a typical week of your childhood?" Sherry suggested.

Doug was receptive to the idea. "I can do that. Well, I think I can. I don't think I could have talked about those memories just a few years ago, but I can more or less get at them now."

"Go ahead." Sherry wasn't impatient. She simply wanted to move him forward, but the story would take multiple sessions.

## A Typical Week in Childhood

*July 26, 2007, in session*

A typical week started with church on Sunday. That's already been described, so after church the Baigns visited a relative, usually Jim and Grandma Baign. At one point, every grandparent, aunt, uncle, all six Baign cousins and two second cousins lived in California within 100 miles of each other. They'd visit them all. Fun!

On Sundays, the family strolled on the beach or in a park after lunch— few crowds got in the way in the 1960s—then went back to church. Dr. M dedicated evening services to warning against the evil world, so Douglas learned the big sins early on: don't dance, play cards, go to the movies, drink, smoke or have sex outside of marriage.

Mondays, he'd eat eggs and toast for breakfast, and bacon if mom had extra money in the cookie jar, walk to school, stutter and lisp when called on in class, get bullied at recess while his teachers called him retarded, eat a PB&J and an apple for lunch, walk by the taco shop on the way home from school (it's still there), turn down the alley, walk into the backyard and pretend to be a dog. Momma May had two.

An hour or so later, Momma May picked Doug up and the two of them played poker while she chain-smoked, cursed her cards, sipped whisky and described her latest conquest at the dance or movie. Six sins for the price of one!

Sherry interrupted. "Just to clarify a point, you listened to Dr. M preach against all the sins on Sunday night then watched your grandmother commit all the same sins by Monday night."

"Yup. Well, five of them. It might take her until Friday night to sleep with a new man. But by Saturday morning I'd come over and watch her boyfriend du noir drop-off a parting gift—cigarettes, costume jewelry or the like. Once May showed me a bottle of pricey Scotch and let me take a sip. Good stuff!" Doug gave Sherry a thumbs up.

"A new man each week. And she described picking him up." Sherry stated flatly.

"Sure. At least one. May certainly completed the set of all the big six sins by Friday night. And she'd be working on the minor sins in between. Screaming, drinking, carousing, getting drunk, which was a separate sin from drinking, and so on. I don't recall that she ever cheated at cards, though. She was honest that way."

"Screaming. Drunk."

"Yup. I suspect, but can't prove, that she got me mixed up with her ex. Grandpa and I share names."

"Your grandmother was emotionally abusing you."

Doug looked puzzled. "Well, I guess you could say that. Seemed pretty normal, really—just the average, everyday screaming at me. Happened all the time."

Anger is not love, love is not abuse. But it was obvious how Douglas had first gotten them conflated.

Sherry took a deep breath, "Go on."

When his mom and dad finally got home, they'd eat dinner as a family. A casserole was common fare. After that, he usually trotted to the back house to play more poker. "I like the game, not that I'm any good at it." If there were no men that night, Doug sometimes fell asleep with Momma May and got molested.

Doug interrupted himself. "Hmm. This is surprisingly easy to talk about. I expected to get emotional at this point, to cry, weep or scream. But nope, no emotions here, so sorry if I sound academic."

"When were you first raped?" is one of the standard questions they ask you when you're an abuse victim. Sherry didn't ask it because the answer wouldn't help any. There is no first memory. Momma May abused Douglas while he was still an infant, before he developed any conscious memory at all.

"How often were you molested?" Sherry asked. That's also a standard question, but it hits a similar difficulty.

He shrugged, "I have no idea. That's like asking how often I had toast for breakfast. I mean, it happened so frequently that it wasn't worth counting. Maybe two or three times a week? Until I was . . . five? six? Less often after that but it still happened until I was nine."

Sherry was aghast. "You were five years old and your grandmother molested you two or three times a week."

"Yeah," Doug responded. "I know now that that's a major problem. But I certainly didn't know it then. Besides," he added. "Momma May asked me to keep it a secret."

"It was a secret." Douglas was annoyed Sherry kept parroting him, but heaven knew that he had trouble speaking too, so didn't visibly react.

"Yeah. Maybe I should slow down a bit."

"Go ahead."

"Momma May owned both houses. She'd been living in the front house, where she and grandpa raised mom and her sibs, before she built the cottage so she simply walked into both houses without knocking, coming in through the side door."

"Your grandmother had no sense of boundaries." Sherry was still incensed.

Douglas chewed his nails, "Yeah. I never thought of it that way, but yeah," Doug repeated himself. "You're right. Dad figured that out and asked her to stay out. She said no, it was her house, but eventually mom and dad got Momma May to knock before coming in. Dad also put up a small fence between the two houses. It was easy enough for someone to walk through the gate, but you could hear them coming.

"Things were better after that, but the gate also worked against me. I can remember being on Momma May's side of the fence and thinking, 'I have to hide my secrets once I walk through the gate.'"

"What secrets were they?" asked Sherry.

Douglas sighed, "Lots of them, but I don't want to talk about it right now. 'Don't' this time as opposed to 'can't'. I don't feel angry or sad or whatever, I'm just worn out. Talking through this stuff is tiring."

"Understandably," Sherry was sympathetic. "We don't have much time left in this session anyway. Do you want to end it early?"

"Let me say one more thing, then let's end it."

"Go ahead."

"Now that I'm past the barriers, it's easy to talk about being abused, because as a kid, it wasn't abuse. I was molested as a baby, I was molested in 4th grade, and Momma May used me as her sex toy off-and-on for the nine years in between. So?

"You asked me to describe a normal week as a kid. That was a normal week as a kid, nothing special about it at all. It's like God created me to be molested."

Something went off in his head—Ding!

"Wait a minute," he said. "That's another schema. In this case, a negative one: 'God created me to be molested.'"

Sherry smiled her approval, "Yes, exactly. We can go into that in more detail next week."

Doug stood up to leave, even though it was still a minute early, then bowed to her. "Thank you for your time. I know I pay you, but I appreciate it beyond just that." He smiled at Sherry then made his own way to the door.

# From Evidence to Memories

*August 9, 2007, in session*

Doug's old convertible could nickel and dime him to death. But it was his, paid for, so he smiled in the heat, the top down, the wind blowing, rock-and-roll music playing on the radio. He was getting better.

And still seeing Sherry. He guessed he'd need to see someone once a month or so for the rest of his life, just to monitor his behavior. So he pulled into the parking lot, enjoying the last notes of "American Pie"— it'd been playing interminably for the last eight miles—and walked into Sherry's office.

"The fact that I can't identify a first memory of being abused doesn't mean I don't remember it at all. It's just that my memory of childhood is muddled."

"Which immediately leads to the question of how much you can rely on it," Sherry replied.

"Exactly. Fortunately, I don't have to. I obtained access to some family records plus four of my relatives —dad, Aunt Cheryl and Uncle Tony and my sister Rose—can confirm key events."

"Let's talk about the evidence of abuse before we talk more about my early memories."

Douglas's great-great grandparents Thorson abused their daughter, great-grandma Schneider. Twenty years later, there's good, but not conclusive evidence that one of great-grandma Schielmann's boarders raped grandma Schneider when she was 14. A generation after that, the courts removed Annette Schneider (Doug's birth mother) from the Schneider household when she was ten because of parental abuse. Court records are useful buggers.

One detects a subtle pattern here. Yeah, verily. The sins of his Schneider great-great grandparents were "visited upon the children unto the third and fourth generation," that is to say, Douglas.

"I'm not having any children, Sherry," he exclaimed. "I try never to even get physically close to them. If there is nothing else I do in my lifetime, I will break the chain."

Sherry looked at him and nodded, "But there's a history of childhood abuse in your family."

"Yup. Would have been nice to know about this sooner, but never mind. And to forestall the next question, you might be wondering if there's that much evidence of abuse in my family, why didn't my adult relatives try to stop it?"

"I was thinking that, yes," Sherry admitted.

In Doug's case, the four adults who could've potentially stopped the abuse were his Uncle Tony and Aunt Cheryl then dad and mom. The answer depends on which adult.

Uncle Tony and Aunt Cheryl knew something was wrong but couldn't prove it, as facts are hard to find in Santa Brisa when the military transfers you from P-Cola to Guam. (Uncle Tony's life story is fascinating and Douglas hoped his cousin would get around to telling it someday.)

But another stop in the endless cycle of transfers was close to Santa Brisa and Uncle Tony swore he knew something was wrong with Grandma May and encouraged his dad to move the family.

That helped. Even if Uncle Tony couldn't pinpoint the problem, it was evidence that there was one. It was evidence that the two primary adults in the situation, Douglas's mom and dad, could have done more than they did. But why didn't they?

"Dad told me," Doug continued, "that he was out of the house lots, which is true. But I don't quite believe him when he claims he didn't know what was going on. After all, Rose remembers mom sitting in dad's lap, crying, begging dad to get us out of there. What was mom telling dad while she sat on his lap?"

"I don't know. And dad won't talk about it. I do know money was tight when I was a kid, so perhaps dad knew what was going on but felt powerless to stop it. His mother-in-law was his landlady."

"Have you thought about asking your father more about it?" Sherry suggested.

"I'd press dad on the issue," he responded, "but bringing it up makes him angry, and it's just not worth it. He's told me all he's going to and that's all I'll ever learn from him. What can I say? I love my dad."

"That takes me to mom and that's a harder story to tell."

He hesitated and stared at the ceiling. He often went blank on these occasions and after 10 or 15 seconds couldn't help but wonder: when did he simply feel blank and when was he having a focal seizure? Then he thought again, 'sufficient unto the day is the evil thereof.' Or as we might say 500 years after King James, don't go borrowing trouble.

"Mom, mom, mom, mom, mom," he repeated. "I've mentioned her but talking about her is difficult. She did some things wrong and I don't like admitting her actions wounded me. It's far easier to think, 'mom was good' and 'Momma May was bad' than to admit that both women are a mix of love and pain.

"Let's skip to talk about Rose instead for the moment."

Sherry blinked, "Why the jump?"

"Mom's dead," he explained. "Unfortunately, but up to now I've been talking about hard evidence: court records you can see, or people you, Sherry, can go talk to like dad or Uncle Tony and Aunt Cheryl. Rose is still alive too, fortunately, so she falls into the category of hard evidence. If we talk about mom, we have to rely on my memory and I don't want to go there just yet."

"That makes sense," Sherry agreed. "So what does Rose remember?"

Before Doug's dad built the fence, Momma May could and did creep into the house through the side door without being noticed. One night, Momma May crept by John and Douglas's bedroom (John got the top bunk) late one evening on her way to Rose's room. Doug woke to her patter of footsteps, puzzled and told John he was going to follow.

"Leave it alone, Doug! She'll know it's you and come in here instead!"

"OK," Doug bounced back to the present. "That's my memory but Rose confirms it. Also, she recently filled in the rest of the story. Momma May came into her room and showed my sister how to masturbate when she was nine years old—by molesting her, routinely.

"Momma May just kept doing it and her tastes were both insatiable and catholic—men, little boys, dogs and little girls like Rose, my sister."

"Dogs," Sherry repeated.

"Yup. Dogs," Douglas confirmed. "That switches over to my memory only, which means I can't confirm it. Want me to continue?"

"Of course. I'll keep what you said in mind, but with confirmation like that from your family, I'm inclined to believe most of your memories. Go on about what you were saying about dogs."

"Okey-dokey. I don't like this memory, but I watched Momma May take off her blouse, naked from the waist up, put dog food on interesting places, then have her pet dachshund lick it off."

Sherry looked ill. "That woman had absolutely no sense of boundaries," she said again. "How old were you?"

Douglas shrugged again, "Maybe eight or nine? Old enough that this is a firmer memory than some of the others.

"Did your real mother, your mom, know what was going on? And if so, was she abusing you, too?" The subject was distasteful to Sherry, too.

He thought about it, looking for the words. This time, Doug found them.

"I dunno. But Mom was an enabler," he said. "My parental relationships until I was nine reminds me of a spy ring. There were three folks inside the ring: mom, Momma and myself, four if you add my sister. Dad was the cutout, the contact between licit and illicit activities. John was out of the picture but probably knew some of what was happening.

"Which means mom may not have abused me, but she certainly knew I was being abused. And she didn't stop it, or couldn't. But she knew."

"You're sure about that."

"Yeah."

Douglas watched mom and Momma May fight over where May was allowed to abuse him—right in front of him, as if he weren't there. The gist was mom didn't want Doug to visit Momma May in her cottage unless mom was present. Momma May was going like . . . how's this going to work again? You want me to take care of Douglas while you're taking classes and you don't want him in my house?

They argued some more over it. Loudly. Finally, mom got Momma to promise to *stop* taking Douglas into the back bedroom, when he was alone with my grandmother. Momma May kept this promise.

"And how many times was I there alone with my grandmother before that argument?" Douglas asked.

Sherry returned a question for a question, "Do you remember any incidents?"

"Dribs and drabs. I can remember sleeping with her. Just sleeping with her, I mean. But it wasn't like I went to her bed because I was scared or something like that. I went to bed with her because she said it was bedtime or nap time. I can remember waking up feeling like I was Momma May's rag doll."

"She petted you?" Sherry asked.

"Some, I think."

"But incidents like that stopped after your mom talked to May."

"Yes, or rather, no. That is, May stopped abusing me in the bedroom. Not that this helped any because I was abused in the living room, too.

"That's another clear memory. May pulled me on top of her in the middle of the floor and showed me where to touch her to make her happy. She cried when I said I'd do anything to make her happy, and said I couldn't just yet. I'd have to wait a few years."

"And you were . . . what? Seven years old?"

"Maybe eight or nine. The thing is I remember enough to know that wasn't the first or only time."

Douglas decided that this was a good time to discuss the value of memories.

Memories can be tricky, even when relatives confirm the events, because the emotional pain distorts your role in it. Doug dreamed about a hot date with Anne the other night then woke up sleepily thinking: Gee, this reminds me of the time I molested my grandmother.

Ding! It's negative schema time: 'I'm evil.' 'It's my fault.' 'I sinned.' Rape victims often blame themselves. Douglas did that Big time.

But let's get something straight. Doug was 8 years old in 1965; Momma May was 53. In exactly what way was he molesting her? It was the other way around. Momma May molested Douglas. It's important to get the pointers straight.

Memories are also tricky because of decay. Did mom do this or was it Momma May? Did Aunt Cheryl say this or was it Aunt Maxine? The separation is crucial because Douglas gets mom confused with Momma May in the first place. Douglas had two mothers, one of whom consistently abused him. Which one? The sands of time move against the separations.

Lastly, memories are inhibited by pain. More than once, Douglas simply stared at the ceiling tiles or looked outside at the garden. It's difficult to go there again.

"But talking about my grandmother is a good way to get rid of her," he ended. "Same as Gothard and there's no use letting hatred poison the system. I need to talk about what memories I have. Next week."

It had been a very tough session, which made Doug all the gladder for a convertible that gave him happiness. He relaxed, turned on the radio, and settled into the driver's seat. This time, his radio was playing a pop song by Barbra Streisand—something about memories.

*August 15, 2007, at home*

*Dear Jacky,*

I just calmed down from another panic attack. I'm not sure if they start from my arthritis, from May, from my apnea, from being too hot in bed, or what. But they sure are disruptive. My heart starts pounding so fast that I worry about getting a heart attack. Then I worry about worrying. The arthritis burns like fire and maybe that reminds of the times I really have been burned. I'm afraid that I'll get cancer, again.

I wanted so badly to cross-dress and play with my Barbie dolls. I could hear this little girl inside me just sobbing and feeling afraid—wanting to hold my hand, wanting to draw in my Barbie coloring book, wanting to feel the satin and caress of my skirt and panties. I don't know what to make of this.

It's easy to get diagnostic. When I get this panicky, my personality divides and I want to hide inside being a girl—being a little girl playing with my dollies. Do I want to comfort the girl that I am without being

293

the girl that I am or want to be? How do I comfort the little boy that I am without becoming the panicked little boy that I am?

Child abuse is so insidious, speaking from the inside of it, partly because it damages the mechanisms humans need to heal the damage in the first place. There's tons of shit up in your head and no way to get it out. The damage can be physical, not just emotional. The brain of a severely abused child is changed.

There's an article about this in *Scientific American*, May 2002. Sexually abused children have a hardware problem. The corpus callosum is abnormally thin, so the child and later the adult is subject to rapid hemisphere shifts in the brain—fast anger, fast recovery.

I feel, or rather, I don't feel, such a blasé shrug about this right now. I am a sexually abused kid. I can write about it, but as an adult it's easier for me to block the rapid hemisphere shifts. On the other hand, it sure does make life dull. After all, you end up stuck in one hemisphere. I can function over here, but it feels so flat, without dimension.

Of course, I could probably let myself feel all the joy and pain too, but then I'd risk flashing out into the other hemisphere and losing control. Oh, hurrah. I'm not blocking out the pain anymore. I'm simply screaming at folks instead.

This still happens. Then Anne gets the brunt of my yelling. Sigh! I'm not entirely healed. The good news is that my therapist finds me to be an interesting case. The bad news is that I don't *want* to be an interesting case because only the boring cases have easy solutions.

Or as mom said while dying of cancer, "Medicine is all very fascinating stuff, except for the fact that it's happening to you." The *Scientific American* article on sexually abused children sure is fascinating. My apologies to Commander Spock.

I want all of me to work together. I want my mind and heart to feed each other, to love each other. I want both brain hemispheres to heal.
*Love,*
*Douglas*

*August 23, 2007, in session*

This time it was Sherry who opened the session. "You said that that your brother John was mostly out of the picture. Why was that?"

Douglas grinned. "Because he's a super-genius. Like House or one of those annoying super-doctors you see on TV, except in John's case he's the real deal."

"Oh?"

"Yeah. The longer story might be worth telling, but the short version is that mom and dad put John into the 1960s equivalent of a Gifted and Talented (GATE) school. That school was over an hour away by bus, so John wasn't home for at least two more hours a day than I was.

"Plus mom and dad hovered over John, grooming his natural abilities. The mentality back then was 'the rich get richer' so talented people got more attention and John has talent running out his nose, plus he's first-born. Momma May had much less chance to get her nasty paws on him than she did with Rose and me."

Sherry nodded and took yet another note. "What's the longer story?" She was naturally curious.

John had been showing signs of genius for a few years, but his parents wanted to confirm his intelligence and get a better fix on it before deciding how to handle the situation.

Everyone in the family was tested and John was found to have an IQ of OMG! In fact, the entire family, including Douglas, tested on the genius scale. But perhaps because he was the youngest, Doug scored just a few points below the others.

"Yeah, I'm the family retard," he said. "Got treated like it too sometimes."

"How did that test impact you?" Sherry asked.

"It's been a mixed blessing," he replied. "On the one hand, I seriously get tired of teachers telling me, 'If you only do half as well as your brother . . . ' yadda, yadda. I attended the same GATE school five years after John and I got that all the time.

"But on the other hand, it's been good for me because I've never felt the pressure and expectations John did. I've never had to worry about being the smartest guy in the room because I already know I'm not. Mostly that's a good thing; helps me relax.

"But opening up the fridge to grab that third hand," Doug grinned, "I get tired of folks underestimating me. Experts keep trying to explain technology to me at work, or theology to me at church or whatever and don't listen when I tell them that (a) I already know, (b) they're probably wrong and (c) here's the right thing instead.

"It might get back to my speech impediment, or being the younger brother of Mr. Super Genius, whatever. Sometimes I feel lost in the shadows even when I'm doing my best to explain things clearly."

He paused. "That might be another schema, though I'm not sure it's a negative one."

"What is?"

"Cassandra," Doug replied. "The Trojan prophetess in *The Illiad* who always predicted the future correctly. But her warnings were ignored because she'd pissed off Apollo and he ordained that her prophecies would never be believed. Then the gods ordered her to tell Troy they were going to lose."

"That doesn't sound fair," Sherry commented.

295

"It wasn't, not that the Greeks were concerned with fairness. But she hadn't done anything to deserve the curse. It was just that Apollo got mad at her because she didn't want to sleep with him or something like that. Been a while since I read that.

"But anyway, the point: I often feel like Cassandra, especially at work, doomed to predict what will happen if we take a given course with no one believing me. I'll tell folks that what they're doing will fail, they'll listen politely sometimes and do it anyway. Then it'll fail."

"Is that something you want to change?" Sherry asked.

Douglas tapped his fingers on his knee. "Maybe. The problem isn't about being right. It's about not being believed and I'm not sure how much I can change that. But perhaps."

"Why aren't you believed?"

"Not positive, possibly because I'm a generalist looking at the whole system and they won't believe someone who is not in their specialty. I could get a BS or PhD in their specialty, I suppose, but sooner or later I'll just deal with someone else in the system who doesn't have the same degree and it's back to the same story. I can't possibly get doctorates in every part of the system, so I'm Cassandra."

Sherry noted the obvious, "There are ways to improve your communication skills."

"I know some and use some. It doesn't seem to be make any difference. Maybe I could get better yet, but it's one reason I prefer to write than talk. I'm better at it and I'm more likely to be understood."

Sherry agreed with him. "That makes sense. Was there anything else you wanted to talk about? We've got a minute or two extra."

He nodded. "I'll make this brief."

Douglas often hid from May behind a patterned magic fan painted with a Japanese garden, house, and white-capped mountains in the background. The fan has a red tassel. Doug held it as a barrier between himself and May, pretending to admire it or to hide his poker tells. The fan let him drift into another world.

She'd yell at him if he didn't fold the fan properly and that gave him an excuse to fuss, bending folds back and forth. He ripped a fan once, but May wasn't as angry as he thought she'd be. She screamed at him, of course, but it must have been her least favorite fan, or maybe she already knew that it was getting old. Anyway, Douglas paid Choko out of his allowance to buy May another one and everything was OK.

He still has that fan. It's one of the few reminders of May he keeps, because he used it to block her out and he bought it fair and square.

"Who's Choko?" Sherry asked.

"Aargh. So many folks to talk about," The topic upset him somehow, "Choko was May's best friend; her family had been confined at Manzanar, the Japanese internment camp during World War II. They met at a department store where Choko also worked sewing alterations."

He thonked his head. "And now I'll need to talk about Manzanar."

Sherry nodded, "Those sound like a good topic for next time."

# The Good, the Bad

*September 6, 2007, in session*

As his sessions gradually shifted to biweekly, Doug grew tired of it all. Sherry once said that counseling is repetitive listening. The patient typically stops coming when they finally bore themselves silly.

A bit cynical perhaps, but repeating oneself does allow stories to sink in, at which point the stories stop controlling you and you finally control them. It's just that some old stories are extremely difficult to discuss even once.

Fortunately, Manzanar, the large Japanese internment camp in WWII, wasn't one of them. Choko gave him a detailed and literally first-hand account of Manzanar well before the incident became a cachet. She was there.

Better yet, Choko was one of the children who wrote letters about Manzanar to a children's librarian down in San Diego, Miss Clara Breed. The letters eventually went into the Smithsonian. The next time Douglas was down in San Diego to visit his grandfather, he asked to visit the library, talked to Miss Breed, then read the original letters—40 years before they were published.

So when Carter opened an investigation in 1980 into the internment, Douglas's going like . . ."Huh? 38 years and you still haven't read your own history books? Let's see here. Hmm. Did we really violate the Constitution when we violated the Constitution?"

Reagan finally issued an apology and compensation in 1988 and this time he's going like . . ."Ah ha! Let's study the obvious for eight more years!" Eight years? Why wasn't something done much, much sooner? Was Miss Breed the only person with her head on straight?

Letters from somewhere unusual became a common theme.

His (birth) mother had met some folks during her trip to Paris and they corresponded. They connected her to a pen pal club and soon she was writing pen-friends in Germany, Taiwan, Singapore and Peru. Then she sponsored a child in Hong Kong through a missionary organization and wrote him, too. He wrote back frequently and the letters just kept coming. Every night his mom would do her school work first, then sit down for an hour or two to write letters.

One evening Douglas went up to her and tried to talk. She listened to his stuttering lisp for a moment, gave him a quick hug then turned back to writing Pengfei in Hong Kong. For the second time that week.

He went and found his Dad. "D-d-d-dad," he asked "Does M-m-m-mom -ha-ha-have a-a-nother sh-sh-sh-un in-in H-hong-K-kong?"

His father laughed. "No. That's just Pengfei. It means 'the flight of the Roc,'" then he explained the mythology and went back to grading science papers.

At least his dad had spent a bit of time with him—more than his mom had—but it still felt dismissive. He needed his mother, not his dad. And he felt abandoned by his mother for someone she'd never met.

Sherry interrupted his storytelling, something she did rarely. "Do you see the common themes?" she asked.

Doug was puzzled. "What themes?"

"Justice. In particular, social justice. Choko's family was treated unfairly then ignored for years. So were you."

He leaned his head back and stared at the white tiles for a moment. "I'd forgotten about Choko," he said slowly. "And I'd forgotten about Manzanar because I'd forgotten about my grandmother. To find one for me is to find the other, to remember the good with the bad.

"The injustice of Manzanar became one of my drivers. All I had to do is look at Choko. I didn't expect to change the government or to suddenly change human hearts, but justice is important to me. Perhaps I can create more justice around me in small ways."

Sherry smiled at him. "Start with yourself. If you can seek justice for Manzanar, you can seek justice for yourself."

He stared at her "How do I do that?"

She rose to leave. "Keep coming here. Find the pieces of your soul that you lost in the fog around Momma May then put them back together."

*September 20, 2007, in session*

Remembering the good with the bad was still a good theme.

Momma May made the best marmalade ever, sort of a Dundee. Her backyard orange tree produced succulent oranges that were a true pleasure by themselves, but when you cut them up to make marmalade, it became OMG! Orgasm à la bouche. Doug never did learn May's exact recipe, but the trick is to leave in the bitterness and not use too much sugar.

May also worked as the chief seamstress at a department store. Wanting to stay ahead of her competition as top dog (her employer used rank stacking) she pulled apart her home sewing machine one day, jury-rigged an extra attachment then jigsawed everything back together again.

Still not satisfied, she repeated the process a few weeks later and MacGyvered the Godzilla of all sewing machines.

Ten years later, she finally found a commercial product that had the same features. Well, almost all of them. But up to then, you simply couldn't buy what she'd designed and built by herself. Or at least, so she claimed.

"My grandmother," Doug declared "was a hardware engineer. Ha! And I learned product testing, my job now, from my grandmother, watching her pull apart a sewing machine, understanding the whole by analyzing items piece by piece. I made design suggestions and kept track of features. Snort.

"Being around May could be fun! She laughed frequently, a raucous cackle of genuine pleasure. She liked gambling, excitement, improvising. Dad is a bit like this too and they shared an odd camaraderie. Dad had more formal training at this than my grandmother did, so May sometimes asked for his help."

"How often did that happen?" Sherry asked.

"Not often. She usually worked it out on her own. Let me tell you a story about that.

"Choko's house was on a street corner. One day a car ran the intersection and smashed into a corner of the house, dislodging it from the foundation. May and Choko fixed it by themselves. They did all the engineering and used dad only as the grunt on the hydraulic jack. She was so proud of that one. Dad could-ah done it all by himself, of course, but dad wasn't there at the time."

Bill Baign very rarely was. Doug has some great memories of his dad during the summer, especially on the family camping trips after summer school—collecting rocks, traveling Route 66, or backpacking in Yosemite. "That's another book, Sherry." But he wasn't there during the school year.

Sherry kept probing. "Do you remember any other good things during that part of your childhood?"

"Yeah," he confirmed. "But before I get there, some memories seem so unbelievable, even when they're corroborated. It feels weird to talk about the world 50 years ago. It was such a different era in so many different ways that it seems like fiction."

"I know that feeling," Sherry agreed. "I moved here in the 1970s."

"OK. That gives you a feel for it, but double that because it's the 1960s.

When Douglas was born, the California ocean was dotted with tiny, beautiful towns up and down the coast—Malibu, Dana Point, Capistrano, Pismo Beach, Cambria, Cardiff-by-the-Sea—with lush beaches between each town.

One of Douglas's neighbors ran into him the other day and talked up the wonderful beach he'd found near Lucia. Had he ever been there?

Yup. But he didn't have the heart to tell his neighbor that it *used* to be a good beach. 50 years ago. Now he can't visit the beach without pushing his way through waves of people and cars.

"I hiraeth the place, especially those uncrowded beaches."

Sherry asked for clarification, "You used that word before but I can't remember the definition."

"*Hiraeth* is the homesick longing for a place that no longer exists."

Sherry nodded. "I can understand that. Go on."

One of Douglas's odder memories is when the family went down to San Diego to visit grandpa when he was five or six. Grandpa took him to Mission Valley to learn how to milk cows.

Now Mission Valley is eight square miles of shopping centers, condos, and high rises. It's a complete zoo, as far as Doug is concerned. You go there to watch humans in their natural mall habitat.

The Tea Room is another odd memory. The one in downtown Santa Brisa has long since been replaced, but back in the 1960s the stylish department store was four stories of posh shopping. The fifth floor was the Tea Room itself, dedicated to serving tea and lunch to weary shoppers and their children or grandchildren. Douglas always looked forward to punching "5" in the elevator.

You could tell what floor you were on by the style of the pillars supporting the ceiling. The pillars in the tea room were green and modern, adding to the rich and integrated whole. The kitchen was on the way to the dining area. Douglas would drool just looking at the platters full of spice pie, deservedly famous, delicious and they went fast!

Small lovely lamps decorated the Tea Room walls and Douglas was fascinated by the colors and shapes they could cast. The children's menu was simple. He had creamed chicken over toast and a Coke—Douglas's only other choice was PB&J. Models wandered around the tables while you ate, displaying the latest fashions in women's clothes.

"One day I decided to be a model," Douglas explained. "The patrons were all women buying clothes for themselves or their children and there were no child models. Pretty simple business model, get one.

"I expected resistance but Momma May was easy to convince and so was the business manager. So off into the back I went and soon I found myself wandering the lunchroom floor—modeling boy's clothing.

"Modeling, I decided very rapidly, was boring. The only mental challenge was noticing who was noticing you and figuring out when to wander by the person's table. Or conversely, avoiding certain tables. Piece of cake or rather, pie. I snagged a free piece of apple that day. Man, that was good stuff!"

There was no particular place for child models to change, so at the end of the shift he found himself in the women's dressing room watching the models changing clothes. The model next to him was shy and commented she was worried about what he'd see between her legs. He glanced at the partially-clad model rather puzzled and said not to worry about it. There was nothing to see. She was reassured, lifted up her skirt, and pulled the rest of her stockings up to her crotch right in front of him. He was eight years old.

Douglas summarized the experience. "I was a male tea room fashion model, probably the only one.

To remember the good with the bad is to remember the bad with the good.

# And the Ugly

Grandpa Schneider, aka Slime Bag to Momma May, was one of several relatives who lived in San Diego. The Baigns visited him once in a while and Douglas liked grandpa. His two daughters from his second marriage weren't that much older than him, so they'd play Marco Polo in his pool together or listen to 1960s rock in Aunt Karen's room. She had the best stereo.

Grandpa would sometimes take Douglas out, just the two of them. They visited Balboa Park, took an insider's tour of San Diego's submarine base, went out on practice maneuvers with the Naval River combat boats in Mission Bay and so on.

"If you don't believe me," he added. "I've got the Super 8s complete with me walking down the gangplank. Grandpa was a sub vet, remember? He knew lots of folks in interesting places and this was the 1960s. I can't speak for my other relatives, but he always treated me well."

Douglas re-entered the reverie of storytelling.

❧❧❧

One day Grandpa took Douglas to the Del Mar Race Track. They bought seats two-thirds of the way up the grandstand and by post time Douglas noticed 30 or so men clotted together near the front row. They were all dressed alike in formal white suits and white hats and stood out from the crowd like a sore thumb.

"Who are they?" Douglas asked Grandpa, pointing them out. "And why are they all dressed alike? All those silly straw hats."

"They're not straw hats. They're called fedoras," said grandpa, "and that's probably Hoover and the FBI." Watching the Del Mar horse races was one of Hoover's few indulgences.

Cool! Any kid in the 1960s knew who J. Edgar Hoover was, so Douglas wanted to introduce himself right away. Just walk right up to J. Edgar and say, "Hi!" Grandpa didn't think this was such a good idea.

"But grandpa!" he protested. "I want them to know who we are!"

"They probably already know. Or at least, they know who I am. Let's not introduce ourselves."

🙰🙰🙰

"Ah well," Doug told Sherry. "My one chance to impress J. Edgar Hoover and it's nixed by grandpa. Yup. Grandpa knew lots of folks in interesting places."

Sherry added a note then asked, "Did you meet any of those 'interesting people' yourself?"

"Yeah. But not through grandpa."

🙰🙰🙰

Momma May knew many of the same folks. The difference was that grandpa had just gotten out of trouble with the local crime scene by dumping his ex-wife into it then moving to a different city entirely, not that Doug understood this at the time. To Douglas he was just grandpa. But when it came to Momma May, the local mob had a deep and abiding interest in protecting their investment.

They wandered into May's house from time to time but usually just got lost in the shuffle of boy toys moving in and out of her house. ("And other places too," he added. "But I digress.")

But Douglas was surprised one day when he brushed past the beads hung across the doorway, walked into the cottage and saw, if you'll pardon the expression, a whole mob. At least four or five men in black suits and fedoras were standing in the living room talking to his grandmother.

The whole black/white game reminded Douglas of *Mad Magazine*'s "Spy-vs-Spy," but this was the 1960s. Subtlety wasn't its strong suit. That was music.

At any rate, Doug overheard them ask May if she knew a way across the border without all that inconvenience of dealing with U.S. Customs. The bureaucracy took too long and was a hassle, something to which he could relate, as waiting in line to get back into the US was a bore.

"You must not be from here," Doug piped up.

One of them looked puzzled and asked, "Why do you say that?"

"Because anyone from Southern California knows there's a big hole in the fence a few hundred yards west of the main entrance," Douglas replied. "You just walk through. Everyone around here uses it." The Baign family had in fact used it once or twice themselves . . . going south, very convenient.

305

"Really?" the mob was interested, but skeptical. But May vouched for Douglas and the route, and a few weeks later they showed up again with smiles on their faces.

"You done good, kid," one of them said, then flipped him a silver dollar—Douglas's share of the take.

~~~~~~~~~~

Doug laughed "I still have that silver dollar in my coin collection, Sherry. The silver alone is worth about 20 bucks. And I have 23 silver dollars. I probably got two or three silver dollars in circulation, maybe even five or ten. But not 23. So it makes me wonder: what else was I doing?

*October 18, 2007, in session*

Sherry started the next session.

"How did you feel as a child being around criminals?"

He nodded. It was a good question to ask.

"Well, they didn't feel like criminals to me. They were just people. I can laugh about it now, but it wasn't funny then. Not because it's 'deadly serious crime business' but because crime was normal. There was nothing to laugh at. It just happened, like being molested. You don't laugh at something normal.

"The normality makes my childhood emotions hard to describe, Sherry, because it's easier to remember something unusual. Molestation, crime and Momma May screaming at me weren't unusual."

"Do you remember any feelings at all?"

He shivered. "Yeah. Terror, fear. There was a constant edge of fear in my life. Fear of being beaten, fear of being caught. Not caught as a crook, being caught as May's seven-year-old boy toy. Being molested was my fault, my shame. It was a secret never to be exposed. I was always looking over my shoulder."

The fear remained as coldness on his skin.

"I also remember the loneliness, feeling very, very lonely. Fear and loneliness were constant companions. Remember that stuffed Dalmatian Momma May made for me?"

Sherry consulted her notes, "That's a long ways back." She flipped some more pages. "The Dalmatian without eyes because you told May that it had eyes all over its body. Is that the one?"

"Yeah. That's the one and that's how I felt. I had eyes all over my body, watching and waiting, looking for people to avoid and places to hide. But with a Dalmatian, there was someone else to watch and guard, to talk to, to give me company. I loved that toy so much."

He paused a moment to look at the garden. The outside was fine. The inside still hurt.

"I feel like there's something missing," he continued. "Like I'm not telling you something, not because I don't want to but because I can't remember, or can't find the words to describe the loneliness."

Words came easier for Douglas now in therapy. But the tenderness, the prickliness of his wounds still clung to him. He couldn't always describe his feelings out loud. He still couldn't talk all the time.

He tried to get at the emotions.

"May was my guardian. She took care of me maybe four hours every day while mom finished college during the day or acted parts onstage at local theaters at night. Mom was a good actress, too! She—my real mom—cared for me . . . oh, say . . . one or two hours a day and on weekends. But May was my guardian.

"Being with May meant fear and loneliness. May screamed at me, got drunk, chain-smoked like a locomotive, and ordered me around like I was her stevedore or clerk, not like her grandchild. May taught me swear words, then mom washed my mouth out with soap when I used them. Not fair, as if childhood ever is, but what are you teaching your child?

"Ha! Thinking of *101 Dalmatians*, May (or maybe mom) was Cruella de Vil. Maybe that's why I liked the movie so much. It was easy to relate to. May was cruel and unpredictable."

*Rudolph the Red-Nosed Reindeer* was another film he liked in the 1960s. He felt like a misfit toy, without the happy ending. Instead, he was whipped for being a misfit, then kept as a misfit so he could be whipped.

"God created me to be a whipping boy. And yes, I mean 'whipping' literally."

Douglas stopped and Sherry raised an eyebrow, "Yes?" she prompted.

"That's another negative schema, isn't it?"

Sherry confirmed his guess, "Right. God did not create you to be whipped or molested."

Sherry shares her shore-side offices with a short lady named Charlene. (Try saying that fast three times running.) That day a few kids were playing loudly in the lobby during Douglas's session while their mom or dad visited Sherry's partner.

"Come with me," Sherry asked Doug. He was curious what this was all about and followed along.

Sherry took him out to the lobby then got the two kids, a brother and sister's, attention, "Please be quiet!" she asked. "You're right outside the door and it might open at any time. You'd be hurt!"

The Sherry took him back into her office and closed the door. "How old were those kids?"

Douglas wasn't sure, "Maybe . . . the older girl was six or seven with a three- or four-year-old brother?"

Sherry nodded, "That sounds about right. Now remember. You were the same age as those children when you were molested. Did God create them to be molested?"

"Of course not!" Douglas was appalled by the idea.

"Then neither were you. It's not your fault. Your grandmother molested you. You were the victim. You're innocent."

It was a revelation. It's one thing to think of yourself as young; it's another to see yourself in another child. Everyone once was young. Everyone was once a child.

One stage for a molested child in forgiving himself is to realize there is no guilt to accrue. You didn't do anything wrong in the first place. You were a child. You're still the same child now, still clutching a stuffed Dalmatian with eyes all over its body—stuttering, scared, and lonely. And innocent.

*November 1, 2007, in session*

Douglas's grandmother May had no aspiration of being a professional criminal. So after she spent seven or eight years doing favors for the Mob, another man in a black fedora showed up in the spring of 1965 and negotiated an offer she couldn't refuse. Do 10 more favors and she'd be done.

"Remember, I was there during the negotiation," he told Sherry, "So yup, it was 10. I have no idea what the favors were but May was in no position to argue, though other positions may have been suggested."

"And no one removed you from the situation?" Sherry asked.

"Who woulda done that? Mom and dad weren't there and May was my guardian. Mom wanted her to keep an eye on me as much as possible."

Sherry shook her head, "Do continue."

❦❦❦

There were a few difficulties. First, another man showed up and treated the first particular black hat with deference. #1 was a Bigwig; second, #1 Bigwig was insistent on keeping the transactions, whatever they were, *sotto voce*. So how to conduct business quietly under the table directly in front of the noses of the family who lived there (Douglas's)? Tricky, that.

Douglas thought about it a bit and chimed in, "Why not do this on Saturdays? Mom and dad will be tied up for the next several Saturdays with Rose, and John is out visiting friends."

Then #1 Bigwig mulled it over and asked May: "Who will take care of the kid on Saturdays?"

"He meant me, Sherry."

Sherry nodded. "Yes, I followed that."

"Junior," I suggested, meaning junior Mob dude.

"I need him as lookout in the front yard."

"No problem. I'll stay with him." It seemed like a simple solution and it was so arranged. #1 Bigwig and May conducted business 10 times at or in the back of grandmother's cottage during the spring and early summer while Junior and Douglas took lookout.

The first week Junior was wary about anybody walking down the street. Douglas started ID-ing folks to allay his suspicions. Maria was in the de Tio family next door, for example, or that crazy old lady Mrs. Anderson lived across the street, as did the Mendez family.

"I liked the Mendezes, Sherry. They cooked terrific Mexican food, and I almost knocked over their piñata at a party one year. Great family!"

By the third week, Junior could identify all the homies for himself, so they could relax and chat while May and #1 Bigwig did whatever they did in the back.

"Good guy, Junior. I sorta miss him."

May was free of her debt and the Mob by late summer, and Junior became one of May's regular clients. In the meantime, mom and dad and the rest of the family were never the wiser. They'd never met #1 Bigwig, and as far as they were concerned, Junior was just another one of May's satisfied boyfriends du noir.

❦❦❦

"You should have been removed from that situation based on the criminal activity alone," Sherry commented.

Douglas shrugged. "Mom probably didn't know about that end of it—the molestation, yes, the crime, no. Dad wasn't there and my grandmother was part of the problem."

"My point," Sherry said, "has nothing to do with the practicality of the situation. My point is that you were in a toxic and dangerous adult situation that was damaging you."

It wasn't clear he understood the significance of her comment. "That's why I'm here, I guess."

Sherry just shook her head again, "Did your grandmother's criminal behavior stop?"

"After that? Uhhh. Mostly yes, I think," Douglas responded.

May remarried five or so years after the Baign family left her property then began to reform. She stopped smoking, stopped drinking, read the Bible, went to church, and began treating her step-children and step-grandchildren really well. When she finally died, her step-grandchildren stood up at the memorial service and talked about how wonderful a grandmother she'd been—the only real grandmother they'd ever known.

"I kept my mouth shut and should get a Nobel Peace Prize for that alone.

"In the meantime, what about the boy? What about the kid who was whipped and molested? Does he ever get a chance at redemption?"

"What about him?" Sherry asked. "What happened to you next?"

※ ※ ※

Douglas ran up to Junior a month or so later as he walked under the orange tree and gave him a big hug. They chatted a bit and he told Douglas his fantasy. He'd spent time alone with Momma May and now he wanted to spend time alone with mom. That way he could brag about having mother and daughter—as if, for anyone who's seen photos of mom when she was 33, he needed further motivation. He'd pay well.

It made sense to Douglas. He went and found May, who rounded up mom and the three of them had a confab. Mom wasn't thrilled about the idea, but May pointed out that she desperately needed the money, which would in turn help the kids.

"What about Billy?" mom asked. Douglas pointed out that there was no particular reason to tell dad what she was doing, and they discussed plans further. Finally, a date and time was arranged when Junior could enjoy mom's company in private.

※ ※ ※

"At the age of eight," Douglas told Sherry, "I had just pimped out my own mother, the great lady who was buried as a church icon. And my mother was that desperate to leave the situation to protect her kids."

"You should not have been consulted for that decision," Sherry was adamant. "Either your mother or grandmother should have removed you from the discussion immediately. And they didn't. The same logic applies with being a lookout for the Mob or with suggesting ways to smuggle. You should not have been a party to their behavior."

But rather than remove Douglas from a life of crime at age eight, his grandmother pulled him into it. That isn't his fault. That isn't his guilt.

# And The Evening And The Morning Were The Last Day

# Sunset

"I'm retiring," Sherry said. The words didn't surprise Douglas for some reason. Sherry was older than he was.

"When?" he asked.

"At the beginning of the year; the landlord wants to raise the lease rates by then anyway."

"Will I still be able to see you?"

Sherry nodded, "Yes. I won't be taking any new patients, but you clearly don't fit into that category. I'm telling you now because I won't be in this office in January. We'll have to meet at my husband's office." Sherry's husband was a lawyer.

"OK," Doug confirmed, "I'll have to know where that is."

"I'll give you the address later. Let's go back to therapy. We're far enough along that we can begin to summarize. How do you feel?"

The question would have irritated him five years ago. Now he just scratched his head. "After six and a half years of therapy? Blank, empty, unfinished. Blank is good. Especially when compared to depressed and suicidal. Empty is also an improvement; unfinished, not so much."

"We'll have more time to continue and finish, if you like," Sherry comforted.

"For which I thank the good Lord."

Sherry prodded him. "Can you say more about how you feel now?"

Douglas thought it over. Sherry retiring changed things in unexpected ways. He needed to think about retirement himself as his job was seriously getting him down and he had no intention of falling back into suicidal depression. So how did he feel?

"I'm still struggling with putting it all together," he said slowly. "Some of my stories feel so odd that it makes me wonder if anyone will really believe them. Besides, coming from such an odd angle at life, I see things that others don't. How do I convince them that my stories are real?

"For example, I ran into one of my Hosanna High friends from the 1970s the other day. We sat down for coffee nearby to swap lies and it turns out he'd been to L'Abri close to the same time frame I went. He

315

spent a few days there, had a great theological discussion at the dinner table and merrily went on his way feeling spiritually enriched.

"I try to do exactly the same thing and end up being mocked and belittled. What am I, a space alien?"

Sherry looked him over. "You don't look green to me. Besides, your third arm is in the refrigerator."

They both grinned.

"You've been through a lot of life events," Sherry continued, "that most people don't go through. It's not a wonder that you see things differently. But that doesn't invalidate your viewpoint, so don't worry about how other people see you. It's a question of how you see yourself."

That made sense. It'd probably take time for him to accept it, but that didn't worry him. The grind of therapy can produce some patience.

"What are you still struggling to put together?" Sherry asked.

"The pieces of my life before L'Abri." He didn't wait for Sherry to ask for more details. "When we first started therapy, I thought I only had to worry about two pieces—before and after L'Abri,

"But now I worry about four pieces: everything that happened to me in my very early childhood—molestation, crime and so on with Momma May; late elementary school and junior high; high school through L'Abri when I was 20, then everything after L'Abri."

Sherry rephrased her question to probe, "And you don't feel like you can put those pieces together."

Doug thought about it, "I kinda understand the last two pieces, junior high through L'Abri, at least in the sense that it's an order of events: junior high, Hosanna High, Leanne, UCSB, Deirdre, JECU, L'Abri. The first thing happened, the second thing happened.

"But everything falls back to Momma May, to my mother, to being an abused child, or even to just being a child. That's not so easy to talk about, because I don't have any chronology."

"You don't think you should just call her 'May'? Sherry asked. "She wasn't much of a mother."

"That's what Anne suggested," he responded. "Maybe later I'll do that, but for now I mean Momma May. My words don't have the force without speaking of her as my mother. My other mother. When I was a child, my mother, my Momma May, abused me."

He paused. "Dang I keep saying that. My apologies. But everything is so disordered in my head about being a child, beyond just being childhood memories, I mean. It's like I gotta say the same thing multiple times to just get the lines straight."

"Are there any other pieces of your childhood that are important?" Sherry asked. "At least, of those pieces you remember."

Douglas's mind drifted back to hiding in the canyon across the street from Momma May's house. He also remembered lots of cats. Butterscotch was his favorite, a beautiful cat about that color. And he remembered losing John's Flexi Flyer and playing in the garden mud under the trellis. Those memories were strong, but didn't feel important. Yet there were a few other memories that did.

"Maybe. I can remember seeing a skeleton walking down the street, for example. I know it wasn't a skeleton, but that's what my brain recorded. I hid behind the bushes and watched a skeleton walk by. Not a costume. A skeleton, the type you might see at a doctor's office."

"Were you depressed as a child?"

"I never thought of that before but yeah, probably so."

"Then that's probably a normal hallucination; normal for a depressed child, I mean."

"Yeah," he sat silently for a moment. "That's about all we can discuss for today, though, isn't it?"

"Yes," Sherry responded. "You're making good progress."

She kept saying that, but it didn't feel like it today. Perhaps it was the thought that Sherry was retiring, even though it didn't yet remove part of his support system. Douglas felt lonely and afraid.

*November 29, 2007, in session*

Douglas had finally learned to talk to Sherry despite feeling embarrassed, but it wasn't easy.

"I dreamed last night of 20 or 30 boys dancing in a circle," he started. "And I watch another man who was me get an erection about two feet long when he saw the boys and he was going to find and rape one.

"I am the rapist. I am the boy dancing near the fire. I am the watcher. And I want to weep over it all. Just weep and weep and weep."

He finally started to cry. It'd been eight months since the last time he had cried, and that had been when he first described being molested to Sherry.

Sherry let him cry some then gently asked. "What are you crying about?" His response came all at once.

"I don't feel like I can control what I say," he said. "I could talk about anything and I don't know what I'll talk about. Maybe I'd talk about the secret Momma May asked me to keep, the secret about my being her catamite, her whipping boy. Her call-girl prostitute and victim. I might even talk about that.

"But I can't talk about that secret, and I must talk about that secret.

"It gets all confusing again. I believe that I'll die if I talk about being her call-girl prostitute and I'm very, very scared. I believe that I'll die if I don't talk about it, and I'm worried that I'll lose my nerve when trying to talk about it. I believe that both me's in those last two sentences are making a mountain out of a molehill. But 'both of me' are very real to me. I believe in this."

Sherry followed the feelings, the gestalt. Doug was describing his pain.

"Ha!" he choked out. "It all reminds me of one of dad's T-shirts: 'Everyone has to believe in something. I believe I'll have another chocolate-chip cookie.' Well, not very many after his heart surgery. But it's true for dad. He really is like that, at least a little, and I'm proud of my father.

"But I am not my father. I don't believe I'll have another chocolate-chip cookie. I'd say that I'd have to get a different T-shirt, but I don't even believe in wearing them. I believe I have to find my own answers.

"It makes me feel sad again to think of that little boy. I feel sad because I see a hurt little boy. But what is sadder is that the hurt little boy that I am feels sad. I feel sad."

"Stop there, please," Sherry asked. Doug complied.

"Go back and repeat what you just said," Sherry directed.

"'I feel sad.'"

"Before that."

"I'm not sure I can repeat it exactly," Doug delayed while mustering his strength.

"Just whatever you can."

"OK. 'I feel sad because I see a hurt little boy. But it's even worse to know that I am the hurt little boy. I feel sad.'"

"And that makes you cry."

"Yes, I am the hurt little boy and I feel sad. It makes me cry."

Sherry explained the significance. "You're admitting it to yourself and that can be used to knit yourself together. You are the hurting child; you are the strong man here in session."

He thought it out. "I'm getting better," Douglas said. It was no longer something just said to encourage him. It was something he was starting to believe.

"Yes."

"You asked me last session how I felt."

"Yes."

"And I said that I feel blank, empty, and unfinished. A guess is that the 'adult me' feels OK and the 'child me' feels sad. Right now, they're about balanced to blankness, but this is unfinished business."

"Yes."

"You think I'm a strong man, too?" Douglas asked.

"It takes strength to admit your pain," was Sherry's response.

"That sounds like something Anne once said. She once suggested that I learn to say that I am a healing man. She was trying to encourage positive self-talk, and she has a point.

"But it's very, very difficult to understand that you are healing and really grok it, to cherish the healing, without first understanding that you are wounded and to grok and cherish that. I think it is difficult for me to say that I am healing because it is difficult for me to say that I am wounded.

"To say that I am wounded is to confess that I have a secret. I am Momma May's little gigolo slave girl. And I am a Man who chooses not to be, but chooses to be free.

"My goal here in therapy, Sherry, is to be able to say the one without first having to say the other, and once I am in fact free, to know the choices of my freedom and to choose among them wisely."

*December 13, 2007, in session*

It was the last session for a month or two while Christmas and New Year's passed and Sherry moved out of her offices. She opened the session by referring to her notes.

"Back in April you said: 'My mother raped me. I am not at the point of forgiveness. I am at the point where I realize that it hurts and that I can let myself cry.' By which you meant your Grandmother."

"But it wasn't until last session that you actually cried. Can you talk more about that?"

Douglas thought about it. "Sometimes therapy is so exhausting," he started, "that there's no room left for tears. And sometimes, I can't help but wonder. 'Maybe I'm not as far along in my therapy as I think. Maybe I'm not at the point of tears, but at the point of just trying to admit that it happened.' You can't cry at the facts if you're still denying them."

"You cried last session," Sherry pointed out. "And that means you're no longer denying the facts. How do you feel now?"

"You keep asking that question," Doug said wryly.

"It's a good question," Sherry asked. "As therapy moves along you're in different places. So how do you feel right now?"

"Right now?" he answered. "Right now it feels like a separate person somehow. Like it wasn't really me being raped. It felt that way when I used to cut myself. 'No, it's not really me doing this. It's another person.'

"I can understand why a murderer or rapist might plead innocent quite honestly. They didn't do it. It was someone else and O.J. just happened to be the only one there at the time. I believe this."

He paused to take a breath. The words were coming out in a cascade.

"It was me, it was me, it was me, it was me. I was raped. I was seduced. I was fucked. Momma told me to lie down on top of her then

319

showed me where to touch her to make her feel good. Momma made me wear a dress while she sized it for my sister. She was so happy to see me look like a girl. Momma lay on top to fondle me. I want to remember this. I need to remember this."

What once may have been a whisper came nearly as a shout.

"Oh, Lord! It was me, it was me, it was me."

He paused a few seconds, then continued. "I don't want to forget this, bury this, pretend it never happened. The way out of my wilderness is to admit that I'm in it.

"It's so confusing. There is such a strong urge to deny it. Momma May loved me. She's a good person. My family can't be like this. I believe in them, trust them, admire them, depend on them. I have to believe in my mother, I have to trust my mother, I have to, I have to, I have to. There's a certain babyishness to it because that's what I was thinking when I was a baby. I have to trust my mother."

"You mean your grandmother."

Douglas stopped for a moment, puzzled. "Grandmother? Mother? Both, I guess, but I think I meant my grandmother." He stopped again.

"Go on," Sherry encouraged. "You're doing well."

He wiped his hair back and continued.

"I told Rose once that the problem abused kids have, myself included, is a cross-circuit. You sincerely love your wife or girlfriend. Like anyone else, you want to express your love, so you sincerely want to beat up your wife. Isn't that the way my mother expressed love to me? That's my role model.

"'Afraid, are you?' Yoda once told Anakin, 'Fear leads to anger, anger leads to hate. Hate leads to the dark side of the Force.' Yeah. I've been there.

"I've never hit Anne, not even once. But yeah. I've wanted to. And yeah, I've yelled at her. Physical pain is not the only way to abuse. But she's still with me and I'm still in therapy. Ya gotta start by admitting you have a problem and that takes courage.

"But courage leads to patience, patience leads to love, and love leads to the bright side of the Force. I don't want to hurt my wife. If I can get that far, then I can learn the others."

"Dealing with the scars of abuse," returned Sherry, "is partly a process of learning to separate. I've said this before: Anger is not love. Abuse is not sex."

Douglas picked up on the thought, "To that I can add: Anne is not my mother or my grandmother."

"Yes."

"But understanding myself," he continued, "helps me to understand my birth mom. She was an abused child too, wasn't she? The logic that applies to me applies to her.

"The fact that my birth mom really did love me did not prevent her from wanting to seduce me."

"You mean your grandmother," Sherry corrected.

Douglas turned white, then answered slowly, "No, I meant my birth mom."

Sherry repeated him. "Your birth mother tried to seduce you."

"Yes."

"And you've never mentioned that before."

"I understand that," Doug agreed. "But I get tired of revealing all these . . ." he paused looking for the right words, " . . . mortifying incidents. They're beyond embarrassing, and there's only so many blood cells I can devote to blushing." The attempt at humor didn't help.

Sherry was sympathetic. "I've been through some of it myself. You have to go through therapy yourself to become a therapist, and I had to reveal my own issues."

"Have you ever been tempted to use revelations against a client?"

Sherry wasn't offended by the question. Doug needed reassurance, "Not really. Other than it being very unprofessional, it's good that I'm not emotionally invested in my clients."

"You have no agenda, other than to help people," he translated.

"Yes. Exactly. Of course, it helps that I can also earn money as a therapist."

"Of course," Douglas echoed. "Well, if you can do it then I guess I can, too."

The story itself was simple. One morning when he was about 13, Douglas woke early then stole one of his mom's slips from the hamper. He'd gone back to bed, masturbated, and still had the slip with him under the covers when his mom walked through his door.

She crossed to his bed, laid down on top of him, and asked if she could join Doug under the covers.

"That's inappropriate behavior," Sherry commented. "It may not rise up to the level of sexual molestation, but is at best poor judgment. Did she succeed in seducing you?"

Douglas sighed. "No, we didn't have sex. We cuddled with the bedspread between us but I didn't let her get under the covers.

"Still, I felt like a bad boy to deny her. She persisted for awhile, then finally gave up and left the room. Aargh. In retrospect, the fact that I had just finished masturbating may have saved me, as I didn't feel much desire at that point.

"But that's not the only time something like that happened."

He stopped. Sherry waited a bit then prompted him. "Go on."

"It's just on the edge of my memory, when I was very young, perhaps three or four. Anyway, mom was washing me and my mother played with my penis. My mother kissed my penis. I was a child and my mother kissed my penis. For that matter, both my mothers did that at some point. I don't remember everything that happened. I remember enough.

"But how many times must I remember before I can cry? And how many tears must I shed before I can forget?"

"Choosing to forget is not forgiveness," Sherry pointed out.

Douglas shook his head. "I don't know if I can ever forgive. Right now, I don't believe in forgiveness. But I don't believe in vengeance either."

"What do you believe in?"

"Power. I don't want the pain to control me, nor do I want to forget the pain. I simply want the power to dominate the pain so that it doesn't conquer me—so that I'm in control of my own destiny and that I choose to be free. So that I am more powerful than my mother or my grandmother."

"Then you have learned all you need to forgive," Sherry said.

"What?!" The idea shocked him.

"Remember the two stages of forgiveness," Sherry clarified. "You stated them yourself: (1) admit something happened and (2) admit it hurts and that it hurts you.

"The third stage," Sherry said, "is simply not to let the pain control you. You don't empower the abuser. You empower yourself. Do you think you can forgive?"

Douglas thought long and hard about his response. "Yes," he said finally. "I love my mom. My Momma raped me. I hate my mom.

"But I will never, ever let that control me. She has already controlled me too much. I will not let that happen again. My destiny is mine.

"But the only way that I can gain power is to admit the truth. *Que pasó, pasó.* What happened, happened. And what happened, happened to me."

*April 4, 2008, El Diablo, Arizona*

*Dear Jacky,*

Dad is dying. I knew that already but needed this vacation to wrap my head around it. But now his time is counted in days and there's so little I can do about it. He's had COPD for two years.

I remember that mom said every day was a gamble—I could have died before she did, purely by accident. Sadly, there are just too many ways to die.

Dad is dying. It became hard for him to exhale properly when he hurt his spine recently and now he's just getting a $CO_2$ buildup. When he finally got into the hospital, he had more than three times the $CO_2$ level to kill. It's sometimes hard for people to die.

Sad, mad, glad, scared, ashamed.

My emotions are often mixed and hard for me to express. That's why Sherry suggested that I combine just those five basic emotions when it's hard for me to describe my feelings—sad, mad, glad, scared, ashamed.

No big surprise, I'm feeling all of those. But it's the PD thing—a Fundamentalist is only suppose to rejoice. 'Dad's graduating! He's going to a better place!' No grief, no anger, no sadness, no fear, no shame. Just praise-the-Lord gladness.

I was once a Fundamentalist. I am no longer.

So I'm sad that dad is dying. Yeah, right. It sounds like a soap opera. "Oh dear, I'm sad Dad's dying." If I grabbed a thesaurus, maybe I could elevate "sad" into more poetic words—gloomy, down, blue, miserable, dejected, despondent. But no word can capture the pure wrench of death.

Dad's nurses said that he told them he'd seen mom, who invited him to join her. Dad's been married to Gwen nearly 20 years and he's still that deeply tied to mom in his heart. Every great love story, and my parents had one, ends in death.

Damn. I'm sad.

I'm roiling mad that dad is dying. This wilderness getaway allowed me to escape Santa Brisa—the traffic, crowds, airplanes and sirens' blare. I'm always standing guard, defending myself against the world's banging intrusions. I constantly itch toward anger.

I love the quiet peacefulness here in El Diablo. Who would suppose that "The Devil" could somehow be so comforting? But even listening to children playing in the park, normally something cheerful even back home in Santa Brisa, became grating. It's just too much sensory overload with death so heavy on my mind.

Rose called me here on my cell. Dad is dying.

I'm angry about it! I feel like everyone will put still more demands on me—to take care of the body, ready the estate, sprinkle ashes, prep the memorial service.

Yet it's hard enough for me to be sane even when things are normal. I've thought about suicide too much lately. I've thought about self-destruction. It simply takes too much effort to push those thoughts away and to inch forward just a little.

You bet I'm angry! Wouldn't you be? It seems that everything piles up on me more and more. Cope, walk away, manage to get away, then Death meets you at the pass.

Go away. I don't want you. I hate you. I hate you, Death. This is not your place. I defend this spot, my spot, my land. This is not your place. You have no place here for me. Go away.

I'm not glad dad is dying, but sometimes I worry that I am. He whipped me. He lied. He yelled at me. He withheld information I needed. And he wasn't there for me when I needed him the most.

Still, I'm not glad. He also loved me, hugged me when I needed him the most. He nourished me, encouraged me, taught me so much. I love my father. I love my dad.

He's dying and I'm scared. Fundamentalists aren't supposed to be scared of death, but seriously now, who isn't?

I'm scared, Jacky. I'm so scared. I'm scared that I'll fall apart again. Scared that I'll embarrass myself at his memorial service. Scared that I'll fail Anne, fail the rest of my family when they need me and expect me to be rational. But I'm not entirely sane in the first place. Can't they just back off?

Dad is dying. I'm ashamed, ashamed it's so very hard for me to cope with it. I'm so ashamed.

Oh, yes. "She's in a better place," they told me when mom died. Yeah, right. Maybe so, as if that could take the pain away. As if that could ever take away my anger or stop my tears.

"Praise God!" they scream in chorus. It's PD shouting, "Rejoice Evermore!" Well, what the heck does that mean? I'm not PD. Perhaps I praise God more with my tears than with a shout.

My dad is dying. You bet I'm sad, mad, not glad, scared, and ashamed. What I need is a hug, to love, to make love, to be close to my wife—to be close enough to believe a little in life, not death.

*With Love,*
*Douglas*

*April 13, 2008, at home*

*Dear Jacky,*

Dad died a few days ago. When mom died, I grieved all at once. Dad had been slowly dying for a few years and we knew it was coming, so I tried grieving in advance. Neither approach has worked. There's just no good way to deal with death.

But dad told me one more story near the end, the story of how our family finally escaped from Momma May. The story fills in some gaps, but doesn't answer everything. It is, however, probably all I'll ever get.

Mom and dad usually attended Wednesday night service at Lands Baptist. But this Wednesday, they decided to drive around as they talked things over. Driving and talking was a habit of theirs, of our family's. In their wandering, dad took a random turn down a dead-end street.

Naturally, he turned around in the cul-de-sac. That's when mom noticed a "For Rent" sign facing in the opposite direction.

She took down the number, called, and the very next day put down the first and last month's rent without so much as talking to dad. That's probably the only time she ever did anything without consulting him first. When dad told me the story, he said he had no idea where mom got the money to cover the rent.

I didn't tell him that I already knew.

*With much love,*
*Douglas*

# Sunrise

*April 23, 2008, at home*

*Dear Jacky,*

We chatted about depression and anxiety in our Bible study tonight, an appropriate subject two weeks after dad died. Sigh! One person suggested that spiritually growing as a Christian meant realizing that problems like depression were OK.

But where do you see the biblical verse, I asked, "And God created depression. Then God looked upon it and said, 'Lo, this is very good!'" Being cast out of Eden was never a good thing.

Growing as a Christian, I said, is learning that it's OK to feel grief or anger. Your problems aren't OK, but you are. Thank God, I finally left fundamentalism behind.

Am I still depressed? Do I still want to die? I love and miss my dad, but my story here revolves around women. So it's time for a survey of the women in these chapters of my life: mom and Momma, Leanne and Deirdre. Or as I can finally say, "May," not Momma.

My mother died from breast cancer 20 years ago. I miss her desperately. Somedays I wear her Huguenot cross and I still cry. There will never, never be enough time to tell her how much I love her. Yes, she made mistakes but she worked to correct them. My grandmother never did.

May, a heavy smoker, died from emphysema. I don't miss her at all. But no matter how I look at it, my mother died twice, mom and Momma. That still hurts.

Deirdre and I have remained out of contact. I did hear that she's a nurse up in the state of Washington somewhere. I still don't know how to deal with the pain. Do I forgive her or does she forgive me? Do I really want to talk with her again, to ask those lingering questions about L'Abri from so long ago?

When I'm honest with myself I say yes, I'd like to talk. But it doesn't really matter what I do with her answers. It's just important to know what they are so I can finish that chapter—to respect my teenage self, then let him be the man I am today.

Leanne and I are also out of contact. I do know more of her than I do of Deirdre and definitely want to talk with her again. It's not just that Lee was my first love, but that I owe her an apology, pure and simple. She touched me in so many ways: healed my heart, burned my heart, held my heart, kept my heart.

And I hurt her.

While my head knows what happened to our relationship, it's my heart I need to answer. I wanted to make love to Leanne—to hold her, claim her, cradle her, surrender to her.

I couldn't because my guardian stood in the way and my desire exploded as an attack. I lost my temper, lost control of myself. Anger, love, abuse, sex. The abuse learned from May kept me from knowing the difference. I wanted to love Leanne, so I attacked her instead.

I need to ask Leanne to forgive me. It doesn't matter if she forgives me or not; it's the asking that will work to heal, perhaps the both of us.

Do I still love Leanne? The answer should be clear, my Jacky. Yes, I do; emotional dead end or not, I dearly love Leanne. But driving into a dead-end street sometimes can make just the right kind of turnaround in one's life. It's all about rising above to see the dead end as an arrow that points your way through.

Where am I in this turnaround? I'm both a 50-year-old man and a sexually abused 8-year-old boy. You don't suddenly stop hurting. What happens, little by little, is that you get better at coping with the pain, anger, shame and confusion.

According to some disturbing stats, about 35 percent of sexually abused boys become child sexual abusers themselves. That's three times the average risk of boys or adults who were never abused. We were attacked, we get angry, we counterattack—a child. So it goes round and round and round.

It's still hard for me to separate love from anger or joy from hatred. There's such a nightmare mishmash of feelings. We love our abuser before the abuse and we love her afterward. They're your mom or your grandmother, the woman who raised me as her son. Love doesn't go away that easily. The abuser may treat us well to make up for the abuse. Your mother loves you, your mother abuses you, your mother loves you. Round and round and round.

Yea. We hate it and we're angry. We are angry at those we love while we love and hate them. Is it love or is it anger? I know when I am angry, but sometimes it feels like it's just another part of love. It's so confusing. Sometimes I want to hurt the people I love and part of me still thinks: isn't that the way it's supposed to be? That's what happened to me.

I hate it, I hate it, I hate it! I don't want to hurt my loves. What reading the psych lit doesn't show you is the pain. But I can tell you a little about the Marquis de Sade. Do you want to know about his darkness? I can tell you about his black little heart because I can tell you about *my* black little heart.

I attacked Leanne. I never hit her, but I yelled at her, screamed at her, belittled her, belittled myself. I hurt her. I hurt myself. I was cruel.

Now I hurt because I committed evil. 'I saw a red door and wanted to paint it black.' I did not want to hurt Leanne with my hateful words because I loved her deeply, but that's why I hurt her when my heart was painted black.

Sometimes I still throb with pain. Sometimes I still just want to end it, to commit suicide. Sometimes I want to abuse someone else so that I can find relief. Sometimes I hide inside computer games.

At other times, I can face the pain. I can write about it here, my Jacky. I can write to you and show you my anger, my confusion, my hatred. Sometimes I can turn the pain away from myself and turn it into words.

And each time I write, a little pain goes away. A little blackness fades. Then I have the courage to look once more and realize that my heart was never black. It's the scattered colors of morning sun, to pierce me with its light.

And I welcome that light to refract into the prisms of my heart. My fear no longer shields me and slowly but surely, the light bends into love. For when I refract all the colors of my heart, then my heart is white.

I still tire easily, my dearest, dearest Jacky. But with these chapters and with these words, I've washed away my deepest pain. And at last, I feel clean. I am free again and it gives me hope.

*With my greatest love,*
*Douglas Baign*

# An Afterword

# Statistics

A 2005 San Diego study (Dube et al., *American Journal of Preventive Medicine,* June 2005) of child sexual abuse indicates that 14 to 40 percent of child sexual abusers of boys are female. A separate international study, drawing on research from 22 countries on child sexual abuse, estimates that 7.9 percent of boys under age 18 are molested (Pereda et al., *Clinical Psychology Review,* June 2009). If we accept those figures then roughly 1.1 to 3.1 percent of *all* boys less than 18 years old are sexually molested by women.

Sherry's estimates differ from those suggested by these studies. She once related that she had handled about 300 sexual abuse cases. Of those, 30 were men and just three of the men had been sexually abused by women—1 percent of her *cases* rather than 1 to 3 percent of all boys.

It's not clear if the difference is due to under-reporting or to other factors.

# A final word or two

Except for Catholic priests and the schoolboys in their charge, little attention has been given to sexually abused boys. But those children may bear that trauma well into decades of adulthood. Perhaps traditional gender roles and ways of looking at child sexual abuse keep many of their stories in the closet. In the meantime, the role of females as sexual abusers has been largely swept under the rug.

The hush-hush or rarity factor, whatever it may be, can make therapy difficult for both therapist and patient. There simply isn't that much psychological literature on the topic. How does one progress?

I wrote this manuscript in part to provide clues to that question.

The #MeToo movement popularly focuses on adult women who have been abused in their everyday and workaday lives. It has helped people to talk about when men abuse women.

That doesn't erase the traumatic events of my childhood or of those close to me looking the other way. Boys are abused too. And we can be abused by women.

But as boyhood sexual abuse victims untangle themselves from the fear, shame, confusion, and anger to tell our own stories, once kept in the dark basements of our lives, perhaps we will witness a change here, too.

As for cross-dressing, well, I'm unlikely to make a Best Dressed list, but I recently bought an expensive, sexy prom dress. I didn't realize how much fun those can be. I'm still a little awkward wearing it, but cross-dressing can be a pleasure, not a sin. Most of the stigma I once felt is gone.

All the key adults in this story have died, except Gothard: mom and dad, Momma May, Dr. M, PD. My sibs and I are all that's left, plus their children and grandchildren (I have none).

My sister 'Rose' still suffers complications from her accident 40+ years ago. She has also been in therapy, struggles with depression, and remembers being abused by my Grandmother.

'John' doesn't remember May abusing him, but did have therapy for Reverse Narcissism - pleasing other folks too much and not taking care of himself. He told me recently that he still gets nightmares revolving around 'not being good enough,' with the time frame of his dreams our years with May. It looks like he caught the fringes of my grandmother while Rose and I caught the brunt, probably because he wasn't around her nearly as often as we were.

My cousins on that side of the family did spend a few years in Southern California, but were military brats and spent most of their childhood elsewhere. They remained unaffected.

My wife Anne and I currently attend a Lutheran church that's as far left on the Christian spectrum as I can get without denying the deity of Jesus. I knew I was in the right church when I saw a sign in the church dining room that read:

"Jesus died to take away your sins. Not your mind."